Yin and Yang in the English Classroom

Yin and Yang in the English Classroom

Teaching with Popular Culture Texts

Edited by Sandra Eckard

ROWMAN & LITTLEFIELD
Lanham • Boulder • New York • London

Published by Rowman & Littlefield
A wholly owned subsidiary of The Rowman & Littlefield Publishing Group, Inc.
4501 Forbes Boulevard, Suite 200, Lanham, Maryland 20706
www.rowman.com

Unit A, Whitacre Mews, 26-34 Stannary Street, London SE11 4AB

Copyright © 2015 by Sandra Eckard

All rights reserved. No part of this book may be reproduced in any form or by any electronic or mechanical means, including information storage and retrieval systems, without written permission from the publisher, except by a reviewer who may quote passages in a review.

British Library Cataloguing in Publication Information Available

Library of Congress Cataloging-in-Publication Data Available

ISBN 978-1-4758-0688-5 (cloth)
ISBN 978-1-4758-0689-2 (pbk.)
ISBN 978-1-4758-0690-8 (electronic)

This book is dedicated to my mom and dad, Paula and Bill Eckard. They are the reason I am the learner—and the teacher—that I am today.

When I was a little girl, some of my best moments were sitting at my kitchen table with my mom. She spent countless hours teaching me to read, to write, and to think critically. Every time I use the process of elimination, I can still hear her voice in my head, telling me to cross off the answers that I know are not true. (This process works well for life decisions, too.) My mother had struggled in school, and her biggest fear in life is that I would be laughed at or ridiculed because I couldn't read well enough or couldn't raise my hand with confidence. Thanks to her, I loved every year of school and graduate work.

My father was a public school teacher, and his students to this day still stop him to tell a funny story of their class experience, repeat one of his famous puns, or simply say that they know math because of him. I remember that even when I was a child, I knew that not everyone got a "thank you" like my dad; he was special. He cared. He taught me by example that spending time honing your skills as a teacher does pay off. Students value how you help them.

Together, my parents were my own personal yin and yang. My mother taught me the yin: learning is something not to be taken for granted; you should inhale all the knowledge you can. My father taught me the yang: that it's not just knowing the material, but how you teach it that can make all the difference. I hope I blend their gifts in a way that makes them proud.

Contents

Preface ix

Acknowledgments xi

Introduction 1

I: Literature Fundamentals and Pop Culture Connections 5

1 Entering a Noir World in the Classroom through Detective Fiction and Film Analysis 7
   Mary T. Christel

2 A *PTI*-Inspired Pedagogy: Appropriating Sports-Talk Discussion Protocols to Facilitate Literature Study 31
   Luke Rodesiler

3 Whose Side Is He On?: Teaching Complex Characters with Novels and Films 49
   Carmela Delia Lanza

4 The Graphic Novel as Historical Marker: Making "History Readable" through Reader-Response Theory 63
   Carissa Pokorny-Golden

5 The Truth Is Out There: Using Science Fiction as a Springboard to Teach Literature 79
   Sandra Eckard

6 Hacker Heuretics and Intertextuality in Video Games and English Language Arts 95
   Hannah R. Gerber

II: Developing Writing and Critical Thinking Skills with Popular Culture — **109**

7 Make It Work: What We Can Learn About the Writing Process from Watching *Project Runway* — 111
   April Brannon and Elle Yarborough

8 Up, Up, and Away: Superman in the Composition Classroom — 123
   Alex Romagnoli

9 Popcorn and Movies for All: Four Reasons Films Work in Developmental Writing Classes — 137
   Salena Fehnel

10 The Heroine's Journey: Writing and *Buffy the Vampire Slayer* — 147
   Jennifer Marmo

11 Speed Dating an iPad until the Break of Dawn: Creative Techno-Feminist Pedagogy for Stephenie Meyer's *Twilight Saga* — 161
   Laura Patterson

12 Composing Digital Found Poetry in Secondary English Language Arts Classrooms — 173
   F. Blake Tenore and Katelynn Collins-Hall

About the Contributors — 189

Preface

When I first began thinking about this text, it looked extremely different. I originally wanted something that could offer some new approaches to teaching—something with popular culture, which is my passion. I've had success using various themes like *Superman*, *Firefly*, and *Buffy the Vampire Slayer* in the college classroom, and I thought, why not make a book that allows great college and high school teachers to share their favorite pop culture lessons?

What I couldn't predict was not just the variety of the submissions that I received, but also the sheer creativity. Suddenly, I had a mountain of great ideas that needed some thread to sew them together into a unified piece. This step is where I struggled the most—what to do once I had submissions. Thanks to much brainstorming with friends and colleagues, I realized the path that I was on was to merge—not separate—the concepts of *what* to teach and *how* to teach it.

While I have read numerous articles, anthologies, and texts on teaching with popular culture, not many actually offer tips and activities that you can pull from the pages and use that day in your classroom. That synthesis became my goal—to create a text that was not only grounded in theoretical underpinnings, but also one that was equally balanced with strategies for implementing the theory and making it work for today's students.

I hope that this text offers you not just insight into why video games, science fiction, film, technology, and graphic novels are useful for the classroom, but also intriguing activities that you actually use or modify for your learners.

Acknowledgments

This book would not be possible without the love and support of my dad. Although he was unsure what I was working on, really, he was always there to encourage me and listen. He is my greatest supporter.

I would also like to thank the contributors to this collection for all of their drafts and revisions as the book came together as a unified piece. Their work inspired me as I read each draft! Last, I would like to thank my friends who provided laughs, encouragement, and support as I tackled this project: Salena Fehnel, Melissa Geiger, Kim McKay, Courtney Tolino, and Nancy VanArsdale.

Introduction

The essence of yin and yang centers on the tension between two halves of a whole that are both divided and connected; it is their struggle that helps to achieve a balance, a precarious balance, between two different parts that require each other to move toward completion.[1] This concept that the two halves are equally necessary provides the foundation for this book.

With many theoretical texts and a plethora of teaching texts on the market today, this book, *Yin and Yang in the English Classroom: Teaching with Popular Culture Texts,* aims to help unify these two parts of our field: theory and pedagogy. This book is designed with you, the reader, in mind; keeping with the concept of *halves* working together to achieve a *whole*, several features in this book work together to achieve unity.

While many theory-based articles argue that much needs to be done to improve language arts studies, they offer insight into problems and make a call for reform. Many exciting strategies are often presented in newsletters, next to the copier, or in articles that focus on teaching—but may often lack the theoretical underpinnings, and research, required for a thorough examination of the problems or strategies.

This text, however, aims to merge the two; each chapter will provide both an examination of the issues, or common obstacles, connected to teaching literature or writing. Then, the authors will also offer step-by-step activities that will be ready-made for use in the classroom. Both the *yin* and the *yang* of theory and practice, then, will be part of each chapter in this collection.

Further, the balance of *yin* and *yang* can be found throughout the text, as this book is divided into two halves—the first section focuses on the teaching of literature, while the second half is geared to teaching writing. Next, each chapter itself is divided equally as well. The first half of each chapter has two sections: The Set-Up and Review of Literature. This half is specifically designed to provide an overview of the issue or concept. For example, one chapter might focus on common skills, while another might address a common problem in a high school or college classroom.

The second half of each chapter focuses on a new strategy or a new way of tackling the issue in the classroom. Each chapter has out-of-the box thinking—and each uses a nontraditional approach to teaching traditional skills. This second half contains practical examples and activities that a teacher could take directly into the classroom immediately. The Classroom Connections and Final Thoughts provide insight into how the activities—all using popular culture in some way—can be useful additions to any teacher's toolbox.

In the first section, "Literature Fundamentals and Pop Culture Connections," each of the six authors focus on how to engage students in meaningful critical thinking while tackling literature studies with nontraditional texts. The goal of these chapters is not to replace traditional classroom activities and projects—like lectures, discussions, exams, and papers—but rather to supplement the classroom environment with some new strategies. The activities presented could be modified in many ways, including using different pop culture media or by crafting shorter versions of activities.

Mary T. Christel offers a new approach to literary elements like *tone*, *mood*, *character*, and *point of view* by integrating the genre of film noir into the classroom. The second chapter, by Luke Rodesiler, focuses on integrating discussion-based learning by using the popular ESPN show *Pardon the Interruption*. Equally compelling, the third chapter focuses on teaching the element of *character* by using complex film and novel characters in "Whose Side Is He On?: Teaching Complex Characters with Novels and Films."

In addition, Carissa Pokorny-Golden focuses on how to develop reading skills and introduce historical fiction with graphic novels. "The Truth Is Out There: Using Science Fiction as a Springboard to Teach Literature" offers a unique unit on science fiction as a bridge to teaching *setting* and *character*. And last, Hannah R. Gerber presents how video games—and the learning styles that gamers apply—can be incorporated into the classroom to improve critical thinking skills.

The second half of the book, the yang to the yin of literature, focuses on new strategies for teaching writing and developing critical thinking skills. Each chapter offers something a little bit new, from graphic novels to various uses of technology. The first chapter in this section uses the ever-popular *Project Runway* to model the steps of the writing process. Next, in "Up, Up, and Away: Superman in the Composition Classroom," Alex Romagnoli focuses on how the use of the specific comic texts can help build literacy and writing skills.

In "Popcorn and Movies for All," Salena Fehnel tackles how to use film to build both motivation and skills with developmental writers. Next, Jennifer Marmo, shares how teaching the epic and the hero's journey should include *Buffy, the Vampire Slayer* to help students understand all the traits that build a heroic protagonist while building writing skills.

Laura Patterson connects two very popular pop culture items, the iPad and the *Twilight* phenomenon, offering new classroom writing activities that increase discussion with "Speed Dating an iPad until the Break of Dawn: Creating Techno-Feminist Pedagogy for Stephenie Meyer's *Twilight Saga*." And last, F. Blake Tenore and Katelynn Collins-Hall present a teacher-student perspective on the advantages of writing digital found poetry.

While not every pop culture item—or every strategy—may work for every classroom, the ultimate goal of this textbook is to help inspire readers to think outside the box and consider adding a little something new to a tried-and-true teaching philosophy. In the end, inspiration and motivation are two key parts to finding balance—your own *yin* and *yang*—in teaching.

NOTE

1. Martin Palmer, *Yin & Yang: Understanding the Chinese Philosophy of Opposites and How to Apply it to Your Life* (London: Piatkus Books, 1998), 1.

BIBLIOGRAPHY

Palmer, Martin. *Yin & Yang: Understanding the Chinese Philosophy of Opposites and How to Apply it to Your Life.* London: Piatkus Books, 1998.

I

Literature Fundamentals and Pop Culture Connections

Chapter One

Entering a Noir World in the Classroom through Detective Fiction and Film Analysis

Mary T. Christel

THE SET-UP

A lone figure emerges from the shadows, living by his wits and his own enterprise, defying established authority. He waits, observing the bleak urban landscape, poised to redress the wrongs of weaker mortals that require both his skill and his muscle. This is the essence of the hard-boiled, noir detective who emerged in print in the 1920s and 1930s and then lurked on the silver screen in the 1940s and 1950s.

The rugged individualism and self-reliance of the western hero, the cowboy, gave way to an urban loner who dealt with lawlessness in an expanding metropolis rather than establishing law and order on a vanishing western frontier. Anxiety certainly colored the hopeful expectations of nineteenth-century western expansion that served as a cinematic emblem of all that was possible in pursuing the American dream. As fewer empty spaces remained on the American frontier in the early twentieth century, the urban landscape became the new arena of criminal opportunity requiring an idiosyncratic, flawed hero who could confront greed and corruption because he knew it all too well and could easily succumb to its allure.

Initially, this new American antihero becomes realized in the form of the noir detective, who does not act and react in a manner that is consistent with the traditional, morally steadfast hero. As defined by Film Noir Studies, the antihero is often confused or conflicted with ambiguous morals, or character defects and eccentricities, and lacks courage, honesty, or grace. The antihero can be tough yet sympathetic, or display vulnerable and weak traits. Specifically, the antihero often functions outside the mainstream and challenges it.[1]

Since this antihero emerges after World War I and in the midst of the Great Depression, audiences were and are able to identify with his adaptation of rugged individualism and self-reliance that even Herbert Hoover promoted in a 1928 campaign speech designed to energize a nation to take matters of economic and social development into their own hands by not relying on government leadership and intervention.[2]

Most students examine the promises and perils of the American dream through literary works such as *The Great Gatsby*, *The Grapes of Wrath*, and *Death of a Salesman*. These acknowledged canonical masterpieces provide students easily accessible American dream themes to extract and explore. But, lurking in the pulp fiction of the early twentieth century are the hard-boiled detective heroes, or antiheroes, who share many qualities that characterize an adolescent from any era: alienation, anxiety, restlessness, rebelliousness.

These traits characterize an American dreamer whose ambitions have been perilously tarnished. The noir detective, through choice or circumstance, finds himself cut loose from the norms of society and plies his trade outside of conventional law enforcement agencies. He must rely on his own wit and strength while navigating the seamier edges of society. This genre of fiction and film does not always yield easy answers about the rewards and costs of being that rugged individual during a time of economic depression and, later, a second world war.

The best of the film noir genre includes the movies that owe their genesis to the popular fiction of Dashiell Hammett and Raymond Chandler. Hammett's Sam Spade in *The Maltese Falcon* is the epitome of the simmering rational detachment of the "Continental Op" developed in Hammett's earlier series of short stories, while Chandler's Philip Marlowe in *Farewell, My Lovely* is more intuitive, less predictable in his ability to maintain that rational detachment.

Filmmakers' fascination with noir characters has persisted over time. Even John Huston, the screenwriter and director of *The Maltese Falcon*, revisits the genre more than thirty years later in his neo-noir film, *Chinatown*. In 2006, a twenty-something filmmaker, Rian Johnson, imagines the world of Spade and Marlowe coming to roost in a twenty-first-century California high school in *Brick*, a neo-noir he wrote and directed as his first feature length film.

Johnson's film is a clear indication that the adolescent loner, gifted with keen observation, deductive reasoning, and tenuous emotional detachment, is not so far removed from the gumshoe of 1930s and 1940s pulp fiction, which makes the study of the genre all that more accessible and intriguing to young adults.

The study of noir detective fiction and film can yield a rich analysis not only of the genre's thematic preoccupations. It also provides a context for the examination of the conventions of the genre: its cast of stock characters, the development of highly atmospheric settings, as well as the impact of point of view in both the print and film versions. All of these elements are the staples of careful literary analysis that can be applied to film study along with attention to the tools unique to the cinematic form.

This approach could easily become part of a survey of American literature to examine the 1930s and 1940s through an atypical range of texts that complement some of the literary "usual suspects": Fitzgerald, Steinbeck, and Hemmingway. A fully developed, stand-alone unit focusing on detective fiction could include examining twentieth-century American detective fiction by placing it in the context of its nineteenth-century American and European origins as well as linking it to its influence on contemporary fiction, film, and television. For reluctant readers, the study of detective literature and film provides texts that meet students at their interest and reading levels in a fashion where more typical choices do not succeed.

REVIEW OF LITERATURE

Providing Context: From Genteel Consulting Investigator to Hard-Boiled Detective

When considering the origins of the detective story, Oedipus the King could be considered the first amateur detective, as he vows to uncover the circumstances of the death of Thebes's former king, Laius, and to expose the murderer that the reader knows will result in an inevitable tragedy of recognition, of patricide and incest, for Oedipus himself. The true genesis of the genre obviously arrives much later and coincides with the advent of professional law enforcement and methodical crime detection in the nineteenth century.

The most influential detectives of this era come from the imaginations of Edgar Allan Poe and Arthur Conan Doyle. Both of their consulting investigators, Poe's C. Auguste Dupin and Doyle's Sherlock Holmes, represent the gentleman detective who combines deductive reasoning and disciplined speculation, which allows each to penetrate the mind and motives of professional criminals.

The gentleman detective avoids getting "his hands dirty" or resorting to any kind of brute force that would put him on par with the criminal element he strives to expose and bring to justice. These investigators approach their task like a scientist.[3] The classical detective represents a generally "well ordered society [where] occasional problems could be solved with deductive reasoning."[4]

John G. Cawelti points out that the aim of a classical detective story involves "the introduction of the detective and the presentation of the crime, through the investigation, to a solution and apprehension of the criminal."[5] These stories focus squarely on understanding the crime and restoring social order. It is only with the enormous popularity of Sherlock Holmes that the investigator himself moves front and center in the minds of the reading public and, later, moviegoers.

The hard-boiled detectives created by Hammett and Chandler cannot help but combine the intellectual skills of their predecessors with cunning street savvy, enabling them to use the tactics that cultivate a callous or brutish detachment from the moral mainstream. Cawelti differentiates the direction of a noir plot from its classical detective counterpart in two ways: "the subordination of the drama of solution to the detective's quest for the discovery and accomplishment of justice; and the substitution of a pattern of intimidation and temptation of the hero for the elaborate development in the classical story of what Northrop Frye calls 'the wavering finger of suspicion' passing across a series of potential suspects."[6]

Sam Spade and Philip Marlowe therefore immerse themselves in the shadowy underworld of the criminal mastermind by physically entering that world more fully than Dupin and Holmes do and get their hands both physically and morally dirty.

In its earliest form, the hard-boiled detective is a remote character, a cipher. Hammett's first private investigator (P.I.) is the "Continental Op." He has no proper name, just a label: the Continental Operative (or "operative" from the Continental Detective Agency). He is a man judged purely on his action, not on a conventionally defined personality or identity. In a way, he is like Poe's Dupin who does not have the flair or idiosyncrasies of Doyle's Holmes. Though unlike Dupin, the "Continental Op" is a man hardened by the criminal world he infiltrates. His code is one of self preservation above all—at any cost.

Thomas Schatz defines this type as one who operates "more by instinct than by intellect . . . submerged inside a sordid, malevolent urban setting and generally resorted to violence in order to survive."[7] Here, the detective is a type rather than a dimensional character, perhaps anticipating television's interchangeable cast of detectives and district attorneys (D.A.s) on a contemporary television crime procedural like *Law and Order*. In a sense it really doesn't matter who solves the crimes or prosecutes the criminals, just so they have the appropriate credentials, experience, and opportunity.

Both Spade and Marlowe find themselves in California, the former in San Francisco and the latter in Los Angeles. Both of these urban landscapes harken back to their association with the American frontier of the nineteenth century. San Francisco was the center of the California Gold Rush and home to the notorious Barbary Coast red-light district. It was the port that played host to ships from the exotic Orient loaded with immigrants, treasure, and modern-day pirates.

Los Angeles was the city of dreams, the home to a fantasy factory called Hollywood. Dupin's Paris and Holmes's London are the cultural and social antithesis of America's west coast urban landscapes. In America, the detective would find a newer, more dangerous kind of corruption in an allegedly classless society with a lack of enduring history or genteel traditions.

Understanding Noir Characters and Conventions

The easiest way to understand any genre is to know it through the characters that populate its world. Cawelti notes, "Like the classical story, the hard-boiled formula develops four main character roles: (a) the victim or victims; (b) the criminal; (c) the detective; and (d) those involved in the crime but incapable of resolving the problems it poses, a group involving police, suspects, and so on—in effect, the set of characters who represent society in the story."[8] The study of detective noir, in literary or cinematic form, can yield a fruitful discussion of gender roles that populate Cawelti's four categories of characters.

The male roles encompass the private investigators, law enforcement allies, criminal masterminds, their hired "muscle," as well as gullible marks, fall guys, and patsies. These types can be defined in the following manner:

- **Hard-boiled detective**—usually veteran of the police force; leaves due to disgrace or frustration with operating within the bureaucracy of the law; not above going outside the law as a private investigator; a loner disappointed by life.
- **Detective's professional partner**—someone to assist the P.I. in his investigation; many times has a hidden agenda that could block the P.I.'s success or discredit him; might be valuable to the P.I. due to greater intelligence but lesser degree of ruthlessness in comparison to the P.I.
- **Law enforcement ally**—a cop, a former partner, or friend who is still on the inside and can provide the P.I. with assistance or a warning about ethical behavior.
- **Mastermind**—the person behind the crime or the con; can come from a fairly sophisticated class of society; can match wits with the P.I.; sometimes exhibits signs of depravity.
- **Mastermind's ally**—generally not as intelligent or depraved as the mastermind; usually provides more "underworld" connections; sometimes sexually ambiguous.

- **The muscle**—generally not very bright, but gives the mastermind the ability to get what he wants by brute force; sometimes takes on role of "fall guy" due to lack of intelligence.
- **The patsy**—someone who unknowingly has some sort of unlawful behavior pinned on him (sometimes her); sometimes the patsy is a willing victim in order to be a part of a criminal group or plot, or to gain or maintain the love of a femme fatale.
- **The fall guy**—similar to the patsy but he (or she) has to "pay" either with his (or her) life or with a potential prison sentence.
- **The mark**—someone who is easily targeted by criminals and can provide them, knowingly or unknowingly, with a variety of resources to commit a crime or complete their plan.

Within that assortment of both principled and unsavory types, there is a range of power, skill, and intellect afforded these male characters, allowing them to act or to be acted upon.

The range of female characters tends to focus more narrowly on those who observe, support, inform, or succumb to male authority, which include the "Girl Friday," virtuous ingénue, and grizzled dame. Only the "femme fatale" is able to find a position of power by using her considerable feminine charms of appearance and sexuality, intellectual prowess, and tawdry past to assert and maintain control over the men on either side of the law. That narrower range of behavior within the female roles can be defined more specifically as:

- **The femme fatale**—the dark and dangerous woman who is connected with the mastermind in some way; is seductively appealing to the P.I. and always a sexual temptation; she could bring on the P.I.'s moral or professional downfall.
- **The "Girl Friday"**—the female ally to the P. I. who is usually a secretary or a low-level assistant; she is sometimes boyish in appearance to create a contrast to the highly sexualized femme fatale; tends to have a great affection for the P.I. but understands that their relationship is platonic or professional.
- **The virtuous ingénue**—a young woman who is caught in the web that the mastermind spins; she is potentially a victim of the plotting and she provides a more wholesome love interest for the P.I. and some moral redemption for him.
- **Grizzled dame**—usually an older woman whom the P.I. relies on for information, who tends to double cross him or leads him on a wild goose chase.

The men in this unforgiving world do not have many options for reliable or trusted feminine comfort and companionship, and as the only woman with a formidable and seductive aura of power and influence, the femme fatale (or femme noire) is the consummate manipulator and betrayer. But, she ultimately is undone by the P.I. because she doesn't have the physical strength, criminal resources, or emotional moxie to outwit and outplay her adversary, who routinely operates outside of the normal bounds of the law and accepted morality.

These characters find themselves bound together in both perpetrating and solving a crime that forms this noir narrative. Cawelti identifies "[t]he typical hard-boiled pattern of action [as]: the detective is called in to investigate a seemingly simple thing, like a disappearance; his investigation comes up against a web of conspiracy that reflects the presence of a hidden criminal organization; finally, the track leads back to the rich and respectable levels of society and exposes the corrupt relationship."[9] Within this formula, the hard-boiled noir detective will test and compromise his moral code as well as become increasingly more vulnerable to the seduction of the criminal world.

CLASSROOM CONNECTIONS

Preparatory Short Viewing Activity: Applying Stock Characters and Conventions

As with any form of genre study, the reader or viewer needs to understand "the rules of the game." There are two ways to come to that understanding: the first would be through discovery and the second would be through application. If black-and-white films and detective stories are extremely foreign, exotic, or off-putting for students, then it is reasonable and helpful to select the application process. It would be practical to begin with reading a short story or even watching a television episode to establish and apply the genre's conventions.

An installment of the ABC television police procedural *Castle* (season 4, episode 13 "The Blue Butterfly") features a storyline that flashes back to a crime committed in 1947, allowing for an easy identification of character types before moving on to a more complex or less familiar application. Have students screen the episode and match the cast of modern-day police investigators, the criminals, and the people in Richard Castle's personal life (his mother and daughter) with the stock noir characters they assume in the flashback sequence to the crime committed in 1947 that needs solving in the present day.

Students should note defining mannerisms, costuming, and interactions between character types that bring the noir world alive and make it distinct from the present-day police procedural shows they are more accustomed to watching. Students should also apply Cawelti's template for mapping out the action of the noir plotline to determine how much of the formula can be addressed in an hour-long television police procedural, another crime genre that depends on its own conventions and formula.

Once students understand the context and can apply rules of the detective noir genre, then "the game's afoot," as Mr. Holmes would say, and it is time to expand that knowledge through further reading and viewing experiences.

Teaching the Detective Genre: Reading the Novels and Viewing the Films

A unit devoted to the study of detective fiction and film noir could cover the study of the novel and film, *The Maltese Falcon*; the novel *Farewell, My Lovely* with its film adaptation *Murder, My Sweet*; and culminate with *Brick*, a modern neo-noir set in a high school.

This approach would allow students to discover and explore the conventions of a popular culture form in its "golden age" as well as tracing its influences through a contemporary film iteration.

Some attention must be paid to looking at the hard-boiled detective by placing that prototype within the context of the "gentleman detective." That could be accomplished in several ways. First, by reading stories that feature Holmes and Dupin or second, by showing clips from film or television adaptations featuring those characters to create quick reference points for later discussion and comparison.

The ideal way to examine the films along with literary origins would be to read the book first and then screen the film with an attention to literary adaptation techniques: fidelity to the source material, compression of time, development of point of view, selection and compositing of character and incident. Development and adaptation of plot and character would be the emphasis of this approach.

In the absence of a "traditional" literary source, the study of *Brick* would focus on how that screenplay selects and adapts elements from the two classic prototype novels and their film adaptations. The shooting script for *Brick* is available as a downloadable PDF at www.rcjohnso.com/brickscript/BrickScript.pdf. And, Johnson also created a graphic novella version of the story that is available to download at www.rcjohnso.com/brickscript/BrickNovella.pdf.

Setting the Focus for Reading the Novels and a Screenplay or a Graphic Novella

As students read *The Maltese Falcon* and *Farewell, My Lovely*, have them focus their attention on the central detective as well as a specific supporting character. Instruct students to highlight or underline and annotate key passages that involve their assigned supporting character. Readers should note how their character is introduced, including what is learned about his or her physical appearance, temperament, background, and motives as they apply to the case Sam Spade or Philip Marlowe is pursuing.

Students should continue to mark scenes that involve their supporting character as well as any scenes where the detective reflects on their relationship or what the detective knows about this character. Crucial questions for students to keep in mind as they read: How does the supporting character's interaction with the detective help the reader better understand that central character? How does that character fit one of the stock characters or stereotypes that populate noir detective film? Is the character purely one "type" or does he or she represent a blending of several types? By taking on this reading focus, students would then become experts on their supporting character.

Assigning students a concentrated focus that includes the central and a supporting character during the reading process empowers them to become the expert whose knowledge encompasses both the scope of the novel by following the detective, the central character, as well as a specialized perspective through tracking a supporting character. Students' impressions of characters can be formalized through a series of journals or blog postings. The questions previously posed could become topics for student writing.

Students can certainly create their own questions and topics. A second level of focus and analysis during the reading process should bring attention to how fully each novel illustrates the narrative pattern identified by Cawelti.

Reading the screenplay or graphic novella as the literary analog to the film, *Brick* would help students consider carefully how stock characters and genre conventions are applied to a familiar setting and set of circumstances. Students could also read one of the texts, paying careful attention to the noir slang that is integrated in the dialogue.

Since that slang is so anachronistic, creating a lexicon of those words and their definitions would help students regard those colloquialisms as less remote. Definitions can be gained by examining the words in context as they appear in *Brick* as well as in *The Maltese Falcon* or *Farewell, My Lovely*. A very comprehensive glossary of noir slang compiled by William Denton can be accessed online at www.miskatonic.org/slang.html.

Once students begin to screen the film adaptations, their task will shift to how faithfully the screenwriter, director, and actors bring each character and the narrative formula to the screen. While viewing the film, students should take notes regarding how the supporting character is introduced into the film's narrative, the degree to which that character helps to advance the plot, how the character's interaction with the detective helps to develop his character, and the impact of an expanded or reduced character's role in the narrative. As a culminating activity that could result in a written response, students should select a passage from the novel to discuss how it is rendered on screen or why it is omitted. An exemplar of passage selection and related analysis is offered in the next section.

Sam Spade on the Page and the Screen: A Study in Terse Style and Stoic Heroism

The film version of *The Maltese Falcon* (1941) remains extremely faithful to the novel, since the style of the novel is incredibly lean, and sections of dialogue from the novel are transposed directly into John Huston's screenplay. The structure of the film follows a series of conversations in various interior spaces: Spade's detective agency office, Brigid's sitting room, a hotel lobby, the Fatman's hotel suite, and Spade's apartment. Only a handful of scenes place Spade, his ill-fated partner Archer, or the criminals on the street.

A more focused way to examine films' literary origins includes analyzing selected passages from the novels prior to viewing the films. To begin that examination, a good focal technique is point of view. The voice-over narrator is a convention usually associated with the detective film, so it is surprising to discover that *The Maltese Falcon* as a novel and as a film does not adopt this technique. The narrative stance of the novel is very reportorial, which allows for an easy, direct adaptation to film.

Chandler permits Philip Marlowe to narrate his own tale, and he is a narrator guilty of embellishment, hyperbole, and bombastic comparisons: "he looked about as inconspicuous as a tarantula on a slice of angel food cake" or "[t]here was a sudden silence as heavy as a water-logged boat."[10] The preservation of the source material's point of view is a crucial factor in how each film develops its tone and approach to its characters.

An examination of Hammett's style should focus on the opening chapter that introduces the reader to Spade, his secretary, his partner, and their prospective client. The chapter begins with a description of Spade himself that is specific, detailed, and establishes him with the provocative detail that "[h]e looked rather pleasantly like a blond satan."[11] The following questions should frame the discussion of this opening passage:

- What kind of impression is made comparing a character with "satan"?
- Why make satan "blond" when in human form one would expect him to be physically dark?
- Why include "pleasantly" to modify and qualify that provocative comparison to a figure of evil or moral mischief?

Obviously, Hammett is setting up a sense of wry irony and incongruity from the start.

For those readers who immediately associate Sam Spade with his cinematic embodiment in the form of Humphrey Bogart, the assertion that he is a "*blond* satan" is also surprising. Other details related to Spade's appearance associate him with a typical stereotype of the devil like a "hooked nose."[12] These features make Spade strangely and clearly demonic, so the reader needs to consider how this connection muddies the moral waters of what would be the central character.

This strangely links him to Sherlock Holmes, whose drug use typically is underplayed or sanitized in various early film adaptations to position him as the consummate rational gentleman detective. With Sam Spade, Hammett establishes a tradition of presenting the twentieth-century private detective with an Achilles's heel or moral feet of clay that does have roots in Sherlock Holmes's initial literary presentation.

In the opening chapter, Hammett also effectively establishes other characters through similarly precise, economical physical details. Spade's secretary Effie has a "shiny boyish face" that signals she would not be of any romantic or erotic value to Spade. Effie tells him that Miss Wonderly is a "knockout," which clearly establishes the client's value as a professional prospect and romantic interest.[13] Conversations between Joel Cairo and Spade as well as between Spade and "the Fatman" yield insight into Hammett's control of his prose to provide just enough details to "show" rather than to directly "tell" the readers what is transpiring and to allow them to form judgments about the characters and their motives.

Examining how the novel concludes makes for an interesting, perhaps surprising, comparison with its film adaptation. Many detective noir novels end by plunging their characters into a nihilistic fate that is antithetical to classical Hollywood endings, which tend to focus on reconciliation and redemption. For example, in the film adaptation of *The Maltese Falcon*, John Huston adds an allusion to Shakespeare's *The Tempest* in Spade's remark, "the stuff that dreams are made of" when Police Detective Polhaus asks him about the black bird as Spade hands over the evidence and Brigid O'Shaughnessy to him and Dundy.[14]

The final shots of the film focus on a close-up of Brigid visually imprisoned by the shadows from the elevator's grate and a medium shot of Sam solemnly descending the staircase with falcon in hand. Justice is served, but Sam Spade can only take the cold comfort of sending Brigid away rather than succumbing to her seductive charms. In the novel, Spade returns to the office to confront the consequences of sending Brigid to jail in a conversation with incredulous Effie who is reading the newspaper account of Brigid's apprehension. The scene ends with the arrival of Iva Archer, his partner's widow and Spade's jealous paramour.

If students are reading the entire novel or selected chapters and viewing the film, a close rereading of the novel's final chapters or scenes would help students to identify and analyze the changes that the screenwriters made to the source material. Students could then engage in speculative discussion of the decision to radically change the ending of *The Maltese Falcon*, which eliminates an epilogue scene that places Spade back in his routine of debriefing the case with Effie and facing the consequences of his adultery with the arrival of the newly widowed Iva Archer.

The novel's ending seems anticlimactic in comparison to the film's final shot of Spade descending the staircase with the lead bird in hand. Students could research changes to the novel by seeking out existing film production notes, critics' reviews of the film, or by viewing helpful "extras" on DVD editions of the film.

Brendan Frye, a Purely Cinematic Creation: The Reluctant Twenty-First-Century Gumshoe

In 2006, Rian Johnson brought the world of the 1940s gumshoe to life in a typical contemporary California high school in his film *Brick*. How Johnson toggles the worlds together is immediately clear in the film's title. In the world of the gumshoe or shamus, "brick" would refer to a lack of intelligence or perceptiveness: "Are you thick as a brick?" In a more contemporary era that word has a connection to a quantity of drugs: a brick of cocaine.

In the world of the film's high school age detective, Brendan Frye, both meanings of the word apply. Brendan is revealed as a loner sitting in a deserted part of the campus, eating lunch on his own and relying on a similarly isolated nerd nicknamed "the Brain" for a bit of advice or a little legwork. Johnson cleverly combines the smoldering detachment of Sam Spade with the recklessness and bravado of Philip Marlowe as Brendan is thrust into the role of amateur sleuth when he discovers the body of a former girlfriend, Emily, in a drainage tunnel at the beginning of the film.

The narrative backtracks to "two days previous" to allow the viewer to follow Brendan to that moment of discovery until the plotline connects the death of Emily to a drug-dealing ring that brings together all the various high school stereotypes: the drama vamp, the befuddled stoner, the hair-trigger muscle, the boastful jock, the upper-crust beauty—all in the thrall of a mysterious adult known as "the Pin."

Johnson integrates jokey allusions to the film's 1940s origins in his screenplay and art direction. Even though it is 2006, none of the kids have a cell phone except for the Brain, and it belongs to his mother, so Brendan relies on the conveniently placed phone booth to make crucial calls. The Pin's curbside home mailbox has a black bird as its distinctive ornament. Laura, the stylish upper-crust girl, is costumed with hats and hair ornaments that evoke a retro, 1940s style. The slang of the film is clearly informed by the patter of Spade and Marlowe: cops are referred to as a "bulls"; a talkative suspect is told to "gum it" or keep quiet; something that is easily done or deduced is "duck soup."

The final confrontation between Brendan and Laura is modeled on the first scene between Spade and Brigid in his apartment right down to the line, "It was you angel." The meshing of these two worlds seems oddly discordant yet in the end strangely satisfying. Brendan's socially and morally chaotic world is replaced by a new order where the bad guys and girls are appropriately punished, though Brendan's ability to emerge from his outsider status in clearly in doubt.

Even though *Brick* garnered only mixed reviews, it does illustrate the enduring legacy of the hard-boiled detective in American popular culture. Even less-than-hard-boiled modern law enforcement, like the New York detectives of television's *Castle*, dons the fedoras, double-breasted suits, and engages in Chandleresque patter to walk on the wild side. For all of the seediness and clichés of that world, it still has its mystique and allure that explores an alienated, urban hero who finds some level of personal and social justice on the other side of polite, lawful social norms.

Analyzing a Neo-Noir Text

An analysis of the film in combination with the study of *The Maltese Falcon* and *Murder, My Sweet* films would focus on how *Brick* uses the typical stock characters and plot conventions of the classic noir detective novel and film. Even though writer-director Rian Johnson cites the novels of Dashiell Hammett and Sam Spade as his central inspiration for his high school gumshoe, there are heavy doses of the reckless Philip Marlowe in Brendan Frye. Since Brendan is a teenager, Johnson noted in an interview:

> In putting this character in high school, I felt it was important to add a very personal element, that of lost love. So our detective is not just doing this because it's his job (though in ten years or so he'll probably be at that point) but because it's the only way he knows how to deal with having his heart broken.[15]

Actually, Brendan's romantic vulnerability is not really that far removed from the lust that fuels many decisions his adult counterparts make. Defining Brendan through his broken heart for Johnson "became about the emotional experience of being a teenager," which makes the transposition of the noir elements in the high school demimonde more than a stylistic exercise and clever mash-up.[16] Brendan's character can be analyzed on first viewing in the following manner:

- How does Brendan acquire the role of investigator?
- What resources must he rely upon to see this investigation to the end?
- Select sequences and interactions illustrating how Brendan exhibits the cool detachment of Sam Spade and the reckless bravado of Philip Marlowe.
- How is the final confrontation between Brendan and Laura informed especially by the dialogue exchanged between Sam and Brigid in the film version of *The Maltese Falcon*?

Post Reading and Viewing Activity: Writing Focus on Character

Once students have completed the reading and viewing for this unit, a written analysis is means to pull together their experience in understanding the elements that brand any narrative as a detective noir. The topics offered here focus on the two most iconic characters of the genre: the hard-boiled detective and the femme fatale.

Essay Topic 1: The Film Noir Detective

This genre developed a new breed of detective. "The classical detective was . . . part of a generally well-ordered society whose occasional problems could be solved with deductive reasoning." Think Sherlock Holmes. But, the hard-boiled detective frequently discovers that crime is part of the natural corruption of human nature and cannot be readily solved. He operated "more by instinct than by intellect . . . submerged inside a sordid, malevolent urban setting and generally resorted to violence in order to survive."[17]

Compare and contrast how Sam Spade, Philip Marlowe, and Brendan Frye illustrate this character type. Select one extended sequence for each character that helps to illustrate how each fits the type, but also brings something unique and different to it as well. In your discussion of each sequence integrate examples of three cinematic techniques that reveal how dangerous each man's world can be.

Essay Topic 2: The Femme Fatale

One of the most critical differences between women in this genre and other genres is how dangerous they can be in a morally dark, criminal world. How does *The Maltese Falcon* and *Murder, My Sweet* present its femme noire or fatale in a manner that is fairly typical of the genre? Select a sequence from the selected film that shows the femme fatale at work and how her behavior is supported through the setting's décor, lighting, costumes, props, and physical behavior. Also focus on how a femme fatale might be set against a "good girl" to play up the natural contrast. How "good" can any girl be in this kind of world? What happens when there isn't this kind of foil or contrast present?

Then, examine how *Brick* adapts the figure of the femme fatale. How easy or difficult is it to pick up who fills this role? Select one character that serves this purpose at various points in the film and link her to a particular sequence as you did with the first film paying attention to the setting's décor, lighting, costumes, props, and physical behavior.

A Second Approach for Analysis: Focusing on Film Noir as a Cinematic Style

For many classrooms it might be impractical to assume that this unit would cover the novels in their entirety along with the films. Students can acquire a sense of the genre conventions and character types from viewing "The Blue Butterfly" episode of *Castle*. They could also read excerpts from *The Maltese Falcon* and *Farewell, My Lovely* to experience the central characters in their "print versions." If the films are the centerpieces of the unit's focus, then attention to cinematic style of film noir needs to be given greater emphasis. An ideally realized unit would be able to balance the two approaches: literary adaptation and cinematic style.

Thomas Schatz provides a useful discussion of the narrative and cinematic characteristics of film noir in *Hollywood Genres*. He reminds us that the genre received its name from French film critics who were the first serious admirers of the these "B movies," and "film noir" literally means "black film" or "dark film." These films are "dark" both in visual techniques and narrative style. Shot primarily in black and white, these films emphasized a shadowy, sinister urban landscape.

Characters also reflect the darker aspects of human nature. Thematically, the films emphasize the corruption of the American dream. Hollywood was beginning to respond to a world that was on the brink of self-destruction, since it possessed the atomic bomb. Film noir techniques gradually find their way into melodramas, westerns, gangster films, and psychological thrillers.

Film scholar and writer-director Paul Schrader identifies seven recurring techniques of film noir that are helpful in examing the narrative cinematic conventions of the genre:

1. the majority of scenes are lit for night;
2. as in German Expressionism, oblique and vertical lines are preferred to horizontal lines;
3. the actors and setting are often given equal lighting and emphasis;
4. tension in a scene is revealed by static arrangement of characters;
5. there is almost a Freudian attachment to water (. . . other reflective surfaces);
6. there is a love of romantic (voice-over) narration; and

7. the complex chronological order reinforces feelings of hopelessness and lost time.[18]

The *American Cinema* series provides a video segment on film noir that runs about fifty minutes and covers the conventions of the genre as well as traces the development of the films from their cinematic origins to the present (circa 1995). That exploration of the genre effectively traces the influence of psychology and the impact of the post–War World II era on the development of noir films that extend beyond the detective as the typical noir protagonist. Lita Burke offers the most compact delineation of the rules of the genre in a three-minute film entitled "Film Noir for Writers."

If the examination of adaptation from print to screen focuses primarily on the films themselves, the filmmaker's application of the genre's distinctive visual style is crucial to fully appreciate the noir world created in that medium. Students need to explore the tools that are unique to the filmmaker in bringing the printed page to life. Mise en scène is especially evocative in these films and requires analysis of camerawork, lighting, décor, costuming, and figure movement.

When considering the creation of the signature mise en scène of film, the level of realism or formalism present is an essential factor to assess. Generally noir films rely heavily on a formalistic approach to mise en scène that borrows a great deal from expressionism and "stresses the importance of form over content."[19] A formalist approach does not strive to replicate reality. It is much more selective or symbolic, and it can even border on the surreal. A number of sequences in *Murder, My Sweet* illustrate this technique as dictated by its source material's melodramatic prose style. *The Maltese Falcon* on the other hand leans more toward realism with subtler touches of formalism, also dictated by Hammett's prose style.

If students need to acquire a basic set of terms to analyze cinematic style in a more precise manner, a useful list compiled by David T. Johnson can be found online at faculty.salisbury.edu/~dtjohnson/filmterms.htm. And, students could screen Lita Burke's short video, "Film Noir for Writers" (litaburke.com/worlds/film-noir-world/film-noir-for-writers-video/) and apply basic film terms to analyze shot composition and editing as a warm-up to viewing and analyzing the feature-length films.

Setting the Focus for Viewing Feature-Length Film Adaptations/Cinematic Style

Students would watch each film in its entirety with a viewing focus to guide that initial examination of the text. Focus questions would have students track specific characters and plot elements to give necessary attention to the narrative components of the film. Some sample questions to apply to the characters of *The Maltese Falcon* would include:

- Define how Spade's relationships with the following women are developed in the opening section of the film. How does his relationship with each of these women define his values, his regard for women: Effie Perrine, his secretary; Iva Archer, his partner's wife; Miss Wonderly (aka Brigid O'Shaughnessy), his client?
- How does the introduction of each woman suggest the noir stock character they will play based on her appearance and mannerisms?
- How do Kasper Gutman, Joel Cairo, and Wilmer Cook reflect stock noir characters that populate the criminal underworld pursuing the "black bird"?

That first viewing would also focus on how the central crime or mystery is introduced, how it ensnares the detective, and how the detective ultimately outwits the mastermind behind the crime. In *The Maltese Falcon* and *Murder, My Sweet*, there is a priceless object that needs to be recovered that motivates murder and betrayal as its whereabouts are uncovered. Finally, attention should be paid to the locales that the detective and the criminals must occupy and navigate including the detective's office, public spaces of the cityscape, and the private lairs of the criminal element. How do those environments both reveal and conceal their secrets and set the stage for pivotal encounters between characters and events that drive the plot?

A second set of questions would require students to pay attention to specific cinematic tools: lighting, character movement or blocking, camerawork (including angle, distance, and movement) and how their application advances a realistic or formalistic approach. Questions that focus on cinematic techniques for one of Spade's interrogations of Brigid that deserves special scrutiny would include:

- How does the general lighting of the scene complement the fact that Miss Wonderly, now Brigid O'Shaughnessy, wants to "come clean" and be truthful?
- Describe two shots that reflect that Brigid wants to appear to be vulnerable and helpless as she appeals to Spade for his help.
- Why is there an "insert" included late in the scene as Brigid goes for the money to retain Spade's services? What does it reveal to confirm something about her story?

These questions would be best addressed after the initial screening of the film. Sequences like the interviews with Miss O'Shaughnessy and, in the next segment, Mr. Gutman, are better considered in isolation by reviewing these key scenes that require more complex analysis.

In order to examine the realistic approach that director John Huston takes in his film adaptation of *The Maltese Falcon*, students should analyze two key conversations that Spade has with Kasper Gutman, or the "Fatman," after watching the film in its entirety. The first interview can be found at 51:11–55:15 and the second at 56:53–64:10 on a standard DVD of the film. These two scenes track the development of Spade and Gutman's cat and mouse game of acquiring and concealing crucial information about the historical importance and monetary value of the falcon, let alone its possible whereabouts. Both scenes play very much like they were meant for the stage.

There is little physical movement between the two characters, but subtle movements speak volumes about who is in control. Students can screen and rescreen the sequences with attention to the placement of the camera (angle, distance, movement), shot content (one versus two people in a single shot), editing (the duration of shots), the use of light and shadow as well as the movement of the characters. If students are unaccustomed to the analysis of cinematic techniques, the techniques can be assigned to groups of students to equally distribute the focus. Sample questions could include:

- Why is this sequence shot in such bright, general lighting with few highly defined shadows?
- How would you describe the physical distance that is maintained between Spade and Gutman during their conversation? What does it suggest about their regard for one another?
- At which points in the scene are individual shots held for longer or shorter duration? How does the conversation dictate the pace of the editing?
- Select and describe several shots that indicate who is really in control of the situation, Spade or Gutman. When does the scene rely on "one shots" and "two shots"?
- How is Gutman shot from time to time in a manner that makes his image distorted? Why is this an appropriate technique?

Both of these sequences lean toward realism over formalism that makes *The Maltese Falcon* seem like a filmed stage play rather than a formalist expression of the seedier world of other noir classics like *Murder, My Sweet*. Students should be asked to consider how the realism of this approach suits the character of Sam Spade, who tends to be a very no-nonsense detective as opposed to the more histronic Philip Marlowe.

The study of *Murder, My Sweet*, the first of several film adaptations of Chandler's *Farewell, My Lovely*, exposes the viewer to the formalistic end of the film noir spectrum as well as to the use of voice-over narration. The voice-over technique naturally derives from the first-person point of view used in the novel and the retrospective nature of how the film's narrative is plotted. The film begins with Marlowe being interrogated by the police and he recounts the events that led him to his present sorry state, accused of shooting a woman and apparently blinded as a result. The events of the film will literally and figuratively bring things to light.

As they did when viewing *The Maltese Falcon*, on a first viewing of this film, students would track how central and supporting characters fill out the "usual suspects" of the noir character types, and how the central investigation is set up and further complicated. They would also focus on the use of voice-over narration during select sequences. Crucial questions to pose to analyze the impact of the narration include:

- To what extent does the voice-over narration augment or contradict what the viewer witnesses on the screen?
- To what extent is the detective a reliable narrator of his own experiences?

Since students will have already viewed a noir film that did not rely on the detective as voice-over narrator, they could discuss why the use of that technique would not be in the spirit of the original novel (if they have read an excerpt) or the film. They could also try their hand at writing voice-over narration for one of the existing scenes in *The Maltese Falcon* to "try it on for size" (a Philip Marloweism).

In order to examine the film's cinematic style, Philip Marlowe's Los Angeles is typified by the sequence where he regains consciousness in a suspicious sanatorium that is rendered in vividly surreal detail in the novel in chapter 25 and translated into nightmarish images in the film adaptation. Access "Trapped in a Net" at 45:18–50:40 on a standard DVD version. The sequence's reliance on highly expressionistic techniques can be examined through the use of the following questions:

- What kinds of visual (images, special effects, editing) and sound techniques are used to depict Marlowe's hallucinations?
- What visual transition brings the viewer back to "reality"?
- Why leave the superimposed images of the web and smoke over Marlowe once he does regain consciousness?
- What does the voice-over narration help to clarify or elaborate for the viewer?

The more expressive techniques employed in *Murder, My Sweet* point the way to how later noir films will utilize highly formalistic lighting, camerawork, and décor to reflect the chaotic world of the alienated detective and the urban criminal underworld bathed in low-key pools of murky light and shadow that pick up the rain puddles dotting a deserted alleyway or the hard-edged shadows of venetian blinds against a stained wall of peeling paint.

Examining the visual style of each film brings into focus the unsettling atmosphere or mood created by the physical environment, one of the hallmarks of this genre. Even in the scenes of showcasing the bright, opulent wealth of Mr. Grayle's grand mansion or the Fatman's posh hotel suite, there is an undercurrent of tension and decadence that is made apparent through subject arrangement, formalistic camerawork, and dramatic shifts in lighting. Many times students gloss over detailed description of setting in a print text to arrive at character interaction, what they consider the meat of the narrative, not fully grasping the importance of literally setting the stage of the world that supports the character interaction. Close viewing supports close reading and vice versa.

In discussing his approach to repositioning an iconic genre in a new context, Rian Johnson noted:

> The decision to set it in high school was, initially at least, just to give it a different set of visual cues, so you couldn't just take a glimpse at guys in hats and shadowy alleyways and switch your brain into "I know what this is" autopilot mode. I wanted people to experience the genre in an unexpected way.[20]

A sample set of viewing questions to explore the connections between these two pulp fiction detective texts would include:

- How do the dialogue and visual details draw the viewer's attention to time elapsing?
- Even though the film is shot in color, how do certain sequences capture the physically dark world of film noir through the use of setting, lighting, camera filters, and camera angles?
- Select a sequence that best illustrates how Brendan's loss of control of the investigation is reflected through sound, lighting, camerawork, and subject arrangement.
- Compare the final conversation between Brendan and Laura with the final conversation between Sam and Brigid in *The Maltese Falcon* considering elements that include camerawork, lighting, dialogue, and costuming to evaluate how director Rian Johnson evokes the elements of a classic noir scene.

Once students identify and analyze the ways *Brick* draws on the hard-boiled detective stories of Hollywood's golden age, they should consider if Rian Johnson's affection and affinity for the genre yields a loving, well-crafted homage or a postmodern mash-up that really does not become a satisfying sum of its parts.

Post Viewing Activity: Focus on Cinematic Style

A culminating activity in the examination of this trio of detective films should include students addressing one of the following topics in a formal essay that pulls together all they have gleaned from reading and viewing.

Essay Topic: Entering the Dark World of Film Noir

Since one of the main interests of this genre is bringing the viewer into the underworld of crime and setting a mood around that world through the use of formalistic elements of mise en scène, discuss how *The Maltese Falcon* or *Murder, My Sweet*, and *Brick* illustrate how a director and his cinematographer use varying degrees of realism and formalism in how they create their "dark world."

Choose one scene from each film that provides the best example of how three elements of mise en scène are integrated in a realistic or formalistic way to dramatize that criminal or dangerous world. Make sure that you use very specific examples of each of the three techniques. Also consider how black and white versus color film affects the mise en scène of these films and the creation of mood.

FINAL THOUGHTS

Literary and cinematic traditions obviously do not exist in a vacuum. Contemporary fiction, film, and television draw on the rich resources of the past. The study of the noir detective can facilitate the examination of the promise and fallacy of the American dream as representative of popular fiction and film texts that emerged and gained popularity during the Depression and the postwar period of the 1940s.

These texts can provide a platform for examination of how a genre builds a set of clearly definable and durable conventions addressing setting, plot, character, and point of view that would augment the study of genre fiction as one of several genres treated, canonical texts covered in a survey of American literature as well as an investigation of detective literature's origins in the nineteenth century and the adaptation of pulp fiction novels to twentieth-century Hollywood films.

Students could follow the dark noir trail into other genres such as Philip K. Dick's science fiction novel *Do Androids Dream of Electric Sheep?* as adapted into Ridley Scott's neo-noir sci-fi film *Blade Runner*. Students might also enjoy television series such as CBS's *Elementary* and PBS's *Sherlock* that updates and transplants Conan Doyle's consulting detective to the twenty-first century. Another option might be the Sherlock Holmes films featuring Robert Downey, Jr. set in a less genteel nineteenth-century London. So, the game remains "afoot" for curious readers. As Dupin and Holmes reflected and refracted the values and manners of their era, so do the hard-boiled detectives of the Golden Age of Hollywood and the pulp fiction of the pre–World War II era.

NOTES

1. John J. Blaser and Stephanie L. M. Blaser, "Film Noir and the Hard-Boiled Detective Hero" (Film Noir Studies, last modified 2008).
2. "Herbert Hoover, 'Rugged Individualism' Campaign Speech" (Digital History, accessed March 15, 2014).
3. Thomas Schatz, "The Hardboiled-Detective Film." *Hollywood Genres: Formulas, Filmmaking, and the Studio System* (New York: Random House, 1981), 124.
4. Ibid., 125.
5. John G. Cawelti, *Adventure, Mystery, and Romance: Formula Stories as Art and Popular Culture* (Chicago: University of Chicago Press, 1976, accessed on March 15, 2014).
6. Ibid.
7. Schatz, 125.
8. Cawelti.
9. Ibid.
10. Dashiell Hammett, *The Maltese Falcon* (New York: Vintage Crime/Black Lizard, 1992), 4, 7.
11. Ibid., 3.
12. Ibid., 3.
13. Ibid., 3.
14. *The Maltese Falcon.* Directed by John Huston. Warner Brothers/Turner Classic Entertainment, 1941/2006. DVD.
15. Tim Ryan, "Interview with *Brick* Director Rian Johnson" (Rotten Tomatoes, Accessed March 15, 2014).
16. Ibid.
17. Schatz, 125.
18. Schatz, 116–17.
19. Graham Roberts and Heather Wallis, *Introducing Film* (New York: Oxford University Press, 2001), 5.
20. Ryan.

BIBLIOGRAPHY

Blaser, John J., and Stephanie L. M. Blaser. "Film Noir and the Hard-Boiled Detective Hero." Film Noir Studies. Last modified 2008. www.filmnoirstudies.com/essays/detective_hero.asp.
"The Blue Butterfly." *Castle*. Season 4, Episode 14. Directed by Chuck Bowman. Los Angeles, CA: ABC Studios, 2013.
Brick. Directed by Rian Johnson. Los Angeles: Universal Home Entertainment, 2006. DVD.
Burke, Lita. "Film Noir for Writers." Posted January 12, 2013. litaburke.com/worlds/film-noir-world/film-noir-for-writers-video/. Video.
Cawelti, John G. *Adventure, Mystery, and Romance: Formula Stories as Art and Popular Culture.* Chicago: University of Chicago Press, 1976. Accessed on March 15, 2014. faculty

.washington.edu/cbehler/teaching/coursenotes/hardboiled.html/.
Chandler, Raymond. *Farewell, My Lovely*. New York: Vintage Crime/Black Lizard, 2002.
Denton, William. "Twists, Slugs and Roscoes: A Glossary of Hardboiled Slang." Accessed on March 15, 2014. www.miskatonic.org/slang.html%20Miskatonic%20University%20Press/.
Digital History. "Herbert Hoover, 'Rugged Individualism' Campaign Speech." Accessed March 15, 2014. www.digitalhistory.uh.edu/disp_textbook.cfm?smtID=3&psid=1334.
"Film Noir." In *American Cinema* series. New York: The Annenberg/CPB Collection, 1994. Video.
Giannetti, Louis. *Understanding Movies*, 12th ed. Needham Heights, MS: Allyn and Bacon, 2010.
Hammett, Dashiell. *The Maltese Falcon*. New York: Vintage Crime/Black Lizard, 1992.
James, P. D. *Talking About Detective Fiction*. New York: Vintage, 2009.
Johnson, David T. "A Short List of Film Terms for Beginning Students in Film Courses." Accessed on March 15, 2014. faculty.salisbury.edu/~dtjohnson/filmterms.htm.
Johnson, Rian. "Brick: the treatment/novella type thing." Accessed on March 15, 2015. www.rcjohnso.com/brickscript/BrickNovella.pdf.
———. "Shooting Script of *Brick* by Rian Johnson." Accessed on March 15, 2015. www.rcjohnso.com/brickscript/BrickScript.pdf/.
Kaminsky, Stuart M. *American Film Genres*. 2nd ed. Chicago: Nelson-Hall, 1985.
Krueger, Ellen, and Mary T. Christel. *Seeing and Believing: How to Teach Media Literacy in the English Classroom*. Portsmouth, NH: Heinemann, 2001.
The Maltese Falcon. Directed by John Huston. Warner Brothers/Turner Classic Entertainment, 1941/2006. DVD.
Murder, My Sweet. Directed by Eward Dmytryk. Los Angeles: RKO/Turner Classic Entertainment & Warner Home Video, 1945/2004. DVD.
Naremore, James, ed. *Film Adaptation*. *Depth of Field* series. New Brunswick, NJ: Rutgers University Press, 2000.
Neale, Steve, ed. *Genre and Contemporary Hollywood*. London: BFI Publishing, 2002.
Roberts, Graham, and Heather Wallis. *Introducing Film*. New York: Oxford University Press, 2001.
Ryan, Tim. "Interview with *Brick* Director Rian Johnson." Rotten Tomatoes. Accessed on March 15, 2014. www.rottentomatoes.com/news/1646686/interview_with_quotbrickquot_director_rian_johnson/.
Schatz, Thomas. "The Hardboiled-Detective Film." *Hollywood Genres: Formulas, Filmmaking, and the Studio System*. New York: Random House, 1981.
Sobchack, Thomas, and Vivian C. Sobchack. "Genre Films." In *An Introduction to Film*. 2nd ed. Glenview, IL: Scott, Foresman and Company, 1997.

Chapter Two

A *PTI*-Inspired Pedagogy

Appropriating Sports-Talk Discussion Protocols to Facilitate Literature Study

Luke Rodesiler

THE SET-UP

The world of professional sports is a major player in popular culture and in the lives of today's adolescents. Professional sports are a fixture on television, attracting record-breaking viewership numbers with championship events.[1] Sports are also the subject of some of the world's most popular video games,[2] and the intersection of the sports world and the music industry, another major player in popular culture, has been explored through various documentary films in recent years.[3]

Those who doubt the place of professional sports in the lives of today's youth need only to take a brief stroll through a local public high school to see large numbers of adolescents sporting the jerseys of their favorite athletes and donning t-shirts, hats, and other accessories that pledge allegiance to their favorite professional and collegiate sports teams. For many youths, the sports world plays a prominent role in their out-of-school lives, as students participate in organized or pick-up sporting events, read about the outcomes of local and national games, simulate their favorite sports through a video-game console, discuss their favorite team's outlook for the upcoming season, manage teams in fantasy sports, or watch their favorite athletes on television once the school day ends.

On television, discussion about the sports world is as prevalent as—if not more prevalent than—the games themselves. Sports-talk programs like ESPN's *First Take* and *Around the Horn,* television shows featuring sports columnists discussing their views on the latest events in the sports world, are commonplace on the television viewer's guide. *Pardon the Interruption* is one such sports-talk program and one of the most widely acclaimed shows airing on ESPN.

Known widely by loyal viewers as *PTI*, *Pardon the Interruption* is a long-running, Emmy-winning television program in which hosts Tony Kornheiser and Michael Wilbon, former sportswriters for the *Washington Post*, discuss a variety of hot-button topics from the day in sports. Airing weekdays, each episode of *PTI* features a segment that follows one of several structured protocols intended to facilitate exchanges between the hosts as they predict the outcomes of sports-related storylines, critique the moves made by head coaches, and evaluate the performances of athletes competing in popular collegiate and professional sports.

As secondary English teachers consider ways to facilitate discussion among students reading shared literary texts, discussion protocols like those featured on *PTI* stand to provide the kinds of structures teachers can leverage to facilitate group talk that promotes sharing varied viewpoints and considering multiple perspectives while also offering a nod to students' interests in popular culture and a point of reference for the kinds of literacy practices in which students are asked to engage during class discussion.

Drawing from a cultural capital model, which acknowledges the ties between popular culture and students' social and cultural experiences,[4] adapting *PTI*-inspired protocols to support literature study is an effort to recognize students' interests in the world of sports and sports programming. As Marsh and Millard asserted, "a general sensitivity to [popular] culture . . . will allow teachers to create more powerful language work from the currency of pupils' own preoccupations."[5]

In this case, drawing upon the cultural appeal of a popular sports-talk television program to guide classroom discussion is intended to promote literacy learning by providing familiar structures for discussing subjective topics like those that often arise when talking sports and studying literature, respectively.

Though an episode of *PTI* may serve as a text worthy of critical study in its own right—for example, an exploration of the ways masculinity is conveyed through the loud, inflammatory discourse that arises between the show's hosts from time to time seems quite appropriate—the focus in this chapter is not on incorporating *PTI* as a cultural text for critical study. Rather, the focus of this chapter is placed squarely on appropriating discussion-based protocols employed on a popular sports-talk television program to engage students in group talk that advances the study of literature.

Just as hosts Kornheiser and Wilbon use *PTI*'s featured protocols to give structure to their discussions about topics from the sports world, teachers may appropriate those protocols to facilitate structured discussion-based literature study in the English language arts classroom and to support students as readers of rich literary texts by providing frames of reference that may be familiar to students who are consumers of and participants in sports culture.

REVIEW OF LITERATURE

The ideas in this chapter build upon scholarship that addresses the value of using discussion as an instructional method in the English language arts classroom and the benefits of tapping students' cultural knowledge and experiences to support literacy learning.

Discussion in the English Language Arts Classroom

Over time, much has been made about distinguishing between various types of group talk, including conversation, debate, and discussion. So which type of group talk results from the protocols featured in this chapter? It seems that classifying the group talk *PTI*-inspired protocols foster as "conversation" does not quite fit, for the protocols seem to offer more structure than the group talk philosopher Nicholas Burbules recognizes as conversation.[6]

Scholar James Dillon's strict vision of discussion, which sees the resolution of problems as a key feature,[7] also seems a bit narrow for the group talk generated by the *PTI*-inspired protocols. The protocols featured in this chapter are focused less on problem-solving and geared more toward the critique of literary characters, plot developments, and the like. Furthermore, when embracing Dillon's perspective on discussion, the group talk produced by some *PTI*-inspired protocols might be viewed as arguments or debates, for the protocols do call for students to take a position before discussion commences. Still, not all protocols featured here are intended to stoke debate.

Thus, for the purposes of this chapter, the synthesized definition of discussion offered by Stephen Brookfield and Stephen Preskill seems to describe the group talk produced when employing *PTI*-inspired protocols. Drawing upon the ideas of Burbules and Dillon, among others, Brookfield and Preskill recognize discussion as "an alternately serious and playful effort by a group of two or more to share views and engage in mutual and reciprocal critique."[8] Such a synthesized definition of discussion is fitting, for the *PTI*-inspired protocols described in this chapter make room for both seriousness and playfulness, allow for multiple students to express their views, and focus on the critique of common texts, as noted previously.

The benefits of using discussion as a pedagogical method are well documented. Scholars recognize discussion as a key method of developing understanding. For example, Judith Langer lauds literary discussion in the English language arts classroom for its capacity to enrich understandings by positioning students to examine multiple perspectives: the author's, their own, and those of their peers.[9]

In a similar fashion, Arthur Applebee recognizes the cultivation of diverse perspectives through discussion as an approach that is characteristic of effective instruction.[10] Furthermore, as Brookfield and Preskill contend, when teachers engage students in discussion they "show respect for students' voices and experiences"[11] and promote "habits of collaborative learning,"[12] each a worthy outcome regardless of one's pedagogical leanings. With such potential, discussion-based instructional approaches have much to offer students and teachers in the secondary English language arts classroom.

Bridging the Classroom Curriculum and Students' Funds of Knowledge

The thought of adapting sports-talk protocols to support discussion-based literature study is informed by scholarship that advocates bridging the formal curriculum of the classroom with students' *funds of knowledge*.[13] Scholars have posited that making connections between students' funds of knowledge, the cultural knowledge and practices students bring with them from beyond the classroom walls, and the classroom curriculum, including the knowledge and practices typically privileged in schools, stands to support student achievement.[14]

Henry Giroux and Roger Simon even contended that "[e]ducators who refuse to acknowledge popular culture as a significant basis of knowledge often devalue students by refusing to work with the knowledge that students actually have."[15] By accounting for students' knowledge of popular culture—including sports culture—teachers can offer students resources and frames of reference that stand to support literacy learning.[16]

The value of bridging classroom curricula and students' funds of knowledge is evident in the scholarship of Ernest Morrell and Jeffrey Duncan-Andrade.[17] Documenting a unit in which students studied popular music alongside canonical poetry, Morrell and Duncan-Andrade argued that "Hip-hop can be used as a bridge linking the seemingly vast span between the streets and the world of academics."[18] Including Hip-hop as a genre of poetry written in response to postindustrialism, Morrell and Duncan-Andrade built a curricular bridge by first engaging students in the practice of analyzing Hip-hop texts and then carrying that practice over to the study of canonical poetry of the Elizabethan Age, the Puritan Revolution, and other mandated historical/literary periods.

Morrell and Duncan-Andrade described how, for example, the study of "If I Ruled the World" by Nas, a modern Hip-hop artist, enriched students' understandings of metaphor, which students then carried over to the study of "Kubla Khan" by Samuel Taylor Coleridge, an eighteenth-century English poet.[19] In this way, Morrell and Duncan-Andrade exhibited how students' knowledge of and interests in popular culture stand to provide accessible frames of reference and resources that can facilitate literacy learning.

As Hall, et al. noted, "When students consume popular culture texts—print or nonprint—they do not just consume particular storylines and ideas; they also absorb structures that they recognize and that help them participate in future textual interactions."[20] As viewers of sports-talk programming and as participants in sports-centered discussions of their own, many students bring to the classroom funds of knowledge that can inform their participation in whole-class and small-group discussions.

PTI-inspired protocols stand to extend the bridge between students' cultural and academic experiences. Understanding the kinds of evaluations, comparisons, and predictions made on *PTI* about storylines, figures, and developments in the sports world stands to assist students in carrying out similar practices as they consider the plots, characters, and relationships depicted in the literature of the classroom.

Just as students might consider games they have watched, articles they have read, prior knowledge they may have, and their own personal experiences before making predictions about developments in the sports world, so too will they weigh their prior knowledge, personal experiences, and what they have read to date before making predictions about how events will unfold in the literature at hand. Bridging the discussions about sports that students watch and, in many cases, take part in outside of the classroom and the discussions of literature that take place inside the classroom stands to support students in constructing new knowledge in the English language arts.

CLASSROOM CONNECTIONS

This section features seven *PTI*-inspired protocols that have been appropriated to facilitate discussion among students, to nudge them toward richer understandings of classroom texts and of their own lived experiences. Each protocol includes a title, a brief overview, a five-point procedure, and sample prompts. The sample prompts are based upon popular American literature that might be used in a typical secondary English language arts classroom. The following seven titles are referenced:

- F. Scott Fitzgerald's *The Great Gatsby*
- Arthur Miller's *The Crucible*
- Harper Lee's *To Kill a Mockingbird*
- Mark Twain's *Adventures of Huckleberry Finn*

- Ken Kesey's *One Flew Over the Cuckoo's Nest*
- John Steinbeck's *Of Mice and Men*
- Tim O'Brien's *The Things They Carried*

The *PTI*-inspired protocols presented in this chapter address four tenets of classroom discussion as recognized by McCann, Johannessen, Kahn, and Flanagan.[21] First, in an effort to promote discussion, each protocol frames prompts in ways that push students to evaluate and synthesize ideas that arise in the text in question and in their own lived experiences. This approach stands in stark contrast to the practice of nudging students to seek out "correct" answers buried in the pages of the text. Instead, students are invited to examine the text closely and to draw upon their respective funds of knowledge to support them in making sense of the text at hand.

Second, by accounting for the time needed for students to gather their thoughts before engaging others in discussion, each protocol is designed intentionally to help students prepare for thoughtful discussion. With an approach akin to the writing-to-learn strategies advocated by scholars such as Duane Roen,[22] students are encouraged to generate thoughts about a text through writing before sharing those thoughts publicly with their peers.

Third, rather than limiting the number of students who may participate, each protocol allows teachers to include as many students in the discussion as contexts allow. As noted above, scholars such as Applebee and Langer encourage teachers to welcome the exploration of multiple and varied perspectives in the classroom. The protocols featured here are intended to support teachers in doing just that.

Fourth and finally, as many as half of the protocols have built-in answer choices that may help facilitate discussion. For example, the structure of a protocol like "Toss Up," which nudges students to choose between two options related to a topic in the text at hand and to defend their positions by drawing upon their understandings of the text and their own life experiences (e.g., "Is R. P. McMurphy's placement on the ward the result of a crafty ruse that allows him to complete his sentence in relative comfort, or does it seem to be an appropriate placement, given what you know about the character?"), provides a pair of options for students to build upon as discussion is initiated.

Readers of this chapter are encouraged to look for evidence of the four tenets outlined above as they examine the design of each *PTI*-inspired protocol detailed below.

Fair or Foul

The "Fair or Foul" protocol calls for students to assess whether actions, situations, or events that have occurred in the text at hand are acceptable (fair) or not (foul) and defend their positions by drawing upon the text and their lived experiences.

Procedure

- The teacher presents an action or situation that has occurred in the text at hand.
- Students assess whether the action/situation is "fair" or "foul."
- Students gather their thoughts in writing, justifying their assessments by drawing upon their understandings of the text, the context of the situation, and their lived experiences.
- The teacher invites students to discuss the prompt with one another.
- The process is repeated with new prompts as time permits or until topics are exhausted.

Sample Prompts

- *The Great Gatsby*

  - Engaging in illegal enterprise to get ahead in life à la Jay Gatsby: Fair or foul?
  - Drawing distinctions between "old money" and "new money": Fair or foul?

- *The Crucible*

  - Lying in an effort to protect a friend or loved one à la Elizabeth Proctor: Fair of foul?
  - Refusing to confess in order to protect your name, even if it means being put to death: Fair or foul?

Fortune Teller

The protocol for "Fortune Teller" prompts students to speculate about the occurrence of future events in the text at hand and draw upon their understandings of the text and their lived experiences to justify their thinking.

Procedure

- The teacher presents a prompt that features an event or situation that *might* occur in the text at hand.
- Students consider the potential for the future event or situation happening.
- Students gather their thoughts in writing, drawing upon their understandings of the text and their lived experiences to defend their thinking.

- The teacher invites students to discuss the prompt with one another.
- The process is repeated with new prompts as time permits or until topics are exhausted.

Sample Prompts

- *To Kill a Mockingbird*

  - Do you see Tom Robinson going free?
  - Do you see Jem's fears regarding his father's safety being realized?

- *The Great Gatsby*

  - Do you see Daisy giving up the wealthy lifestyle she has with Tom Buchanan to rekindle her relationship with Jay Gatsby?
  - Do you see Jay Gatsby living happily ever after with Daisy Buchanan?

Good Cop/Bad Cop

The protocol for "Good Cop/Bad Cop" is similar to the "Fair or Foul" protocol, though paired students or paired groups of students must take opposing positions on a single event or development in a text, either in defense of it (Good Cop) or against it (Bad Cop), drawing upon the text at hand and their lived experiences to justify their positions.

Procedure

- The teacher presents an event or development that allows students to take opposing sides.
- Students select a role, either Good Cop or Bad Cop.
- Students make their cases in writing, rationalizing their thinking by drawing upon their understandings of the text at hand and their lived experiences.
- The teacher invites students to discuss the prompt with one another.
- The process is repeated with new prompts as time permits or until topics are exhausted.

Sample Prompts

- *Adventures of Huckleberry Finn*

  - Case #1: Huck Finn faking his death to escape from his father.
  - Case #2: Huck Finn helping Jim, a runaway slave.

- *One Flew Over the Cuckoo's Nest*

  - Case #1: R. P. McMurphy failing to join Cheswick in his stand against Nurse Ratched.
  - Case #2: Chief Bromden smothering R. P. McMurphy.

Odds Makers

The "Odds Makers" protocol is similar to the protocol for "Fortune Teller," except students are asked to make predictions in the form of a percentage about the likelihood of a future event occurring in the text at hand, rationalizing their predictions by drawing upon the text and their lived experiences.

Procedure

- The teacher presents a prompt that features an event or situation that *might* occur in the text at hand.
- Students make a prediction in the form of a percentage about the likelihood of the future event/situation occurring.
- Students gather their thoughts in writing, defending their predictions by drawing upon their understandings of the text and their lived experiences.
- The teacher invites students to discuss the prompt with one another.
- The process is repeated with new prompts as time permits or until topics are exhausted.

Sample Prompts

- *Of Mice and Men*

  - What is the likelihood that George, Lennie, and Candy will fulfill their shared dream of living and working on their own farm?
  - What is the likelihood that Lennie can avoid the wrath of Curley and his mob?

- *Adventures of Huckleberry Finn*

  - Knowing what we do about Huckleberry Finn, what is the likelihood that he can continue living the civilized life under the guardianship of Widow Douglas?
  - What is the likelihood that Jim successfully secures his freedom?

Report Card

The "Report Card" protocol calls for students to evaluate various events or situations from the text at hand as presented by the teacher, assign letter grades, and rationalize their evaluations by drawing upon the text at hand and their lived experiences.

Procedure

- The teacher presents a prompt that features an event or situation that *has already occurred* in the text at hand.
- Students assign a letter grade to the event/situation.
- Students gather their thoughts in writing, justifying their grades by drawing upon their understandings of the text at hand and their lived experiences.
- The teacher opens the floor, inviting students to share their grades and rationales and to discuss each other's ideas.
- The process is repeated with new prompts as time permits or until topics are exhausted.

Sample Prompts

- *The Things They Carried*

    - Reluctant to go to war, Tim O'Brien heads to the Canadian border. What's the grade?
    - Tim O'Brien ultimately goes to war because he is too embarrassed not to go. What's the grade?

- *Of Mice and Men*

    - George continues to befriend and look after Lennie, despite the trouble Lennie causes him. What's the grade?
    - George kills Lennie before Curley and his men get to him. What's the grade?

Toss Up

The "Toss Up" protocol calls for students to choose between two options related to a topic in the text at hand and defend their positions by drawing upon their understandings of the text and their lived experiences.

Procedure

- The teacher presents a prompt that allows students to choose from a pair of options related to the text at hand.
- Students choose between the two options.
- Students gather their thoughts in writing, rationalizing their selections by drawing upon their understandings of the text at hand and their lived experiences.
- The teacher invites students to discuss the prompt with one another.
- The process is repeated with new prompts as time permits or until topics are exhausted.

Sample Prompts

- *One Flew Over the Cuckoo's Nest*

  - Is R. P. McMurphy's placement on the ward the result of a crafty ruse that allows him to complete his sentence in relative comfort, or does it seem to be an appropriate placement, given what you know about the character?
  - Who is to blame for the death of Billy Bibbit: R. P. McMurphy or Nurse Ratched?

- *The Things They Carried*

  - What takes a heavier toll on soldiers at war: the weight of the physical burdens they must carry or the weight of mental burdens (i.e., fears, anxieties, etc.) they carry with them in a figurative sense?
  - What's more important in the composition of a story based on real events: happening truth or story truth?

What's the Word?

The "What's the Word?" protocol calls for students to select a word to complete a statement about a character, relationship, event, or other element of a text and defend their selection by drawing upon their understandings of the text at hand and their lived experiences.

Procedure

- The teacher reads a prompt consisting of a partial sentence structured in a way that it nudges students toward taking an informed position about an event, character, or development in the text at hand.

- Students choose an apt word or phrase to complete the sentence in a thoughtful manner.
- Students gather their thoughts in writing, rationalizing their word choice by drawing upon their understandings of the text at hand and their lived experiences.
- The teacher opens the floor, inviting students to share their words and rationales and to discuss each other's ideas.
- The process is repeated with new prompts as time permits or until topics are exhausted.

Sample Prompts

- *The Crucible*

  - Mary Warren folding in court under the pressure of accusations from Abigail Williams and the other girls is _____.
  - John Proctor tearing up his signed confession is _____.

- *To Kill a Mockingbird*

  - Tom Robinson's conviction is _____.
  - Boo Radley rescuing Scout from the attack of Bob Ewell is _____.

FINAL THOUGHTS

In addition to addressing core tenets for facilitating discussion, the *PTI*-inspired protocols detailed above support students as readers of rich literary texts. Researchers have stressed that reading is a complex task that draws upon a host of cognitive strategies,[23] and *PTI*-inspired protocols may foster a number of strategies that support students as active readers: (a) making connections; (b) making predictions; (c) evaluating texts; and (d) tapping prior knowledge and previous experiences.

PTI-inspired protocols may support students in making the text-to-self, text-to-text, and text-to-world connections that Cris Tovani and other literacy scholars contend support comprehension.[24] Invited to draw upon the text at hand and their lived experiences, students may be moved to make text-to-self connections as they rationalize their positions in "Good Cop/Bad Cop" or as they justify their selections in "Toss Up." Likewise, a protocol such as "What's the Word?" opens the door for students to compare the developments of one text to the happenings in another text they have read (e.g., describing Chief Bromden's smothering of R. P. McMurphy as "Smallish" and then drawing parallels between the merciful act in Kesey's *One Flew*

Over the Cuckoo's Nest and George Milton's compassionate killing of Lennie Small at the close of Steinbeck's *Of Mice and Men*).

In addition, a protocol like "Fair or Foul" seems apt for students connecting the happenings in a novel to events playing out in the world at large (e.g., decrying Jay Gatsby's efforts to get ahead through illegal activity by recalling the fallout of notable professional athletes admitting to the use of performance-enhancing drugs in recent years). In this way, *PTI*-inspired protocols may aid students in making the connections that support comprehension, and that's before the work of discussing ideas with other students even begins.

As Langer explained, when entering a literary orientation, readers often find themselves "reaching toward a horizon of possibilities"[25] as they speculate about what is happening in the text and make predictions about what is yet to come in the pages to be read. Specific *PTI*-inspired protocols, such as "Fortune Teller" and "Odds Makers," invite students to make predictions based on their understandings of the text at hand and their lived experiences.

For example, if predicting whether or not Tom Robinson will go free in *To Kill a Mockingbird*, students must consider the novel's setting, weigh what they have learned about racism during that time in that specific region, and speculate what the possible verdicts might mean for other characters and for the development of the remainder of the novel. Considering such aspects—and contemplating the perspectives offered by others—is sure to inform the meaning students make of the literature they read.

Evaluating a literary text and the characters, events, and relationships it presents is another active reading strategy endorsed by scholars.[26] Multiple protocols presented in this chapter position students to form opinions and make evaluative judgments about what they have read. For example, in response to the "Report Card" protocol, students must assess the developments of a novel, pass judgment in the form of a letter grade, and explain their position by drawing upon their understandings of the text and their lived experiences.

When making evaluations, students are likely to find themselves employing other cognitive reading strategies. Students might monitor the development of the plot, question a character's motivations, and predict the fallout of a character's actions to inform their evaluations. In this way, *PTI*-inspired protocols stand to foster a wide range of active reading strategies.

Undergirding the cognitive strategies mentioned above, good readers also tap their prior knowledge and previous experiences as they read.[27] Every one of the *PTI*-inspired protocols stands to help students consider their prior knowledge and past experiences in relation to the characters, events, and relationships depicted in the literature studied. Whether drawing connections between texts, making predictions regarding the evolution of characters' relationships, or evaluating a character's actions, students are encouraged to do so in light of the knowledge they have constructed over time and their own lived experiences.

The *PTI*-inspired protocols detailed above are intended to be flexible. They may be used to explore a wide range of texts that far exceeds the seven titles referenced above in the interest of providing recognizable examples. Beyond print-based texts, the protocols may also be used to explore nonprint texts, including major motion pictures, short films, and episodes of television programs. Regardless of the text in question, *PTI*-inspired protocols offer teachers a creative way to structure group talk that promotes critical reading and collaborative meaning-making.

In line with the flexible nature of each protocol, English language arts teachers may opt to adapt the suggested procedures to fit their own unique contexts. For example, though intended to facilitate group talk, each protocol may be reduced to steps one through three in situations where time for rich discussion is limited or in circumstances where attending to focused writing is the lesson's aim.

Conversely, though each protocol accounts for students writing in order to think carefully about their responses to a prompt, teachers may encounter situations in which they determine that facilitating discussion without providing such writing time would be appropriate. However, as McCann, Johannessen, Kahn, and Flanagan suggest, providing time for students to write in response to a prompt may go a long way toward facilitating thoughtful classroom discussion.[28] Thus, though the protocols are flexible, teachers might want to think carefully before deviating from the recommended procedures.

Additionally, as appropriate, teachers might consider having students work with a partner or in small groups to complete the second and third steps of each protocol collaboratively before facilitating a whole-class discussion. Again, each teacher ought to make such decisions based on the needs of students in the unique context of the classroom. Ultimately, the *PTI*-inspired protocols are intended to offer structure without being overly rigid, allowing teachers to facilitate group talk in ways that will meet the needs of all students.

NOTES

1. Maury Brown, "Game 1 of the NBA Finals Generates Record TV Ratings for ABC," *Forbes*, June 13, 2012, www.forbes.com/sites/maurybrown/2012/06/13/game-1-of-the-nba-finals-generates-record-tv-ratings-for-abc; Scott Collins, "Super Bowl 2014 was a Blowout—and Most-Watched TV Show in History," *Los Angeles Times*, February 3, 2014, articles.latimes.com/2014/feb/03/entertainment/la-et-st-super-bowl-2014-most-watched-tv-show-in-history-despite-blowout-20140203.

2. Roger Bennett, "EA Sports FIFA Soccer's U.S. Boom," *Bloomberg Businessweek*, September 20, 2012, www.businessweek.com/articles/2012-09-20/ea-sports-fifa-soccers-u-dot-s-dot-boom; John Gaudiosi, "EA Sports Kicks off NFL Season Early with Record Madden 13 Sales, Players Talk Virtual Game," *Forbes*, September 4, 2012, www.forbes.com/sites/

johngaudiosi/2012/09/04/ea-sports-kicks-off-nfl-season-early-with-record-madden-13-sales-players-talk-virtual-game.

3. Luke Rodesiler, "More Than a Game: Examining Sport and Society with ESPN's 30 for 30," *Screen Education* 64 (2011): 76.

4. Margaret C. Hagood, Donna E. Alvermann, and Alison Heron-Hruby, *Bring It to Class: Unpacking Popular Culture in Literacy Learning* (New York: Teachers College Press, 2010), 29.

5. Jackie Marsh and Elaine Millard, *Literacy and Popular Culture: Using Children's Culture in the Classroom* (Thousand Oaks, CA: Sage, 2000), 2.

6. Nicholas Burbules, *Dialogue in Teaching: Theory and Practice* (New York: Teachers College Press, 1993), 112.

7. James T. Dillon, *Using Discussion in Classrooms* (Buckingham: Open University Press, 1994), 8.

8. Stephen D. Brookfield and Stephen Preskill, *Discussion as a Way of Teaching: Tools and Techniques for Democratic Classrooms*, 2nd ed. (San Francisco: Jossey-Bass, 2005), 6.

9. Judith Langer, *Envisioning Literature: Literary Understanding and Literature Instruction*, 2nd ed. (New York: Teachers College Press, 2011), 54.

10. Arthur N. Applebee, "Engaging Students in the Disciplines of English: What are Effective Schools Doing?" *English Journal* 91, no. 6 (2002): 33.

11. Stephen D. Brookfield and Stephen Preskill, *Discussion as a Way of Teaching: Tools and Techniques for Democratic Classrooms* (San Francisco: Jossey-Bass, 2005), 29.

12. Ibid., 33.

13. Luis C. Moll, and Norma Gonzalez, "Lessons from Research with Language-Minority Children," *Journal of Reading Behavior* 26, no. 4 (1994): 443.

14. Leigh A. Hall, Leslie D. Burns, and Elizabeth Carr Edwards, *Empowering Struggling Readers: Practices for the Middle Grades* (New York: Guilford, 2011), 57.

15. Henry A. Giroux and Roger I. Simon, *Popular Culture: Schooling and Everyday Life* (Granby: Bergin & Garvey, 1989), 3.

16. Anne Haas Dyson, *The Brothers and Sisters Learn to Write: Popular Literacies in Childhood and School Cultures* (New York: Teachers College Press, 2003), 83.

17. Ernest Morrell and Jeff Duncan-Andrade, "What They Do Learn in Schools: Hip-hop as a Bridge to Canonical Poetry," in *What They Don't Learn in School: Literacy in the Lives of Urban Youth*, ed. Jabari Mahiri (New York: Peter Lang, 2004), 247–68; Ernest Morrell and Jeffrey M. R. Duncan-Andrade, "Promoting Academic Literacy with Urban Youth through Engaging Hip-hop Culture," *English Journal* 91, no. 6 (2002): 88–92.

18. Ibid., 89.

19. Ernest Morrell and Jeff Duncan-Andrade, "What They Do Learn in Schools: Hip-hop as a Bridge to Canonical Poetry," in *What They Don't Learn in School: Literacy in the Lives of Urban Youth*, ed. Jabari Mahiri (New York: Peter Lang, 2004), 260.

20. Leigh A. Hall, Leslie D. Burns, and Elizabeth Carr Edwards, *Empowering Struggling Readers: Practices for the Middle Grades* (New York: Guilford, 2011), 57.

21. Thomas M. McCann, Larry R. Johannessen, Elizabeth Kahn, and Joseph M. Flanagan, *Talking in Class: Using Discussions to Enhance Teaching and Learning* (Urbana: National Council of Teachers of English, 2006), 15.

22. Duane H. Roen, "A Writing-to-Learn/Reader-Response Approach to Teaching Antigone," in *Reader Response in Secondary and College Classrooms*, ed. Nicholas J. Karolides (Mahwah: Lawrence Erlbaum Associates, 2000), 225.

23. Deborah Appleman, *Adolescent Literacy and the Teaching of Reading* (Urbana: National Council of Teachers of English, 2010), 13.

24. Cris Tovani, *I Read It, but I Don't Get It: Comprehension Strategies for Adolescent Readers* (Portland: Stenhouse, 2000), 69.

25. Judith A. Langer, *Envisioning Literature: Literary Understanding and Literature Instruction*, 2nd ed. (New York: Teachers College Press, 2011), 28.

26. Deborah Appleman, *Adolescent Literacy and the Teaching of Reading* (Urbana: National Council of Teachers of English, 2010), 14.

27. Ibid.

28. Thomas M. McCann, Larry R. Johannessen, Elizabeth Kahn, and Joseph M. Flanagan, *Talking in Class: Using Discussions to Enhance Teaching and Learning* (Urbana: National Council of Teachers of English, 2006), 53.

BIBLIOGRAPHY

Applebee, Arthur N. "Engaging Students in the Disciplines of English: What Are Effective Schools Doing?" *English Journal* 91, no. 6 (2002): 30–36.

Appleman, Deborah. *Adolescent Literacy and the Teaching of Reading: Lessons for Teachers of Literature*. Urbana: National Council of Teachers of English, 2010.

Bennett, Roger. "EA Sports FIFA Soccer's U.S. Boom." *Bloomberg Businessweek*. September 20, 2012. www.businessweek.com/articles/2012-09-20/ea-sports-fifa-soccers-u-dot-s-dot-boom.

Brookfield, Stephen D., and Stephen Preskill. *Discussion as a Way of Teaching: Tools and Techniques for Democratic Classrooms*, 2nd ed. San Francisco: Jossey-Bass, 2005.

Brown, Maury. "Game 1 of the NBA Finals Generates Record TV Ratings for ABC." *Forbes*. June 13, 2012. www.forbes.com/sites/maurybrown/2012/06/13/game-1-of-the-nba-finals-generates-record-tv-ratings-for-abc.

Burbules, Nicholas. *Dialogue in Teaching: Theory and Practice*. New York: Teachers College Press, 1993.

Collins, Scott. "Super Bowl 2014 was a Blowout—and Most-Watched TV Show in History." *Los Angeles Times*. February 3, 2014. articles.latimes.com/2014/feb/03/entertainment/la-et-st-super-bowl-2014-most-watched-tv-show-in-history-despite-blowout-20140203.

Dillon, James T. *Using Discussion in Classrooms*. Buckingham: Open University Press, 1994.

Dyson, Anne Haas. *The Brothers and Sisters Learn to Write: Popular Literacies in Childhood and School Cultures*. New York: Teachers College Press, 2003.

Fitzgerald, F. Scott. *The Great Gatsby*. New York: Scribner, 2004.

Gaudiosi, John. "EA Sports Kicks off NFL Season Early with Record *Madden 13* Sales, Players Talk Virtual Game." *Forbes*. September 4, 2012. www.forbes.com/sites/johngaudiosi/2012/09/04/ea-sports-kicks-off-nfl-season-early-with-record-madden-13-sales-players-talk-virtual-game.

Giroux, Henry A., and Roger I. Simon. *Popular Culture: Schooling and Everyday Life*. Granby, MA: Bergin & Garvey, 1989.

Hagood, Margaret C., Donna E. Alvermann, and Alison Heron-Hruby. *Bring It to Class: Unpacking Pop Culture in Literacy Learning*. New York: Teachers College Press, 2010.

Hall, Leigh A., Leslie D. Burns, and Elizabeth Carr Edwards. *Empowering Struggling Readers: Practices for the Middle Grades*. New York: Guilford, 2011.

Kesey, Ken. *One Flew Over the Cuckoo's Nest*. New York: Signet, 1963.

Langer, Judith A. *Envisioning Literature: Literary Understanding and Literature Instruction*, 2nd ed. New York: Teachers College Press, 2011.

Lee, Harper. *To Kill a Mockingbird*. New York: Warner Books, 1982.

Marsh, Jackie, and Elaine Millard. *Literacy and Popular Culture: Using Children's Culture in the Classroom*. Thousand Oaks, CA: Sage, 2000.

McCann, Thomas M., Larry R. Johannessen, Elizabeth Kahn, and Joseph M. Flanagan. *Talking in Class: Using Discussion to Enhance Teaching and Learning*. Urbana: National Council of Teachers of English, 2006.

Miller, Arthur. *The Crucible*. New York: Penguin Books, 1995.

Moll, Luis C., and Norma Gonzalez. "Lessons from Research with Language-Minority Children." *Journal of Reading Behavior* 26, no. 4 (1994): 439–56.

Morrell, Ernest, and Jeff Duncan-Andrade. "What They Do Learn in Schools: Hip-hop as a Bridge to Canonical Poetry." In *What They Don't Learn in School: Literacy in the Lives of Urban Youth*. Edited by Jabari Mahiri, 247–268. New York: Peter Lang, 2004.

Morrell, Ernest, and Jeffrey M. R. Duncan-Andrade. "Promoting Academic Literacy with Urban Youth through Engaging Hip-hop Culture," *English Journal* 91, no. 6 (2002): 88–92.

O'Brien, Tim. *The Things They Carried*. New York: Broadway Books, 1998.

Rodesiler, Luke. "More Than a Game: Examining Sport and Society with ESPN's 30 for 30." *Screen Education* 64 (2011): 72–78.

Roen, Duane H. "A Writing-to-Learn/Reader-Response Approach to Teaching *Antigone*." In *Reader Response in Secondary and College Classrooms*. Edited by Nicholas J. Karolides, 225–234. Mahwah, NJ: Lawrence Erlbaum Associates, 2000.

Steinbeck, John. *Of Mice and Men*. New York: Penguin Books, 1993.

Tovani, Cris. *I Read It, but I Don't Get It: Comprehension Strategies for Adolescent Readers*. Portland: Stenhouse, 2000.

Twain, Mark. *The Adventures of Huckleberry Finn*. Berkeley: University of California Press, 2001.

Chapter Three

Whose Side Is He On?

Teaching Complex Characters with Novels and Films

Carmela Delia Lanza

THE SET-UP

In her memoir, *Reading Lolita in Tehran: A Memoir in Books*, Azar Nafisi participates in a discussion with her students on the F. Scott Fitzgerald novel, *The Great Gatsby*. Despite the fact that this takes place in Iran in the late 1970s to early 1980s during a revolutionary time, Dr. Nafisi experiences what most language arts teachers experience while teaching a novel: the need to find a lesson or moral to the story.

Some students in the discussion want to view Gatsby's world as good versus evil, or perceive that one character is the symbol of greed. However, Dr. Nafisi informs her students that "a novel is not an allegory . . . it is the sensual experience of another world."[1] She then goes on to say, "If you don't enter the world, hold your breath with the characters and become involved in their destiny, you won't be able to empathize, and empathy is the heart of the novel. That is how you read a novel, you inhale the experience."[2] If students do not find empathy for the characters, they will not engage in a holistic relationship with the text.

Most high school English teachers at some point during the academic year focus on literary analysis and in particular the study of character. Unfortunately when we look at language arts textbooks for the analysis of character, we are still looking at definitions that create binary relationships: characters who are evil or characters who are good. Often students are asked to make distinctions between characters who are protagonists or antagonists, but what do we do with characters who do not fit into those neatly defined categories?

It is unheard of for a literature textbook to ask students to inhale the literature or to suggest that we have to be open to the complexity of the characters and not view them in a one-dimensional space. Well-created and well-written characters, from the students' readings, offer shades of personality; they are characters who make choices and decisions that often cause others to suffer or may provide moments of forgiveness or salvation. But how are those complex characters taught in a language arts classroom?

Most English teachers know the frustration when having spent weeks on a Shakespeare play or a Charles Dickens novel, the students are still responding with "Spark Note" responses. They are just not getting the nuances of Richard III's deformity and his internal suffering. They are still viewing Miss Havisham as some kind of evil, aging witch, and there is no class discussion on Miss Havisham as a dynamic character who once was a girl with a sense of hope and joy. Of course, popular culture does not always help students when they are bombarded with stereotypes from advertising to song lyrics. In this world of instant gratification, it has become all too easy for students to label and categorize others.

However blaming popular culture and initiating some kind of discussion about the "good old days" of instruction is not the answer. The fault is not popular culture but what we choose to bring into our classrooms for analysis and discussion as part of our ongoing study of canonical literature. From the time students begin their education in elementary school, most language arts teachers rely on the binary relationship of protagonist and antagonist.

This is certainly emphasized in the textbooks used when there are lessons on characterization. Language arts teachers emphasize to our students that the antagonist is the opposite of the protagonist, and what do students learn? They view most (if not all) characters in these binary and therefore simplistic and limiting categories of good and bad, right and wrong, and so forth. At some point educators are hoping for more from their students.

Language arts teachers want students to see the complexities of characters who make choices and must deal with the consequences of those choices. It is imperative that students understand the context of culture, gender, and all the other factors that truly create characters in literature. Perhaps language arts educators need to start questioning these tidy definitions of characterization that are often presented in textbooks. For example in the McDougall Littell's online eleventh grade literature textbook, *ClassZone: McDougal Littell Literature, Grade 11*, the "Analysis Frames" for fiction offers the following questions for character analysis:

> Who are the main characters and the minor characters in this story? What do you learn about the characters through their physical appearance, thoughts, and

speech? What do you learn from the comments of other characters, or the narrator? In what ways does each character react to other people or events? What do these reactions reveal about him or her? What reasons might he or she have had for reacting this way? In what ways does each character change over the course of the story?[3]

These questions focus on factual responses involving "who" or "what," but where are the "why" questions? Where are the questions that lead students to consider the complexities of character and the complexities of human behavior? In the "Evaluate and Critique" section of this worksheet, the student is asked:

Evaluate the main character. Is he or she a good person? A smart person? Do you agree with his or her actions or opinions? Support your evaluation with evidence from the story.[4]

These questions only offer students two choices regarding character analysis—is the character good or bad? And the questions imply there is only one or possibly two ways of viewing the character. That kind of questioning does not promote critical thinking.

Another educational book publisher and distributor, Scholastic, includes a worksheet, "Understanding 'Character' Analysis," that defines a character as "a person, place, or thing in a work of literature." It then asks the student to bring in a "class example" and then a personal example of a character.[5] This is another example of an activity that will not promote critical thinking for students regarding character. Unfortunately many teachers rely on these worksheets for the teaching of character analysis.

There are many lessons offered online for teachers that teach characterization. Unfortunately those lessons do not promote critical thinking and creativity. For example, teachers will find graphic organizers that list characters in the following categories: protagonist, antagonist, minor character, flat character, dynamic characters, static characters, and round characters. Often the graphic organizers ask the students to choose one symbol that represents the character in the novel or story.

Other graphic organizers ask the student to identify the main character, antagonist, and so forth, and then fill in important details on the character in a chart format. These graphic organizers are modeled from the textbooks' approach on character analysis. They are mostly a type of fill-in-the-blank assignment that requires little thought in the response.

There are even lists of character traits that students can access, which indicate whether certain traits are positive or negative. For example, a negative trait would be "poverty in present generation" but a positive trait would be "wealth in present generation."[6] This value judgment would be debatable with many educators and students regarding diversity, inclusion, and socioeconomic issues.

If teachers want to move beyond worksheets and fill-in-the blank charts, they might want to consider the use of film as an effective resource regarding the study and analysis of character. Film can help students understand the depth and nuances of character. When most people think of movies, they can easily refer to many characters who exist and behave in the world because of a myriad of circumstances and experiences.

Even the character Darth Vader, who has transformed into a visual icon of evil, has a history and a context for his violent and ultimately self-defeating actions. At some point Darth Vader's inability to endure loss and suffering turns him into a monster. Yet is there justification in calling Darth Vader the antagonist of the Star War films? Does that character simply fit that category?

Students, who are now experiencing characters like Tony Soprano, in the TV series *The Sopranos* or Walter White in the TV series *Breaking Bad* need more analytical work regarding the analysis of character. Film and television offer characters who make amoral choices but who are also capable of loyalty and love. This ambiguity needs to be addressed in the language arts classroom; it is no longer a world where all characters are either good or bad, and we have really never lived in a world like that anyway.

For example, Shakespeare's King Lear is a man who makes foolish and dangerous choices. He chooses to disinherit his youngest daughter because he is disappointed in how she responds to his question, "How much do you love me?" But he is also an individual who is capable of love, compassion, and vulnerability. Since this is a very challenging Shakespeare play, students can start with the nuances and gray area of character using film and then move on to challenging texts like a Shakespeare play or a William Faulkner novel.

However, it is not enough for a language arts teacher to show a film adaption of a novel and ask the students how is the movie different from the book, or to show a movie in class once a term as some kind of "reward" or "treat." In *Seeing & Believing: How To Teach Media Literacy in the English Classroom,* educators Ellen Krueger and Mary T. Christel comment on how the use of film in the classroom has been vilified and that watching a film at the end of a semester has been viewed as a "dessert after a multicourse repast of reading, writing, and testing."[7] It is also not effective teaching if teachers delegate a "movie day" when they take a sick day.

Often administration mandates that teachers are not allowed to show films before a holiday break or on an early dismissal day. Perhaps this is a consequence of teachers using film to get to the end of a semester. That kind of instruction undermines the important role of popular culture in a language arts curriculum. Popular culture deserves a legitimate space in a language arts curriculum. Students need the ability to read all kinds of texts including film and television. The use of popular culture validates students' lives and interests, and it reflects the complex experience of being human. Therefore, using film to supplement literature studies will help students dig deeper into the many layers of character analysis to craft more effective and thoughtful arguments.

REVIEW OF LITERATURE

The use of popular culture in the classroom continues to be a topic for discussion among educators. In 1996, the National Council of Teachers of English (NCTE) and International Reading Association (IRA) mentioned the importance analyzing visual texts, like film, in their *Standards for the English Language Arts*.[8] These standards were reaffirmed in 2012 by the NCTE Executive Committee. In their 2012 document, NCTE enthusiastically supported the study of film and television in connection to literacy. NCTE stated:

> Being literate in contemporary society means being active, critical, and creative users not only of print and spoken language but also of the visual language of film and television, commercial and political advertising, photography, and more.[9]

NCTE goes on to acknowledge the concern that having students watching films is a passive activity that does not support or encourage literacy. But NCTE argues "we cannot erase visual texts from modern [society] . . . we must therefore challenge students to analyze critically the texts they view."[10] The key is that students need to engage with the visual texts.

If film encourages passivity it may be that students are not given challenging assignments regarding film. It may be that students are simply asked to watch a film and nothing more in an English classroom. If used with thoughtful planning, visual texts give students the skills to analyze literature and to analyze the world around them.

NCTE also addresses how certain texts should be chosen for English programs. NCTE maintains "students benefit from reading texts that challenge and provoke them," and the texts should "reflect the diversity of the United States' population in terms of gender, age, social class, religion, and ethnicity."[11] Popular culture provides complex texts and also reflects the multicultural world students live in.

When teachers bring in rap music, fashion, videos, film, and television shows, students are given the opportunity to discuss issues regarding ethnicity, social class, and gender. In particular, film, Hollywood movies or art films, offers a myriad of texts that can generate writing, reading, and discussion in any English classroom. A plethora of teaching books focused on the using of film in the classroom has grown dramatically in recent years. NCTE has published titles like *Great Films and How to Teach Them, Reading in the Dark, Reading Shakespeare Film First,* and *Reading in the Reel World.* In fact on the NCTE website there is a category for "Teaching with Film in the English Classroom" that is a useful resource and that clearly shows NCTE's support of film and the use of popular culture in the English classroom.

There are some educators who support the use of film in the classroom with reluctant readers or students who have completely stopped reading. In Kjersti VanSlyke-Briggs's article, "Using the Arts to Fend Off Alliteracy," VanSlyke-Briggs maintains that by supporting the traditional readings with texts like film, photography, and interviews, students who were aliterate gained the confidence to engage with the more traditionally academic texts in the classroom.[12]

Along with helping students who struggle with literacy, film is also used as companion texts to canonical works. Krueger and Christel suggest partnering certain films with certain canonical texts like using the film "The Dresser" with Shakespeare's *King Lear* or the film "Apocalypse Now" with Joseph Conrad's *Heart of Darkness*.[13]

Krueger and Christel also offer an activity, "A Way In: Character Dossier Activity," which helps students develop a more in-depth relationship with a character in a novel. They use Charles Dickens's novel, *Great Expectations*, but this activity can be used with any novel or short story. The student must "create a dossier for his character based on textual support" and several journal writings must focus on the character's traits and actions (personal habits, physical appearance, important possessions, etc.) and how the character changes throughout the novel. The student then must do a comparison and contrast to how the character is portrayed in a film by the actor.[14]

For some educators popular culture offers an opportunity for students to engage in texts that are often marginalized and considered unworthy of serious study in a classroom. Ernest Morrell supports the idea that bringing popular culture in the classroom empowers students who often feel disconnected with traditional literature that does not offer a diverse vision of the world. Morrell supports the philosophy that popular culture offers more for multiethnic students, especially students in urban communities.[15] Popular culture bridges the student's everyday life to critical thinking and literacy.

In an interview with Per Seyersted in 1976, Leslie Silko, Native American woman writer, expresses her general disinterest in political groups because, in addressing societal issues like racism, gender rights, and the human injustices, they ignore "all of the personal subtleties and the unique experiences and aspects of this individual's life which have brought this person to this place and time."[16]

This act of ignoring the subtleties of a person can also be said when we look at how characterization is taught in most high school language arts classrooms. Speaking from the writer's point of view, Silko claims "it is much more important to explore all of the possible depths and all of the possible details of a person's life and to range through time—back to a time before the person was born,"[17] and that is exactly what she does regarding the character, Tayo, in her novel, *Ceremony*.

Although *Ceremony* is usually found on college reading lists, it has gained some popularity in the high school language arts classroom. According to Allan Chavkin, the editor of the book, *Leslie Marmon's Silko's Ceremony: A Casebook*, "with the opening up of the canon and with the interest in multiculturalism in recent years, the novel is not only frequently assigned required reading for university students but also for some advanced high school students."[18]

It has been a novel that has appeared on the Advanced Placement literature suggested reading list and has often been included in any high school elective course that focuses on Native American literature. It is one of the few Native American novels that has been reviewed, analyzed, and evaluated beyond its contribution to multicultural literature.

Along with having difficulties with how the novel is structured because of Silko's use of nonlinear time and a shifting narrative, students will also struggle with the main character, Tayo, a young man from Laguna Pueblo in New Mexico who joins the military to fight in World War II. In order for students to connect with the novel and explore themes, they will need to understand Tayo, and that is where an English teacher can use film to introduce students to characterization that is challenging and will encourage critical analysis.

Like other texts from popular culture, film is an effective way to begin an in-depth exploration of a challenging work of literature. It is important, however, to choose a film that is not simply entertaining and simplistic. Although most students feel more comfortable viewing and analyzing visual texts, English teachers must still find intellectually challenging films.

One filmmaker who has offered complex characters in the anime genre is Hayao Miyazaki. While his films are often compared to Disney movies, Miyazaki's films are really not part of the Disney world.[19] Miyazaki's work, like Shakespeare, offers morally complex worlds where nature is not always benign and people must deal with their own personal histories.

Like Disney, there might be a magical world in a Miyazaki film, but it is not a world that detached itself from prejudice, violence, and intolerance. All of this can be seen in one of Miyazaki's anime films, *Princess Mononoke*, which is "notable for its balanced exploration of the conflict between nature and technology."[20] It is also a film that avoids stereotyped and clichéd characters and offers a world of complex interrelationships regarding nature, technology, and spirituality.

Princess Mononoke begins with a battle. A young protector, Ashitaka, is called upon to defend his village against a wild boar-god who is out of control with rage. The boar-god's behavior results from a wound inflicted by some kind of weapon. Ashitaka, after praying for the boar-god to cease, is forced to kill it.

During the battle, Ashitaka is wounded, and this wound contains all the evil and rage from the boar-god. Because of his wound, Ashitaka must leave his home and never return. Ashitaka starts on a journey to discover how and why the boar-god was wounded. This is the start of the main character's journey, and the film, *Princess Mononoke*, focuses on Ashitaka's discoveries and experiences during the journey.

Throughout the film, Ashitaka is seeking a balance in a world that has lost its way. He will defend whomever he believes needs his help or support. When he meets Princess Mononoke or San, she demands that he show his loyalty to her and her fight against Lady Eboshi, but he is unwilling to take sides in this war that involves archetypal forces. Ashitaka cannot fully support San's position of hating all humans because he will not engage in hating any person or community. It is interesting to note that despite the fact that San is human, she does not align herself with the humans in this narrative.

Ashitaka also cannot support Lady Eboshi's pragmatic view that the natural world is only there for humans to dominate, commodify, and consume. Ashitaka is able to accept contradictory viewpoints and also offer compassion to everyone involved in the conflict. He acknowledges San's anger and hatred towards other humans, and Lady Eboshi's egotistical drive for power at any cost, but he will not take a side in this war.

Throughout the film, Ashitaka participates in multiple modalities involving cultural and ethical values. So how would English teachers approach this character? At times Ashitaka engages in violence, and at times he steps in to diffuse any risk of violence. He is an excellent example of a character that shows paradoxes and nuances in his actions and beliefs. After all, the human condition is rich with paradoxes and nuances, and students need to not only notice those paradoxes and nuances, but analyze the complexity of character in film, literature, and hopefully in themselves.

Like Ashitaka, Tayo cannot be easily categorized in a box regarding who he is and what he does throughout the novel. Tayo is not purely good or evil, and his actions and personality traits often blur the defining lines of gender and ethnicity. Tayo returns from World War II, spiritually unbalanced. Unlike Ashitaka who is forced to kill while defending his people or defending innocent people under attack, Tayo commits violence because he is being personally attacked; he is still reacting from an egotistical point of view and has difficulty feeling compassion.

Tayo is not able to walk away from the intolerance and hatred or attempt to resolve the conflict, but instead chooses to engage in it. Yet at the same time, he cries for the loss of his cousin, Rocky, who was tortured by the Japanese and unlike Tayo did not survive the war. In fact throughout the novel Tayo often cries or vomits, which symbolizes Tayo's need to cleanse himself of what he experienced in the war.

Most of Tayo's actions symbolize the struggles he is experiencing in his journey to regain balance in his life. The physical manifestations of his spiritual struggles can be compared to the life-threatening wound Ashitaka experiences at the beginning of the film when he kills the boar that attempts to destroy his village. This wound begins to bleed and ooze whenever Ashitaka commits a violent act in the film or he loses control of his emotions. Both characters take on physically and spiritually the effects of an imbalanced world, and the comparison will help students see their complex characters more clearly.

CLASSROOM CONNECTIONS

An excellent classroom activity that encourages critical thinking is the Socratic seminar. According to Michael Strong, author of *The Habit of Thought: From Socratic Seminars to Socratic Practice*, "Socratic Practice consists entirely of conversations on textual meaning: students are not 'taught' critical thinking, logic, or reasoning. Instead, they develop habits of mind which benefit them in diverse contexts."[21]

Socratic seminars offer teachers the opportunity to nurture critical thinking. It is interesting how teachers sincerely want their students to think but most of what occurs in the classroom is about being "taught at" and does not give the students the space to engage in their own learning. According to John H. Bushman, the author of *Teaching English Creatively,* "we place teachers in the front of the classrooms and ask that they tell the students what they need to know,"[22] and that does not offer a genuine experience of learning. The student is passive and usually does not take any responsibility in his or her own education.

Socratic seminars offer students the opportunity to discuss character in all its complexity. Socratic seminar is not an approach that reduces the study of character to short definitions of types. Socratic seminar is not a teacher-led discussion, but rather a student-led one.[23] It differs from a teacher-guided discussion, which often includes specific questions. The question for a Socratic seminar does not have a "yes or no" response; in fact a good Socratic seminar does not arrive at some ultimate answer. The value of the Socratic seminar is the act of engaging in meaningful conversation.

Because the Socratic seminar is not as structured as other class assignments, students need some preparing before engaging in one. It would be helpful if the teacher offers a mock one for practice where the students could pause and the teacher would offer constructive comments on what is working and what is not. For example, often students like to go off-topic and start discussing social activities, and the teacher can remind them they need to continue to discuss the seminar topic.

Students also learn how to be active listeners in a Socratic seminar. Often, students do not listen to what their classmates are saying, and they are only waiting for a student to stop talking, so they can make a statement. In a Socratic seminar, students should not ignore another student's question; there needs to be a genuine effort to listen and respond.

An effective Socratic seminar connects to several literacy skills including reading, writing, speaking, listening, and thinking. This process begins before the actual seminar. There needs to be some ground work involved before a class can have a dynamic and thought-provoking seminar. Unfortunately, some teachers believe they are having Socratic seminars in their classes when it is really a teacher-guided discussion or even at times a lecture. Some teachers believe a seminar means having students sit in a circle and talk about anything. However, a Socratic seminar should have a plan or script, and it should be challenging enough for the students to discuss for about an hour.

If the teacher would like to organize a Socratic seminar using film to analyze character in a novel, *Princess Mononoke* would be an excellent pre-reading activity for the novel, *Ceremony*. This is an important first step before engaging in a challenging novel. While watching the film, the students should discuss what is happening in the movie and connect the narrative to the character, Ashitaka. The teacher would focus class discussions on whether Ashitaka takes sides regarding the main conflicts in the film, and why he makes certain choices and decisions.

The students may be assigned several writing activities connected to *Princess Mononoke* including the following:

- Write a poem from the point of view of one of the characters in the film.
- Write a journal entry from Ashitaka's point of view and then write a response to it from another character's point of view in the film.
- Analyze one scene in the film regarding literary elements like metaphor, foreshadowing, tone, and symbol.

These activities would then lead to the primary activity, a Socratic seminar, regarding the characters of *Princess Mononoke* with particular attention to Ashitaka. The goal is to create a conversation with students regarding character that does not rely on superficial description such as a black hat being equated with evil. Socratic seminar opens the door for inquiry regarding thematic ideas and philosophical questioning. Students hopefully will begin to question their own preconceived notions on characters in a literature text.

They may begin to cultivate "a deeper understanding of what is known and what is not known."[24]

When the class begins the novel, *Ceremony*, *Princess Mononoke* may be used as a reference point or a guide for the students regarding Tayo's character and what he is experiencing in the novel. Instead of students feeling confused or bewildered by Tayo's behavior, there will be connections made to *Princess Mononoke* and how characters are not simply victims or heroes, good or bad.

In addition, another benefit of this approach is that students will have an introduction to analyzing characters within cultural context. Tayo's contradictions and struggles in the novel are connected to his life as a Native American living in a post–World War II society that continues to express intolerance against his ethnicity. Tayo is ethnically mixed, therefore he is not fully accepted by some of the Laguna Pueblo people, and he is not fully accepted in the white world.

Ashitaka's search for balance is also connected to his cultural context—he is forced to leave his tribe, his people, forever because of his killing of the boar-god at the beginning of the film. Ashitaka is also a victim of racism and witnesses intolerance in others: humans against humans, humans against animals. Both characters must find a way to heal. Leslie Silko asserts that we all "get out of balance and out of harmony with our natural surroundings, and also we can get out of harmony with one another. And then it is quite difficult and painful, but necessary, to make a kind of ceremony to find our way back."[25]

FINAL THOUGHTS

With the work of film and Socratic seminar, students will have the tools they need to view characterization critically and academically. They will be able to make connections from characters in popular culture, who may not always behave as heroes or villains, to characters in literature who may seem incomprehensible at first. With thoughtful class activities and texts that are challenging, written or visual, students will begin to discuss universal ideas and questions. It does not matter if the film is animated or if the novel focuses on a Laguna Pueblo war veteran; students will connect the characters to the universal questioning of what it means to be human.

Most English teachers understand the importance of critical thinking and strive to make their lessons thoughtful and reflective. However, students will not become reflective if what they are reading or watching in class is reduced to one-sentence responses on a worksheet, fill-in responses, and simplistic categorizations of character. By warming up with complex, multidimensional characters in film, students will be better prepared to become the critical thinkers that are engaged and prepared for the modern literature classroom.

NOTES

1. Azar Nafasi, *Reading Lolita in Tehran: A Memoir in Books* (New York: Random House, 2003), 111.
2. Ibid.
3. *ClassZone: McDougal Littell Literature, Grade 11*, www.classzone.com.
4. Ibid.
5. "Understanding Character," *Scholastic,* www.scholastic.com.
6. "Character Analysis and Traits," *Chicago Gear Up,* www.chicagogearup.org/archives/yal/units.
7. Ellen Krueger and Mary T. Christel, *Seeing and Believing: How To Teach Media Literacy in the English Classroom* (Portsmouth: Henemann, 2001), 68.
8. National Council of Teachers of English and International Reading Association, *Standards for the English Language Arts,* (Urbana: NCTE, 2012), 5.
9. Ibid.
10. Ibid.
11. Ibid., 20.
12. Kjersti VanSlyke-Briggs, "Using the Arts to Fend Off Alliteracy," *California English* 15, no. 4 (2010): 14.
13. Ellen Krueger and Mary T. Christel, 80–81.
14. Ibid., 70–71.
15. Ernest Morrell, "Toward A Critical Pedagogy of Popular Culture: Literacy Development Among Urban Youth," *Journal of Adolescent & Adult Literacy* 46, no. 1 (2002), 72.
16. Per Seyersted, "Interview with Leslie Marmon Silko," in *Conversations with Leslie Marmon Silko,* ed. Ellen L. Arnold (Jackson: University of Mississippi Press, 2000), 7.
17. Ibid.
18. Allan Chavkin, "Introduction," in *Leslie Marmon Silko's Ceremony: A Casebook* (Oxford: Oxford University Press, 2002), 7.
19. Christina Hoff Kraemer, "Between the Worlds: Liminality and Self-Sacrifice in *Princess Mononoke*," *Journal of Religion and Film* 8, no. 1 (2004), 1.
20. Ibid., 2.
21. Michael Strong, *The Habit of Thought: From Socratic Seminars to Socratic Practice* (Chapel Hill: New View, 1997), 19.
22. John H. Bushman, *Teaching English Creatively* (Springfield: Charles C. Thomas Publisher, 2001), 136.
23. James P. Downing, *Creative Teaching: Ideas to Boost Student Interest* (Englewood: Teacher Ideas Press, 1997), 81.
24. Michael Strong, *The Habit of Thought* (Chapel Hill: New View, 1997), 85.
25. Thomas Irmer and Matthias Schmidt, "An Interview with Leslie Marmon Silko," in *Conversations with Leslie Marmon Silko,* ed. Ellen L. Arnold (Jackson: University of Mississippi Press, 2000), 148.

BIBLIOGRAPHY

"Analysis Frames." *ClassZone: McDougal Littell Literature, Grade 11*. McDougal Littell. www.classzone.com
Bushman, John H. *Teaching English Creatively.* Springfield: Charles C. Thomas Publisher LTD, 2001.
"Character Analysis and Traits." *Chicago Gear Up.* chicagogearup.org/archives/yal.

Chavkin, Allan. "Introduction." In *Leslie Marmon Silko's Ceremony: A Casebook*. Edited by Allan Chavkin. Oxford: Oxford University Press, 2002.

Downing, James P. *Creative Teaching: Ideas to Boost Student Interest.* Englewood: Teacher Ideas Press, 1997.

Irmer, Thomas, and Matthias Schmidt. "An Interview with Leslie Marmon Silko." In *Conversations with Leslie Marmon Silko*. Edited by Ellen L. Arnold. 146–61. Jackson: University of Mississippi Press, 2000. 146–61.

Kraemer, Christine Hoff. "Between the Worlds: Liminality and Self-Sacrifice in *Princess Mononoke*." *Journal of Religion and Film* 8, no. 1 (April 2004): 1–6. www.unomaha.edu/jrf/Vol8No1/BetweenWorlds.htm.

Krueger, Ellen, and Mary T. Christel. *Seeing and Believing: How To Teach Media Literacy in the English Classroom.* Portsmouth: Heinemann, 2001.

Morrell, Ernest. "Toward A Critical Pedagogy of Popular Culture: Literacy Development Among Urban Youth." *Journal of Adolescent & Adult Literacy* 46, no. 1 (Sept. 2002): 72–77.

Nafisi, Azar. *Reading Lolita in Tehran: A Memoir in Books.* New York: Random House, 2003.

National Council of Teachers of English and International Reading Association. *Standards for the English Language Arts.* Urbana: NCTE, 2012.

Seyersted, Per. "Interview with Leslie Marmon Silko." In *Conversations with Leslie Marmon Silko*. Edited by Ellen L. Arnold. 1–9. Jackson: University of Mississippi Press, 2000.

Silko, Leslie Marmon. *Ceremony.* New York: Penguin, 1977.

Strong, Michael. *The Habit of Thought: From Socratic Seminars to Socratic Practice.* Chapel Hill: New View, 1997.

"Understanding Character." *Scholastic.* www.scholastic.com.

VanSlyke-Briggs, Kjersti. "Using the Arts to Fend Off Alliteracy." *California English* 15, no. 4 (April 2010): 14–17.

Chapter Four

The Graphic Novel as Historical Marker

Making "History Readable" through Reader-Response Theory

Carissa Pokorny-Golden

THE SET-UP

In Hillary Chute's piece "'The Shadow of a Past Time:' History and Graphic Representation in *Maus*," she aptly explains that while "most readings of how *Maus* represents history approach the issue in terms of ongoing debates about Holocaust representation, in the context of postmodernism, or in relation to theories of traumatic memory," it is "the form of *Maus*" that "is essential to how it represents history."[1]

While Chute centers her piece on Art Spegielman's *Maus*, the first graphic novel to win a Pulitzer Prize in 1992, it has become more evident, in the advent of *Maus*, that the graphic novel has become a vehicle for the retelling of historical narratives (whether fiction or nonfiction) in today's secondary and post-secondary education classrooms. The use of the graphic novel as historical marker has become more predominant since the publishing of Spiegelman's *Maus*, as it has been followed by the publication of works such as Matt Phelan's *The Storm in the Barn*, Brian Selznick's *The Invention of Hugo Cabret*, and Marjane Satrapi's *Persepolis*.

Chute states it best by saying, "Comics mak[e] language, ideas, and concepts 'literal' . . . call[ing] attention to how the medium can make the twisting lines of history readable through form."[2] But it is not just comics that make history more readable. Other forms like graphic novels, picture books, and other hybrid forms do this as well.

While *Maus* and many graphic novels may not be considered nonfiction tales entirely (as any good postmodernist would argue that memory is forgotten in the retelling of the past), they do offer a retelling of history that attempts to be honest to the past insofar as the past can be reconstructed. These stories, while told through comic art or as in the case of Selznick's *The Invention of Hugo Cabret* and Matt Phelan's *The Storm in the Barn* "not entirely through comic art," utilize "evocative visuals [to] add much to each story and offer new perspectives to readers" thus adding to their value in the classroom in concert with other forms of print and nonprint media.[3]

Ultimately, the graphic novel, used as a precursor to other more traditional print pieces, for instance, nonfiction or fiction novels or texts, adds an incentive for students' continued reading and study of historical fiction. Graphic novels are also an especially useful tool for teaching students in the inclusion classroom as they can reach students on all levels of reading ability. English teachers today are faced with students of varying abilities and graphic novels can add to these teachers' toolboxes to help with teaching classics and multicultural texts to able readers, reluctant readers, and English as a second language (ESL) students.

The challenges of teaching English using only traditional texts are many. For one, teaching the classics doesn't always guarantee students interest in today's classroom. Anne Trubek in her piece "Books that Make Middle Schoolers Groan" makes it clear that "when it comes to classics, it can be tricky to find stories that resonate with today's plugged-in kids."[4]

For many students, Trubek finds that the graphic novel is "one genre guaranteed to seem fresh and engaging in the classroom," adding that Samantha Webb, a professor of children's and adolescent literature at the University of Montevallo in Montevallo, Alabama, recommends teaching Art Spiegelman's *Maus: A Survivor's Tale* because "*Maus* is a more accessible choice for a unit on the Holocaust, particularly for older middle school students."[5]

Rachel Wilson in her piece "Multicultural Graphic Novels" agrees with Trubek's use of graphic novels in the English classroom, not only to add to student interest in literature in class, but as an "excellent medium in getting reluctant readers to read" and ESL students "reading at a higher level than they normally would."[6]

Wilson mentions Michele Gorman's findings in *Getting Graphic: Using Graphic Novels to Promote Literacy with Preteens and Teens* that "visual imagery in a graphic novel can help the reader 'process the story' and not have the frustration that can trouble these same readers when dealing with a text-only book."[7] Wilson supports use of Spiegelman's *Maus* and Satrapi's *Persepolis* as two examples of "notable multicultural graphic novels" for the classroom "that address the issues that all teens face."[8] Using graphic novels in the classroom, then, can help readers become more engaged with not just the material but with reading as well.

REVIEW OF LITERATURE

The use of historical fiction in the classroom has been on the rise as it provides students with a compelling story (either visual or written discourse), an emotional connection to the characters telling the story, and a stronger understanding of their own and others' diverse backgrounds. In other words, historical fiction causes an "efferent and aesthetic response to literature," what Louise Rosenblatt, proponent of reader-response theory focused on in her seminal work, *The Reader, The Text, The Poem: The Transactional Theory of the Literary Work*.[9]

This efferent and aesthetic response can be brought about by historical narratives alone but used in concert with the graphic novel and its visually attractive package of narrative and text, can add to the students' emotional connection to the story. This connection is imperative, as Mary Taylor Rycik and Brenda Rosler point out in their piece, "The Return of Historical Fiction," as "it is just as important for students to emotionally respond to books as it is to learn from them."[10]

In *Maus*, *The Storm in the Barn*, *The Invention of Hugo Cabret*, and *Persepolis*, historical fiction is brought to life for students eliciting several pathways for discussion through reader response theory. In using graphic novels, their narrative counterparts, and reader-response theory, students can meet several reading and writing goals, at all levels of learning. These learning goals include the Common Core standards for reading informational texts, reading literature, writing, and speaking and listening, as well as the following NCTE (National Council of Teachers of English) standards:

- NCTE Standard 1: Students read a wide range of print and nonprint texts to build an understanding of texts, of themselves, and of the cultures of the United States and the world; to acquire new information; to respond to the needs and demands of society and the workplace; and for personal fulfillment. Among these texts are fiction and nonfiction, classic and contemporary works.
- NCTE Standard 3: Students apply a wide range of strategies to comprehend, interpret, evaluate, and appreciate texts. They draw on their prior experience, their interactions with other readers and writers, their knowledge of word meaning and of other texts, their word identification strategies, and their understanding of textual features (e.g., sound-letter correspondence, sentence structure, context, graphics).

- NCTE Standard 11: Students participate as knowledgeable, reflective, creative, and critical members of a variety of literacy communities.
- NCTE Standard 12: Students use spoken, written, and visual language to accomplish their own purposes (e.g., for learning, enjoyment, persuasion, and the exchange of information).[11]

Overall, using graphic novels in the classroom, along with activities focused on their use with other print texts and literary theories like reader-response, can lead to increased student understanding of historical events, increased understanding of oneself and others in the world, and increased participation in class with other students.

The environment needed for teaching reader-response theory is important to the success of teaching this form of literary theory with historical pieces. Teaching students reader-response theory, especially with the use of graphic novels, requires taking on certain methods of learning and teaching. Robert E. Probst's piece "Transactional Theory in the Teaching of Literature," outlines several important principles to follow in teaching reader-response:

- Invite response. Make clear to students that their responses, emotional and intellectual, are valid starting points for discussion and writing.
- Give ideas time to crystallize. Encourage students to reflect upon their responses, preferably before hearing others.
- Find points of contact among students. Help them to see the potential for communication among their different points of view.
- Open up the discussion to the topics of self, text, and others. The literary experience should be an opportunity to learn about all three.
- Let the discussion build. Students should feel free to change their minds, seeking insight rather than victory.
- Look back to other texts, other discussions, other experiences. Students should connect the reading with other experiences.
- Look for the next step. What might they read next? About what might they write?[12]

Probst's principles clearly demonstrate the importance of allowing students time to interact with the text and one another. The hallmark of reader-response theory, especially Rosenblatt's transactional theory (which relies more on structuralism), is to ensure that students are interacting with the text, its form, and its connection to their own lives. Open discussion with others in class allows for more subjective criticism, allowing "a text's meaning" to "be developed from and out of the reader's responses, working in conjunction with other readers' responses and with past literary and life experiences."[13]

In Probst's principles above, it is especially important to foster an environment of acceptance in the classroom. What Peter Smagorinsky terms "final draft speech" in his text, *Teaching English by Design: How to Create and Carry Out Instructional Units*, cannot be accepted in the reader-response classroom as it incurs students' fear of saying the wrong things or giving the wrong answer to the teacher's questions about a text.[14] Probst points out clearly that "teachers, therefore, do not lead classes carefully along to foreseen conclusions, sustained by critical authority, about literary works."[15]

Instead, teachers must allow students to use exploratory speech, "acknowledging the uniqueness of the reader and each reading, accepting the differences, and crafting out of that material significant discussion and writing."[16] The teacher needs to encourage understanding of differing viewpoints, allowing students to change their minds and add to the narrative understanding of the class. Most importantly, students need to connect their understanding with other texts, looking at what they might read next to further their understanding of a historical event or work.

This need to connect and enhance student understanding of texts like graphic novels with more traditional print texts makes teaching historical graphic novels using reader-response theory a successful strategy for reaching NCTE/IRA goals for teaching in the ELA classroom while simultaneously getting on-level, at-risk, and ESL students interested in reading.

The affective appeal of graphic novels has been well documented by researchers. In a 2012 study of sixty teachers by Lapp, Wolsey, Fisher, and Frey in the *Journal of Education*, they found that the "majority of the teachers believe[d] that graphic novels hold high interest and motivation for readers."[17] Coupled with studies completed by Rakes in 1999, Weiner in 2004, and Frey and Fisher in 2004, Lapp, Wolsey, Fisher, and Frey surmised that "interest" was "increasing in the use of graphic novels as an aid to literacy" in the classroom.[18]

For instance, Lapp, Wolsey, Fisher, and Frey found that Rakes suggests "that students should be taught to read visual images, skills she indicates are of special importance as electronic media increase the amount of graphic information students" encounter, suggesting themselves that "the images, the layout of the page, and the words in a graphic novel interact to scaffold complex concepts and inspire new understanding."[19] They add that "knowledgeable teachers working with readers who struggle, who are on grade-level, or who have advanced reading proficiencies may find graphica suitable as an access point for more traditional literacy instruction."[20]

Similarly, Weiner states that graphic novels "can enrich the students' experiences as a new way of imparting information, serving as transitions into more print-intensive works, enticing reluctant readers into prose books, and, in some cases, offering literary experiences that linger in the mind long after the book is finished."[21] Lapp, Wolsey, Fisher, and Frey, further mention that Frey and Fisher in an earlier study found that graphic novels enhanced the multiple literacies of struggling students as a "limited amount of text was suited to students with lower reading levels while dealing with complex and more mature themes" and "graphic novels appealed to readers who struggle with grade-level texts."[22]

Maus, The Storm in the Barn, The Invention of Hugo Cabret, and *Persepolis* are all good examples of award-winning graphic novels that can be used in classes with students of not only lower reading levels, but those who are reluctant to read, are challenged by learning a new language, or those who find classic English texts boring.

As stated earlier, Spiegelman's *Maus* is considered the seminal text for teaching historical fiction in the classroom. It is the first graphic novel to win a Pulitzer Prize; it is also multicultural in nature as it discusses the effects of the Holocaust not only on Spiegelman's father and mother, but also on Spiegelman himself.

Satrapi's *Persepolis*, a *New York Times* Notable Book and a *Time* Magazine "Best Comix of the Year," is also a well-used text in classrooms across the United States including the city of Chicago as a coming-of-age story detailing life in Iran during the Islamic Revolution. Wilson cites both of these texts in her article "Multicultural Graphic Novels," as giving the reader "a deeper insight into other cultures; in effect, the reader is actually seeing what the writer has seen" and doing so "in a way that almost any student will be able to comprehend."[23]

While a different form of the graphic novel than Spiegelman's *Maus* and Satrapi's *Persepolis*, Phelan's *The Storm in the Barn*, winner of the 2010 Scott O'Dell Award for Historical Fiction, an American Library Association Notable Children's Book Selection, and a YALSA Great Graphic Novels for Teens Selection, works in a similar way to bring back the past history of the Great Depression. Elizabeth Bird in her review of Phelan's book for *School Library Journal*, comments that "Phelan conjures up another time and place" that will allow "today's youngsters" to "really understand how it is to be a child on a farm somewhere and not be of any use at all."[24]

And last, but not least, Selznick's *The Invention Of Hugo Cabret*, a 2008 Caldecott Medal Winner, a 2007 National Book Awards Finalist, a 2007 *New York Times* Best Illustrated Books of the Year, and a Quill Award Winner in the Children's Chapter/Middle Grade Category, is also a strong example to use in the classroom. Bird, who also reviewed this book for *School Library Journal*, adds that "the story is told with pictures that act out the action and then several pages of text that describe the plot elements. The final effect is like watching a puzzle work itself into clarity."[25]

CLASSROOM CONNECTIONS

The opportunities to use graphic novels as historical markers in concert with traditional print texts are endless. Graphic novels can bring "readers closer to the hardships and horrors experienced during political and military conflicts by giving these issues a personal perspective," offering teachers "opportunities to link English and history in their lesson and unit plans."[26] Utilizing frontloading strategies, teachers can introduce more challenging texts with graphic novels.

Journals

For instance, in learning about the Holocaust, students can first be introduced to graphic novels that discuss the happenings of the Holocaust from a historical perspective using reader-response theory. In a high school English class, Art Spiegelman's *Maus* can be assigned before reading Elie Weisel's *Night*. While reading *Maus* in class using Probst's principles discussed earlier, students can journal their feelings about the reading after independently reading or reading out loud as a class.

These journal responses can then be discussed in class each day alternating between partner (think-pair-share) and small-group discussions. Smagorinsky's fishbowl strategy can also be utilized here as well. The fishbowl strategy allows for whole-group discussion in a unique format. Students who will be discussing are placed in a small circle in the center of the room, while the remainder of the class listens in a larger circle around them. "Students who wish to enter the discussion, may, at any time, get up and tap out one of the fishbowl discussants and replace him in the center of the class."[27]

Once students have read *Maus* while writing and sharing their responses in class, students can then move on to reading Weisel's *Night* in the same manner. Having completed the same activities for *Maus* above, students can then write a constructivist comparison-contrast paper comparing the tales of Eliezer and Vladek, discussing the similarities and differences between the two. In this paper students should also explore the relationships between fathers and their sons in these novels, allowing them to add their own experiences with their fathers in light of these texts. If teachers feel uncomfortable using *Maus*, it could be replaced by *The Diary of Anne Frank* instead, allowing students to compare the different gender's views of the Holocaust.

As *Maus* and *Night* are both works of nonfiction that focus on the Jewish culture in both the United States and in the world at-large, they meet NCTE Standard 1 as "students are read(ing) a wide range of print and non-print texts to build understanding of texts, of themselves, and of the cultures of the United States and the world."[28]

Similarly, the activities presented above in teaching *Maus* and *Night* also meet NCTE Standards 3, 11, and 12, in that students are focusing on "a wide range of strategies to comprehend, interpret, evaluate, and appreciate texts" using reader-response techniques like journaling, think-pair-share, small-group, and fishbowl strategies (Standard 3) while participating in "literacy communities" (Standard 11) using "spoken, written, and visual language to accomplish their own purposes."[29] Students of all learning abilities will be able to journal and participate in discussions during class, as well as while writing their papers as per their individualized education plans.

Multimedia Project

Another teaching strategy using Holocaust literature is to have students, in groups of three or four, choose one Holocaust novel (print novel) and one graphic novel or picture book to present in class. Groups need to create a multimedia project (using PowerPoint, Microsoft Word, or Prezi presentation modes) including a synopsis of each text and its author, as well as themes inherent in both texts.

In this way, students analyze both print and graphic texts, comparing and contrasting the ways that these texts share similar or different themes about the Holocaust. For instance, students in a group might choose the novel, *The Boy in the Striped Pajamas* by John Boyne, which details the fictional friendship between two young boys during World War II, one the son of the head of a concentration camp and the other a concentration camp prisoner.

This novel might then be tied to the picture book, *Willy and Max: A Holocaust Story* that tells a story similar to *The Boy in the Striped Pajamas* but in picture book format. Willy's father, a German, owns an antique shop, while Max's family lives in the Jewish quarter of town. The two become friends before the start of World War II and are then separated by it.

Students would then present a PowerPoint, Prezi, or Microsoft Word presentation, giving synopses of both stories and their authors, tying them together through content (i.e., plot structure) and theme. Possible themes discussed might be coming of age, war, and identity.

This project is only one way that the importance of graphic novels can be relayed to new generations of students, reminding them that showing is as important as the telling of a story. All four NCTE Standards, 1, 3, 11, and 12, are reached in this student assignment as well. NCTE Standard 1 is covered by use of print (text) and nonprint texts (picture book) about the Jewish culture while Standard 3 is covered by student group evaluation of each text in a class presentation.

Lastly, Standards 11 and 12 are met through creative use of information in presenting the texts and the verbal presentation itself. Again, students of all learning abilities will be able to work together on this project with each student contributing to the overall presentation of information. By providing a visual example before assigning a more text-oriented format, students will better understand the printed text thereby "hav[ing] the potential to scaffold struggling students into fluent readers and enhance[ing] the literacy experiences of more proficient readers."[30] A copy of a rubric for use with this project can be found at the end of this piece.

Graphic Novels and Historical Perspective

Other examples of graphic novels and or novels with graphic elements that can be used to frontload more traditional print pieces include Phelan's *The Storm in the Barn*, Selznick's *The Invention of Hugo Cabret*, and Satrapi's *Persepolis*. Phelan's *The Storm in the Barn*, a tale of the Dust Bowl/Great Depression could be used in a middle school/high school classroom in concert with other novels discussing that time period in American history.

For instance, *The Storm in the Barn* might be used to frontload John Steinbeck's *Of Mice and Men* in the middle school classroom or along with another Steinbeck piece, *The Grapes of Wrath*, enhancing high school students' understanding of the Depression era in much the same way discussed earlier with *Maus* and *Night*. Other pieces like Karen Hesse's *Out of the Dust* and Michael L. Cooper's *Dust to Eat* would pair nicely with Phelan's *Storm in the Barn* as well.

Extending this further, students could couple readings of *The Storm in the Barn* with one of these texts along with Dorothea Lange's photos taken for the Farm Security Administration during the 1930s of migrant and displaced farm workers, "Migrant Mother," being one of her most popular.

Of course, as outlined using the stories *Maus* and *Night* above, reader-response theory can be initiated in the classroom with the use of think-pair-share, small-group discussion, and fishbowl discussions. Journaling is also important to the learning process when utilizing a graphic novel before a print text. In having students once again work on NCTE Standards 1, 3, 11, and 12 by journaling in class and working with each other in partner, small groups, or large group discussions like the fishbowl, they will better make connections between visual and print texts.

Media Projects

Even more unusual than Phelan's *The Storm in the Barn*, *Maus*, or *Night* is Brian Selznick's *The Invention of Hugo Cabret*, a mixed media work that includes pencil and ink artwork by the author himself coupled with movie stills and black and white photographs. The book can be tied to discussions outside of the English classroom about early 1900s France, early moving picture production, and the early history of the automaton.

The teacher might begin the unit discussing these events with a PowerPoint presentation that covers these topics, incorporating recently adapted movie clips from *Hugo* (2011), the film adaptation of *The Invention of Hugo Cabret*, directed by Martin Scorsese. The work can be easily tied to this movie along with other media pieces that relate to the work of Georges Méliès like the Smashing Pumpkins video for "Tonight Tonight" (1996) from *Mellon Collie and the Infinite Sadness*, and Georges Méliès's silent film, *A Trip to the Moon*.

After the PowerPoint frontloading activity, students in either middle school or high school can independently write journal responses that are shared in class after reading or watching movie clips. Students in high school could possibly create their own silent videos or music videos using the iMovie application while students in middle school might work together to create their own simple flip book. These activities include coverage of NCTE Standard 1 for use of differing text/media formats, Standard 3 for use of various activities that promote discussion, and Standards 11 and 12 in creating a verbal/nonverbal video or flip book presentation in a community using spoken, written, or visual language.[31]

Last, but by no means least, the use of Marjane Satrapi's *Persepolis*, the tale of a young girl during the Islamic Revolution in Iran, offers a view and history of Iran, a tie between an understandable narrative of life in Iran during and after the Islamic Revolution and the United States' current situations with Iran and its ally, Israel. This text is better suited for high school and college students.

Many college professors use *Persepolis*, not only as a graphic novel but also as a text in relation to teaching about Western literature. *Persepolis* has also been adapted into a movie of the same name directed by the author, Marjane Satrapi and Vincent Paronnaud. The movie, in French, available with English subtitles, won The Cannes Film Festival Jury Prize Award in 2007, can easily be used in concert with the book.

In teaching this in class, the book can be introduced in a high school classroom through a WebQuest activity focusing students on several websites discussing the time period covered by Satrapi in *Persepolis*. Students would then discuss their findings, then either reading them out loud as a class, independently, or in groups. Each day of discussion students will be asked to complete journal entries and discuss these with a partner or with a small group. If using small groups, students should present their analysis on a section by reading it to the rest of the class, followed by more class discussion.

At the end of the class, students might be assigned a paper discussing common themes of adolescence found in both Satrapi's Iranian culture and American culture. NCTE Standards 1, 3, 11, and 12 are evident once again in the use of a nonprint/print text, followed by individual written response and discussion.

Additional Theory Applications

While using reader-response theory is clearly evident in each of the classroom applications discussed above, Probst is quick to remind teachers that reader-response theory does "not deny the validity of other approaches to literature" as other "historical, biographical, and cultural perspectives may all yield insight into literature."[32] It is important to keep this in consideration while teaching reader-response theory solely on its own merits.

Other theories work well with reader-response theory, especially postmodernism, which deals well with the implications of the past on modern society. For instance, Spiegelman's *Maus* easily lends itself to both reader-response and postmodern theory as Eric Berlatsky in "Memory as Forgetting: The Problem of the Postmodern in Kundera's *The Book of Laughter and Forgetting* and Spiegelman's *Maus*" points out that history and "its implications in the postmodern world still resonate, particularly . . . in the case of traumatic events and historical incidents that serve as sites of communal and individual identification for oppressed peoples."[33]

Memory plays an important part of Art Spiegelman's retelling of his father, Vladek's story of the Holocaust because *Maus* not only retells Art's father's story but also his own. Satrapi's *Persepolis* also relies on memory and postmodern and postcolonial ideas, as Satrapi is retelling her story of life in Iran and her subsequent escape to Europe during the Iranian Revolution. While this essay focuses on the importance of reader-response theory in historical graphic novels, it is also important to realize that other theories can be used in concert with reader-response theory to enliven and add to the conversation in the classroom.

FINAL THOUGHTS

Don Gallo said it best in his short column entitled "Bold Books for Innovative Teaching" in 2004 when he stated, "Many teachers of English Language Arts remain unfamiliar with the wide range of choices in this genre (the graphic novel), in part because we did not grow up with these novels, in part because our literary sentiments have been trained to avoid anything with illustrations, and in part because many of us haven't known where to start investigating this fascinating new field."[34]

Because of their format, which is both visually and aesthetically pleasing, graphic novels and those texts with elements of the graphic novel draw students into reading including the student at risk, the student with reading disabilities, and the student that just dislikes reading altogether. In an increasingly technologically advanced society, graphic novels reach these students because as Mel Gibson so clearly states in his piece in *The Routledge Companion to Children's Literature*, "picture books, comics, and graphic novels are rich and complex media, combining image and text in different formats, [and] playing on the interdependence of these signifying systems."[35]

Graphic novels do this by "draw[ing] on many sources not just from the arts, like film and painting, but also from popular media and other cultural products."[36] As discussed in this essay, graphic novels can and should be used not only in relation to more traditional print texts to further students' understanding of history and literary theory, but also to strengthen students reading and writing skills through journaling and more constructivist activities utilizing WebQuests and creating presentations, flip books, and videos in the classroom.

The graphic novel (i.e., in either its comic form, storybook form, or hybrid form) can be a vehicle for change and understanding of history by providing students with a visual story (in concert with written discourse), and an emotional connection creating stronger understanding of the past, of their own stories, and of others from diverse backgrounds. More importantly than this though, is the graphic novels' reach to all levels of students regardless of race, gender, or socioeconomic background.

For those students who "simply are not capable of conjuring images in their mind[s] from reading the text," graphic novels "provide images that help students interpret the text as well as denote particular thematic connotations, purposes, or idea[s],"[37] while for on-level learners, they "represent a welcome move away from what they consider traditional 'school reading.'"[38] Accordingly, as Katherine T. Bucher and M. Lee Manning in "Bringing Graphic Novels into a School's Curriculum" state, graphic novels "must represent the best qualities of the literature genre and must be appropriate for adolescents."[39]

The award-winning graphic novels discussed in this piece, *Maus*, *The Storm in the Barn*, *The Invention of Hugo Cabret*, and *Persepolis* have been chosen by reviewers, researchers, and well-respected educational journals as representative of these best qualities. Coupled with other outstanding print texts in the classroom, strong classroom strategies and methods, and the NCTE Standards in the English Language Arts Classroom, Common Core initiatives in the classroom can be met, along with individualized educational programs. Without a doubt, there is no better time to incorporate the graphic novel into the classroom than now.

NOTES

1. Hillary Chute, "'The Shadow of a Past Time': History and Graphic Representation in *Maus*," *Twentieth Century Literature* 52, no. 2 (2006): 200.

2. Ibid.

3. Mark Letcher, "Off the Shelves: Graphically Speaking: Graphic Novels with Appeal for Teens and Teachers," *English Journal* 98, no. 1 (2008): 93.

4. Anne Trubek, "Books that Make Middle Schoolers Groan," *Instructor* 119, no. 1 (2009): 32.

5. Ibid., 33.

6. Rachel Wilson, "Multicultural Graphic Novels," *Library Media Connection* 24, no. 6: 32, Academic Search Complete, EBSCOhost (accessed May 17, 2014).

7. Michele Gorman, *Getting Graphic: Using Graphic Novels to Promote Literacy with Preteens and Teens* (Worthington: Linworth, 2003), quoted in Rachel Wilson, "Multicultural Graphic Novels," *Library Media Connection* 24, no. 6: 32–33, Academic Search Complete, EBSCOhost (accessed May 17, 2014).

8. Rachel Wilson, "Multicultural Graphic Novels," *Library Media Connection* 24, no. 6: 32–33, Academic Search Complete, EBSCOhost (accessed May 17, 2014).

9. Louise Rosenblatt, *The Reader, The Text, The Poem: The Transactional Theory of the Literary Work* (Carbondale: Southern Illinois University Press, 1978), quoted in Mary Taylor Rycik and Brenda Rosler, "The Return of Historical Fiction," *The Reading Teacher* 63, no. 2 (2009): 165.

10. Mary Taylor Rycik and Brenda Rosler, "The Return of Historical Fiction," *The Reading Teacher* 63, no. 2 (2009), 165–66.

11. National Council of Teachers of English, "NCTE/IRA Standards for the English Language Arts," *NCTE (National Council of Teachers of English)*, 2013, www.ncte.org.

12. Robert Probst, "Transactional Theory in the Teaching of Literature," Urbana: ERIC Clearinghouse on Reading and Communication Skills, 1978, ED 284274.

13. Charles E. Bressler, *Literary Criticism: An Introduction to Theory and Practice,* Fifth Edition (Boston: Longman, 2011): 80.

14. Peter Smagorinsky, *Teaching English by Design: How to Create and Carry Out Instructional Units* (Portsmouth: Heinemann, 2008): 10–11.

15. Robert Probst, "Transactional Theory in the Teaching of Literature," Urbana: ERIC Clearinghouse on Reading and Communication Skills, 1978, ED 284274.

16. Ibid.

17. Diane Lapp, Thomas Devere Wolsey, Douglas Fisher, and Nancy Frey, "Graphic Novels: What Elementary Teachers Think about Their Instructional Value," *Journal of Education* 192, no. 1: 26.

18. Ibid., 25.

19. Ibid., 23.

20. Ibid., 24.

21. Stephen Weiner, "Show, Don't Tell: Graphic Novels in the Classroom," *English Journal* 94, no. 2: 115.

22. Diane Lapp, Thomas Devere Wolsey, Douglas Fisher, and Nancy Frey, "Graphic Novels: What Elementary Teachers Think about Their Instructional Value," *Journal of Education* 192, no. 1: 24.

23. Rachel Wilson, "Multicultural Graphic Novels," *Library Media Connection* 24, no. 6: 32–33. Academic Search Complete, EBSCOhost (accessed May 17, 2014).

24. Elizabeth Bird, "Review of the Day: The Storm in the Barn by Matt Phelan," *School Library Journal,* August 21, 2009, www.slj.com.

25. Elizabeth Bird, "Top 100 Children's Novels #39: *The Invention of Hugo Cabret* by Brian Selznick," *School Library Journal*, May 30, 2012, www.slj.com.

26. Robert Probst, "Transactional Theory in the Teaching of Literature," Urbana: ERIC Clearinghouse on Reading and Communication Skills, 1978, ED 284274.

27. Peter Smagorinsky, *Teaching English by Design: How to Create and Carry Out Instructional Units* (Portsmouth: Heinemann, 2008): 33–34.

28. National Council of Teachers of English, "NCTE/IRA Standards for the English Language Arts," *NCTE (National Council of Teachers of English)*, 2013, www.ncte.org.

29. Ibid.

30. Diane Lapp, Thomas Devere Wolsey, Douglas Fisher, and Nancy Frey, "Graphic Novels: What Elementary Teachers Think about Their Instructional Value," *Journal of Education* 192, no. 1: 24.

31. National Council of Teachers of English, "NCTE/IRA Standards for the English Language Arts," *NCTE* (*National Council of Teachers of English*), accessed December 1, 2013, www.ncte.org.

32. Robert Probst, "Transactional Theory in the Teaching of Literature," Urbana: ERIC Clearinghouse on Reading and Communication Skills, 1978, ED 284274.

33. Eric Berlatsky, "Memory as Forgetting: The Problem of the Postmodern in Kundera's *The Book of Laughter and Forgetting* and Speigelman's *Maus*," *Cultural Critique* 55, no. 1 (2003): 101.

34. Don Gallo and Stephen Weiner, "Bold Books for Innovative Teaching: Show, Don't Tell: Graphic Novels in the Classroom," *The English Journal* 94, no. 2 (2004): 114.

35. Mel Gibson, "Graphic Novels, Comics and Picturebooks," in *The Routledge Companion to Children's Literature,* ed. David Rudd (London: Routledge, 2010): 100.

36. Ibid.

37. Elizabeth M. Downey, "Graphic Novels in Curriculum and Instruction Collections," *American Library Association* 49, no. 2 (2009): 183.

38. Katherine T. Bucher and M. Lee Manning, "Bringing Graphic Novels into a School's Curriculum," *Clearing House* 78, no. 2 (2004): 67, *Academic Search Complete*, EBSCOhost (accessed May 17, 2014).

39. Ibid., 68–69.

BIBLIOGRAPHY

Berlatsky, Eric. "Memory as Forgetting: The Problem of the Postmodern in Kundera's *The Book of Laughter and Forgetting* and Spiegelman's *Maus*." *Cultural Critique* 55, no. 1 (2003): 101–51.

Bird, Elizabeth. "Review of the Day: The Storm in the Barn by Matt Phelan." *School Library Journal,* August 21, 2009, www.slj.com.

Bird, Elizabeth. "Top 100 Children's Novels #39: *The Invention of Hugo Cabret* by Brian Selznick." *School Library Journal*, May 30, 2012, www.slj.com.

Bressler, Charles E. *Literary Criticism: An Introduction to Theory and Practice.* Fifth Edition. Boston: Longman, 2011.

Bucher, Katherine T., and M. Lee Manning. "Bringing Graphic Novels into a School's Curriculum." *Clearing House* 78, no. 2 (2004): 67–72. *Academic Search Complete*, www.EBSCOhost.com/. Accessed May 17, 2014.

Chute, Hillary. "'The Shadow of a Past Time': History and Graphic Representation in *Maus*." *Twentieth Century Literature* 52, no. 2 (2006): 199–230.

Downey, Elizabeth M. "Graphic Novels in Curriculum and Instruction Collections." *American Library Association* 49, no. 2 (2009): 181–88.

Frey, Nancy, and Douglas Fisher. "Using Graphic Novels, Anime, and the Internet in an Urban High School." *English Journal* 93: 19–25.

Gallo, Don, and Stephen Weiner. "Bold Books for Innovative Teaching: Show, Don't Tell: Graphic Novels in the Classroom." *The English Journal* 94, no. 2 (2004): 114–17.

Gibson, Mel. "Graphic Novels, Comics and Picturebooks." In *The Routledge Companion to Children's Literature,* edited by David Rudd, 100–11. London: Routledge, 2010.

Gorman, Michele. *Getting Graphic: Using Graphic Novels to Promote Literacy with Preteens and Teens.* Worthington: Linworth, 2003.

Lapp, Diane, Thomas Devere Wolsey, Douglas Fisher, and Nancy Frey. "Graphic Novels: What Elementary Teachers Think about Their Instructional Value." *Journal of Education* 192, no. 1: 23–35.

Letcher, Mark. "Off the Shelves: Graphically Speaking: Graphic Novels with Appeal for Teens and Teachers." *English Journal* 98, no. 1 (2008): 93.

National Council of Teachers of English. "NCTE/IRA Standards for the English Language Arts." *NCTE (National Council of Teachers of English).* Accessed on December 1, 2013. www.ncte.org.

Probst, Robert. "Transactional Theory in the Teaching of Literature." Urbana: ERIC Clearinghouse on Reading and Communication Skills, 1978. ED 284274.

Rakes, Glenda C. "Teaching Visual Literacy in a Multimedia Age." *Tech Trends* 43, no. 4, 14–18.

Rosenblatt, Louise. *The Reader, The Text, The Poem: The Transactional Theory of the Literary Work.* Carbondale: Southern Illinois University Press, 1978.

Rycik, Mary Taylor, and Brenda Rosler. "The Return of Historical Fiction." *The Reading Teacher* 63, no. 2 (2009), 163–66.

Smagorinsky, Peter. *Teaching English by Design: How to Create and Carry Out Instructional Units.* Portsmouth: Heinemann, 2008.

Trubek, Anne. "Books that Make Middle Schoolers Groan." *Instructor* 119, no. 1 (2009): 32–34.

Weiner, Stephen. "Show, Don't Tell: Graphic Novels in the Classroom." *English Journal* 94, no. 2: 114–17.

Wilson, Rachel. "Multicultural Graphic Novels." *Library Media Connection* 24, no. 6: 32–33. *Academic Search Complete.* www.EBSCOhost.com/. Accessed May 17, 2014.

Chapter Five

The Truth Is Out There

Using Science Fiction as a Springboard to Teach Literature

Sandra Eckard

THE SET-UP

According to *The Literary Terms Handbook*, literary elements such as the basic *plot* and the more layered concept of *theme* are called "elements because they are the building blocks of literature."[1] However, finding ways to teach these skills in a meaningful way can be challenging so that students don't just memorize vocabulary, but rather learn how to analyze pieces of writing by *using* the terms.

Many factors influence whether or not students internalize literary elements. First, they may be disengaged with the text because it doesn't seem "interesting." Second, the literature might contain issues or ideas that are universal—but these connections may be hidden beneath settings, language, or events that seem so distant to students that they are turned off before they can find meaning. Last, students may often feel that "school literature" that has literary merit—the texts that are valued by those in authority—are intimidating or difficult to read. Moreover, they might believe that their taste, their ideas about what makes reading fun or relevant, is the opposite—their taste is not relevant.

Scholars have written about precisely this point—that students may feel that they are not part of the "club" or the literary community in schools. Classic pieces of literature—like Shakespeare's plays or Chaucer's *Canterbury Tales*—are often met with a cringe with just one glance at the page.

Having students actually *analyze* the literature then becomes even more challenging.

Breaking down a play, a novel, or even a short story using literary devices to analyze the literature is usually one of the strategies teachers employ to help generate critical thinking and promote deeper insight into a text. However, when analyzing literature that students feel disengaged with, they often provide surface-level comments, especially about what they feel is obvious. Conversations in a classroom not yet warmed up to the terms—and critical thinking—might feel choppy.

Who is the protagonist?

The main character.

What is the setting?

That date.

Instead of viewing the literary devices as a way to think about the context of the literature—what makes the text function successfully and propel the theme—the devices may feel more like "busy work" to students than actual tools that they can use to gather insight. In short, what we use to bring them closer to the text may be creating even more distance.

If instructors want students to join what Frank Smith calls the "literacy club," we need to make tools, and the toolbox, more accessible to students.[2] As Versaci explains, we need to stop thinking of literature—and the successful analysis of text—as something akin to "medicine" that "will somehow make them better people if only they learn to appreciate it."[3] If we want to invite them to the "literature party," we need to build bridges between what they find meaningful and what we, as teachers, think is essential.

Science fiction can help build that bridge for students. A hot trend in young adult literature—and film—today is dystopian fiction that is set in a world that might (or might not) resemble our world but integrates social and political themes that the teen protagonist has to grapple with. *The Hunger Games, Harry Potter, Divergent*, and even *Twilight* are popular young adult literature (YAL) novels that teens gobble up voraciously. Other than a few classics such as *Dr. Jekyll and Mr. Hyde* or *Frankenstein*, not much science fiction can be found in classroom curriculums.

By sprinkling in science fiction, instructors can connect what students like to read with their teaching goals for literature. Science fiction—often thought of as a nonacademic, poor-relative to "real" literature—can help students understand how to accurately use the tools of literary analysis while building a bridge of experience that can help them join the academic literacy club with a solid foundation of skills, more confidence, and perhaps even increased enthusiasm for literature studies.

Creating an introductory unit that centers on one science fiction text—coupled with film versions—can help students build their analytical skills with a compare/contrast model. This unit can serve as a bridge before tackling harder or deeper texts. This chapter, then, will show how using Jack Finney's novel *Invasion of the Body Snatchers*, along with 1956, 1978, and 2007 film versions, can build a successful foundation for literary elements such as *setting* and *character*.

REVIEW OF LITERATURE

Written in 1954 as a serial column for *Collier's Magazine*, Jack Finney's *The Body Snatchers* was widely read and immensely popular. Amid a clamor for more, Finney revised the pieces to make the work a seamless pulp novel in 1955—what is now known as *Invasion of the Body Snatchers*. Designed to be accessible reading for a mass audience, the novel built suspense by interweaving the strange with the normal, painting the picture of an "any town" where aliens disrupt the calm of the everyday with a quiet, while-you-sleep invasion.

Lim argues that Finney's story of "soul-swiping alien forms attempting to take over the planet by replicating and replacing the human population as they sleep" has become "a modern American myth" and "an infinitely flexible metaphor."[4] The tale has transformed over time to reflect the worries of society and is "irresistible to generations of storytellers, given its capacity for alternative interpretations and . . . its ability to reflect a larger cultural and political relevance no matter the period."[5] Despite taut moments and scary images, the novel's theme is of hope in the face of danger as well as the value of independence over conformity.

The novel itself is not a modern alien invasion story that students would be familiar with in terms of structure; it is "not the guns-blazing *Independence Day* type of invasion . . . and it's not the bug-eyed monster SF of fifties movies."[6] Instead, it is a slow-burn story, much more like a thriller or mystery. Students would find the structure of the plot different than modern takes on science fiction, and the symbolism of the pod people's goals—conformity, uniformity, life without emotion—could easily be connected to cliques and teen pressures, bringing in modern issues—and teen angst—as part of analyzing the novel's theme.

Over the years, much has been written about Finney's intentions for the novel. Most often, critics have argued that Finney wrote the novel as a metaphor during the time of the Cold War to symbolize McCarthyism, but Finney himself states that the novel was not crafted with a specific metaphor in mind: "I wrote it to entertain its readers—nothing more."[7] The entertainment factor, combined with a malleable metaphor, creates a text that is ripe for students to make connections with while both reading and analyzing. In short, the novel "makes us *feel*."[8] It is a horror story where the main character "has stepped through the first-person convention and is actually talking to us."[9]

A year after the novel was published, Allied Artists made it into one of the first science fiction films to reach beyond a cult audience. Barry Keith Grant argues in *BFI Film Classics: Invasion of the Body Snatchers* that with "its paranoid plot of emotionless alien duplicates replacing average folk, *Invasion of the Body Snatchers* was the first postwar horror film to locate the monstrous in the normal" world, thus crafting a text that was ripe with opportunities for metaphor and character analysis, along with real-world connections.[10]

Unlike other monster films of the time period, this film—like the novel—focuses on paranoia rather than gore or special effects. Divorce might be the most scandalous element in the film for the audience of the 1950s. The terror in the film results from what you can't see: the inside of the pod people. On the outside, they *look* human; however, they are far from that with what you imagine while watching.[11]

Unlike the novel, with a wounded town picking up the pieces and moving forward optimistically, the 1956 film version by Don Siegel ends differently. Becky—the female lead—has transformed into a pod person, providing an uncharacteristic unhappy ending for the main couple of Becky and Miles. In addition, instead of the hope of the novel, the film concludes with Miles telling his story—and help arriving perhaps too late. It is a cautious ending that "underscores the cost of defiance and truth telling."[12] Analyzing not just the differences in the novel and the book, but also the ways this theme of truth could translate to teens and the price of independence, could work well in a classroom.

In 1978, another cinematic version *Body Snatchers* was released. This film version is definitely a mirror of the 1970s progressive thought: women had careers outside the home, people got therapy to discuss their problems, and living together was now more commonplace. The stark contrast in society—and the element of *setting*—could provide students with interesting avenues to explore how changing the setting changes the literature. The dramatic differences in women's roles—both Elizabeth and Nancy (the updated characters of Becky and Wilma) have careers—could be valuable starting points for examining society and women's roles.

The location was also moved from small town to city, with the events of the 1978 film taking place in San Francisco, California. Not only was this a real town—unlike the fictional Santa Mira—it was a booming city. The contrast in population, culture, and values was evident as the location allowed for the city to become a character in the film, showcasing life in San Francisco with numerous night location shoots.[13]

One more cinematic version is worth including: *The Invasion*. This 2007 film was not beloved by critics upon its release, but it has fared well over time. Many scholars have studied gender as a contrast in this film, especially because of the literary element of *character*. In the film, the protagonist and love interest are switched. Instead of a male lead, the Miles character—the doctor who learns of the invasion and attempts to thwart the plot—is now a woman. Nicole Kidman plays Carol Bennell, a psychologist who is perplexed by her patient's claim that her husband is not her husband.[14]

Nelson asserts that Kidman's character is a manifestation of the issues involved with women with multiple roles as a wife, mother, and worker in the modern age.[15] None of her roles are clean-cut or perfect, as she is a single mother grappling with custody issues with her child's father. This construct becomes the center of the character's dilemma in the film: she can't begin a relationship with Ben Driscoll, her suitor, because of her fear of relationships; she has separation anxiety when Oliver, her son, visits with her ex-husband; and her uneasy alliance with her ex is compounded by the alien invasion.

Carol's fear of loss—of Oliver, of Ben—is central to the story and relatable to most viewers. She states to Ben in a rare emotional moment, "I'm so afraid I'm going to fall asleep. I am going to lose him. I'm going to lose you. I'm going to lose everything that matters."[16] This film "reveals anxiety about the state of the American nuclear family. People once loved become imposters and strangers. The pods only change the stakes of a preexisting family conflict."[17] These issues can be relatable to teens, as many students will also have experienced divorce and family issues as well.

Entertainment Weekly ranks *Invasion of the Body Snatchers* as one of the most influential apocalypse stories ever created, with two versions (1956 and 1978) in the top ten.[18] By using not only the original novel but the film versions as well in the classroom, students can dig deeply into not just the story, but also the *variations* of the story. Each adaptation of Finney's story presents not just a snapshot of American life, but also an evolving portrait of societal change; the characters, issues, and settings change in the films to reflect the real-life changes in the fabric of America.

Therefore, studying science fiction texts like *Invasion of the Body Snatchers* can open up a classroom to a deeper study of both literature and the human condition.[19] While the basis of literary studies is to engage a reader with a text so that they can uncover meaning that will enhance their lives, many times the canon will not correlate to the literature that a student will actually *want* to read. Creating a classroom of real readers means involving them—to some extent—in works that will appeal to them. While our ultimate goal should be to expose students to the great works, we might want to build a bridge to help them get there; as Finch and Westfahl state, "too much literary criticism is in danger of ignoring the reader altogether."[20]

Including pop culture elements, then, can make the lessons literally "pop" for readers.[21] As Adams poses, "Pop culture is what students talk about in the hallways, so why not harness that interest and relate it to learning?"[22] In addition to connecting to students and generating enthusiasm, including pop culture studies as part of the classroom will improve student achievement, increase critical thinking, and develop language skills.[23]

Further, using science fiction can build connections between literature and the real-world, and activities in class that ask students to explore will help students build bridges that will create interest in all areas of learning: "Great science fiction can be a springboard to studies of history, earth and space technology, physical science, technology, government, life science, and the environment."[24] And interest helps students not just memorize, but apply, what they are learning in meaningful ways.

Flannery O'Connor states, "If teachers are in the habit of approaching a story as if it were a research problem, for which any answer is believable so long as it is not obvious, then I think students will never learn to enjoy fiction." Literature instructors need to avoid the "perfunctory and mechanical teaching of literary elements" that can take away the joy of reading.[25] Blending popular culture and science fiction with the study of literary elements in the literature classroom can be one path that instructors can use to achieve student enthusiasm and build a solid foundation for learning outcomes.

CLASSROOM CONNECTIONS

This unit was designed for a college literature and film course that was a three-hour, once-a-week class that met for a traditional semester of fifteen weeks. This unit to build skills was situated at the beginning of the course and ran four weeks, with traditional material to follow, including *Dracula* and *Pride and Prejudice*. All of the *Invasion of the Body Snatchers* films are PG-13 or PG, so they could be used in a high school or a college setting.

Depending on time and needs, this unit could be four weeks (one month), or it could be minimalized with only one adaptation—or even clips from the various adaptations—to suit classroom curriculums and time variants. The activities below are designed to supplement traditional classroom discussion and writing activities. The highlighted activities could be warm-up strategies, exit strategies, or the main lesson of the day, also depending on class length.

Quote Shuffle

This activity could be useful at any stage in the reading process, though it may work best around the midpoint of the novel. Many students do not take effective margin notes or specifically pay attention to how a character is evolving over time, so for characterization—and attention to making notes while reading—this activity can be effective halfway through so that they can then apply these reading strategies to the remainder of the novel.

Provide each student with a 4 x 6 note card and a thin color marker (or two). Based on their reading so far, have each student select one quote that stands out to them. Using the beginning of the book—or, perhaps even something that the class read prior to the novel *Invasion of the Body Snatchers*—model how to think about a chapter and select a quote so that they have a firm sense of what you want them to look for. Directions for selecting a quote might include the following:

- Which character have you been intrigued by the most as you read?
- What insight can you glean about human nature from the story?
- Which passage made you reread it for meaning?
- What dialogue has been thought-provoking for you?

Students should write their quote on the lined side of the card and properly cite it. In addition, they can write in the color marker or use the marker(s) to add flourishes to make the quote appealing to other readers.

After all students have selected their quotes and crafted their cards, give each student a small piece of tape. Have them find a safe spot (like a bulletin board, a chalkboard, or the door) to hang their quotes for others to read. Once all the quotes are hanging in the classroom, have students pick a starting point and go around the room reading each quote.

This step is an effective way to recap the story for some readers who have a hard time with remembering all the details, and it is a great way to have students spend more time thinking about the specific ways that dialogue and internal monologue are useful for building character.

Once everyone has read the variety of quotes, now comes the "shuffle" component of the activity. Have students find one quote card that speaks to them, pull it off the wall, and return to their seats. On the blank back of the card, students can write a reaction to the quote, how it connects to the growth of the character or the plot, or why it "stuck out" as memorable to them.

Once finished, provide each student with a piece of tape to "re-tape" the card on the wall again. This time, they should hang the card with their responses facing outward.

Once more, each student walks around the room, reading the responses, and when finished, they select a response that "speaks" to them. Taking the card off the wall, they return to their seats. Now, using both the quote and the response, bring them into a whole-class discussion to examine the novel—and how to be attentive readers.

If this activity takes too much time, it can be broken into one part per day as a mini warm-up for four days. Students will enjoy the kinesthetic nature of the activity and begin to see the connections between dialogue, narration, and character construction. If this activity is a hit, try it as well focusing on use of description to tackle setting.

Poster Activity

After finishing the novel, gather the class in groups of three to five students, depending on class size. Each group would receive a large piece of poster paper, black markers, and either crayons or color markers. Depending on class size, each group of students would be responsible for creating a poster version of a set of chapters. For example, each group would receive between four and five chapters (depending on number of groups and the length of the chapters).

Using their book, class notes, and their fellow group members, each group would craft a poster that provides the following information about their set of chapters:

- What are the main ideas of the plot that are essential to these chapters?
- How is the setting important to the plot in this set of chapters?
- What do we learn about the characters? How do they grow or become *round characters* as a result of these events in the book?
- What images—look at description of setting carefully—can you include to visually represent the events in these chapters?
- Find at least three quotes that your group believes are important to the growth of the character. Include in some way on the poster. Be sure to cite!
- Discuss all of these items for your poster first, and then, once you have it drafted, create a title at the top to capture the significance of this set of chapters in a meaningful way. Be creative!

This activity is designed to allow students to showcase, creatively, an application of their knowledge of *plot*, *character*, and *setting*—tying in these literary elements to the overall themes of the novel. Students would have the ability to be creative (drawing images, making word art, selecting quotes, creating a clever title) while still providing the teacher with immediate insight into their grasp of the material. Each group member would be able to work on one task independently before sharing with the group as well, keeping each member engaged throughout the activity.

After all groups are finished, have each group hang their poster on a wall in the classroom so that they can share their work visually while presenting their points. Have the groups go in chronological order so that, when finished hanging the posters, the entire novel is on display from left to right. If possible, leave the posters on the wall for the rest of the unit. They can be useful references when comparing the films back to the original novel.

Five-Minute Find

This activity is a great warm-up strategy to prep students for analyzing how the setting and the events of the time influence a work of art. A Five-Minute Find is either a homework activity or, if you have access to computers in your classroom, a completely in-class event.

Have students spend five minutes online researching as many of the words or events that they can in that time frame. Students should take notes or, if possible, print out a resource or two that they prefer. Provide students with directions and key words to look for related to setting—and historical events—related to the time period of the film. With the 1978 version, consider any events that might impact the pessimistic tone of the film such as

- Kent State shootings
- Vietnam War
- President Nixon's resignation
- Watergate

Students can also look up "events in the 1970s" or use one source to springboard to another source that they find interesting. After the five-minute time frame, have students present what they have learned about one facet of the 1970s and connect that, through lecture and discussion, to the tone of the film as part of your set-up for the fears of the time.

This activity can be repeated for each of the three films to help students unfamiliar with the time periods better understand the setting for each of the films.

Journals

As a useful reflection during—or after—watching the films, having students write a timed journal entry can be a great way to tie the images in the movies back to the themes and literary elements in your unit. After discussing important historical connections, setting, and the time period, students would have the film as a visual example of what "small town America" was depicted as on film. As a ticket out or exit activity after watching a film, consider using a five-minute reflective journal entry as a strategy to wrap up the day.

For example, with the 1956 *Invasion of the Body Snatchers,* consider examining *setting* in one entry.

What are your impressions about the setting of *Invasion of the Body Snatchers*? The film is set in 1956 and takes place in a small town. What details do you remember about the setting? How does the time period affect setting? What about the costumes? How do the characters—and their actions—reflect the time that this movie was filmed? You can use your own thoughts on the movie as well as our class notes on setting and historical influences to answer this prompt.

These journal entries could be useful for *character* as well, or as you move through the films, as a way to compare and contrast the differences in *setting* and *character* over time.

Here's another example, this time comparing the 1956 and the 1978 settings:

Think about how the settings are different between both film versions of *The Invasion of the Body Snatchers* that we have watched so far. What do you think is different in the time periods? Think about location, history, and society. In addition, what characteristics of setting do you think are the same, or similar, in both versions? Why? Give a few examples to support your points.

These prompt topics could be created in advance or generated spontaneously after class discussion. Towards the end of the unit, return the prompts to the students so that they could use their ideas to help generate a research topic.

Character Portrait

This activity is designed to help students flesh out details related to *character construction*. Although it could be used at any stage in the unit, this example will be part of the wrap-up after the novel has been read and all of the films have been watched and discussed in class.

Provide students with a sheet of paper, crayons, or thin markers. The paper (standard 8.5 x 11) will serve as the space for students to "paint" a portrait of a character. Students will draw from a basket or simply be assigned a specific character as the subject for their painting. Students will have one of the following twenty-five characters:

- Novel: Miles, Becky, Wilma, Jack, Mannie, Budlong
- 1956 Film: Miles, Beck, Danny, Jack, Teddy, Wilma, Uncle Ira
- 1978 Film: Matthew, Elizabeth, Jack, Nancy, David, Dr. Howell
- 2007 Film: Carol, Ben, Tucker, Oliver, Dr. Galeano, Wendy

If the class size is larger than twenty-five students, feel free to include other characters to increase awareness of minor characters or flat character construction.

The goal of the Character Portrait is to have a student examine all facets of a character, and how the character is built throughout the novel or film. Have students consider all facets of the character such as the initial introduction/description of the character, important quotes, and how the character is important to the plot.

Students would be assigned—or would draw—one character. Using class notes, reading or viewing notes, and their reflections they would build a portrait of the character. Directions should be specific but allow for choice; while some students might want to literally draw the character and place reflections around the picture, other students might be more comfortable being creative in other ways. In other words, a portrait can be built through words or a combination of words and pictures.

Encourage students to pull quotes from their notes and use the vocabulary of *character construction* such as *flat, round, major character, minor character, protagonist,* and *antagonist*. Provide students with requirements for their portraits, such as a physical description of the character, type of character (*major* or *minor*), quotes, growth (*round* or *flat*), and how the character is important in the overall plot. Depending on time constraints, this activity could focus on notes and recall or go more in-depth with possible rereadings (or viewings) of scenes to provide more detail.

The Character Portrait, much like the Poster Activity, can be pinned to a bulletin board to allow students to use the work in the future for written projects. The Character Portrait can be a great discussion starter that not only analyzes a character, but also offers a model that students can use on their own as a brainstorming tool to analyze character on their own.

Chalk Talk

Although the literal device is a chalkboard and chalk, this activity could easily be modified for a white board—or even a bulletin board—depending on classroom materials. A Chalk Talk is a silent activity that uses board responses instead of, or to supplement, classroom discussion.[26] The goal of a Chalk Talk activity is to build in time for students to think and write before talking. It can be especially useful to either evaluate prior knowledge at the beginning of a unit or to assess learning as part of overall closure to a topic.[27]

This Chalk Talk is focused on making connections between ideas and helping the students to see what they know before starting a research project on their own. Divide up the board space into chunks for the following topics: memorable quotes, important characters, historical connections, and themes.

As students walk into the classroom, provide them with the directions for the Chalk Talk. Make sure to include the element of not talking, for the sharing will happen after the Chalk Talk has closed. Students may use their notes and reflections to make any comments, questions, or posts under each of the four categories. They should make at least one post for each.

Once students seem to have tackled each of the boards, push them to start making connections. If someone asked a question, draw a line and answer it; if someone posted a memorable quote, make an arrow and write a personal response. Students can continue to branch off comments and add additional reflections and responses until they have used all the board space or time has been called.

A Chalk Talk is a simple way to tie all of the pieces of the unit together and help students visually see all that they have learned so far. Once the silent portion has concluded, it is a useful way to generate discussion and lead into a cumulative project, such as an exam or a paper.

FINAL THOUGHTS

While not a traditional approach to teaching literary elements, using *Invasion of the Body Snatchers*—or some other science fiction text—might be a promising way to turn students on to literature. Finch and Westfahl assert that "all good literature is subversive, but SF is also concerned with intriguing ideas . . . where we may be forced into situations where the only way to survive is to give up cherished patterns of behavior that served us in the past . . . We may not like that idea, but surely we must think about it."[28] This is, in short, the primary usefulness of blending science fiction into the classroom. The ideas are intriguing and naturally lend themselves to both student interest—goo, gore, or dystopian visions already built in to entertain—and deep literary analysis. *The X-Files* asserted that the truth is out there, but if teachers truly want to find that truth—that belief that our students can analyze the great works well—they might need to be open to alternate paths like science fiction to reach that goal.

Many years ago, Janet Kafka argued in *The English Journal* that "*good* science fiction . . . is especially appealing to teenagers, both male and female, and you might find that with careful selection you can turn on even the most reluctant readers."[29] If our goal as educators is to teach not just the material but the skills as well, science fiction might just serve as the bridge between what *teachers* need and what *students* want to read. If teachers can build a strong toolbox with many tools within that students know how to use, then they have succeeded not just with one book or one classic, but rather with the most important goal: they have helped to create readers who understand how to analyze any type of literature.

NOTES

1. Sunflower Education, *The Literary Terms Handbook* (Lexington, KY: Sunflower Education), iv.
2. Frank Smith, *Joining the Literacy Club* (Portsmouth, NH: Boynton/Cook Heinemann).
3. Rocco Versaci, "How Comic Books Can Change the Way Our Students See Literature: One Teacher's Perspective," *English Journal* 91 November (2001) 61.
4. Dennis Lim, "A Second Look: *The Invasion of the Body Snatchers*," *Los Angeles Times*, July 20, 2012, articles.latimes.com/2012/jul/20/entertainment/la-et-mn-second-look-20120722.
5. Ibid.
6. John DeNardo, "Review: *Invasion of the Body Snatchers* by Jack Finney," *SF Signal*, 2004, www.sfsignal.com/archives/2004/06/review_invasion_of_the_body_snatchers_by_jack_finney/.
7. Maureen Corrigan, "The Sad Lesson of *Body Snatchers*: People Change," NPR, 2011, www.npr.org/2011/10/17/141416427/the-sad-lesson-of-body-snatchers-people-change.
8. Dean Koontz, "Introduction: These Immigrants Don't Need No Stinking Green Cards," in *Invasion of the Body Snatchers: A Tribute*, ed. Kevin McCarthy and Ed Gorman (Eureka, CA: Stark House Press, 2006), 11.
9. Stephen King, "*Invasion of the Body Snatchers*," in McCarthy and Gorman, *Invasion of the Body Snatchers: A Tribute*, 22.
10. Barry Keith Grant, *BFI Film Classics: Invasion of the Body Snatchers* (London: Palgrave Macmillan, 2010), 7.
11. Ibid., 23.
12. Al LaValley, "*Invasion of the Body Snatchers:* Politics, Psychology, Sociology," in *Invasion of the Body Snatchers: Don Siegel, Director* (New Brunswick, NJ: Rutgers University Press, 1989), 15.
13. Anthony Timpone, "The Unseen Body Snatchers," in McCarthy and Gorman, *Invasion of the Body Snatchers: A Tribute*, 129.
14. *The Invasion*, DVD, directed by Oliver Hirschbiegel (2007; Burbank, CA: Warner Home Video, 2007).
15. Erika Nelson, "*Invasion of the Body Snatchers:* Gender and Sexuality in Four Film Adaptations," *Extrapolation* 52, no. 1 (Spring 2011), 51.
16. *The Invasion*, DVD, directed by Oliver Hirschbiegel (2007; Burbank, CA: Warner Home Video, 2007).
17. Erika Nelson, "Gender and Sexuality," 51.
18. "The Ultimate Apolcalyst," The Apocalypse Issue, *Entertainment Weekly*, July 4, 2014, 44.
19. Leo Kelley, *Science Fiction: Patterns in Literary Art*, (New York: Webster, McGraw Hill Publishing), 2.
20. Sheila Finch and Gary Westfahl, "Dispatches from the Trenches: Science Fiction in the Classroom," *Extrapolation* 40, no. 1 (Spring 2000), 28.
21. Caralee Adams, "Lessons in Pop: Does Pop Culture Belong in the Classroom?" *Scholastic Instructor*, (Holiday 2011), 37.
22. Ibid., 37.
23. Derek Greenfield, "Lessons in Popular Culture," *Pedagogy, Culture, & Society* 15, no. 2 (July 2007), 230.
24. Susan Lee Stutler, "From *The Twilight Zone* to *Avatar*," *Gifted Child Today* 34, no. 2 (Spring 2011), 46.
25. Michael W. Smith, and Jeffrey D. Wilhelm, *Fresh Takes on Teaching Literary Elements* (New York: Scholastic Press), 5.
26. Judi Fenton, "Using Chalk Talk in the Classroom: An Opportunity to Have a Conversation in Writing," *Teachers Network*, teachersnetwork.org/ntny/nychelp/mentorship/chalktalk.htm.
27. Ibid.
28. Sheila Finch and Gary Westfahl, "Dispatches from the Trenches: Science Fiction in the Classroom," *Extrapolation* 40, no. 1 (Spring 2000), 28.

29. Janet Kafka, "Why Science Fiction?" *The English Journal* 64, no. 5 (May 1975), 52.

BIBLIOGRAPHY

Adams, Caralee. "Lessons in Pop: Does Pop Culture Belong in the Classroom?" *Scholastic Instructor*, (Holiday 2011). 37–40.

Corrigan, Maureen. "The Sad Lesson of *Body Snatchers:* People Change." NPR. www.npr.org/2011/10/17/141416427/the-sad-lesson-of-body-snatchers-people-change.

DeNardo, John. "Review: *Invasion of the Body Snatchers* by Jack Finney." *SF Signal*. 2004. www.sfsignal.com/archives/2004/06/review_invasion_of_the_body_snatchers_by_jack_finney/.

Fenton, Judi. "Using Chalk Talk in the Classroom: An Opportunity to Have a Conversation in Writing." *Teachers Network*. 2014. teachersnetwork.org/ntny/nychelp/mentorship/chalktalk.htm.

Finch, Sheila, and Gary Westfahl. "Dispatches from the Trenches: Science Fiction in the Classroom." *Extrapolation* 41, no. 1 (Spring 2000). 28.

Finney, Jack. *Invasion of the Body Snatchers*. New York: Simon & Schuster, 1978.

Grant, Barry Keith. *BFI Film Classics: Invasion of the Body Snatchers*. London: Palgrave Macmillan, 2010.

Greenfield, Derek. "What's the Deal with the White Middle-Aged Guy Teaching Hip-Hop? Lessons in Popular Culture, Positionality and Pedagogy." *Pedagogy, Culture, & Society* 15, no. 2 (July 2007). 229–43.

Invasion of the Body Snatchers. DVD. Directed by Philip Kaufman. 1978; Beverly Hills, CA: MGM, 2007.

Invasion of the Body Snatchers. DVD. Directed by Don Siegel. 1956; Chicago, IL: Olive Films, 2012.

Kafka, Janet. "Why Science Fiction?" *The English Journal* 64, no. 5 (May 1975). 46–53.

Kelley, Leo. *Science Fiction: Patterns in Literary Art*. New York: Webster, McGraw Hill Publishers, 1972.

King, Stephen. "*Invasion of the Body Snatchers*." In McCarthy and Gorman, *Invasion of the Body Snatchers: A Tribute*, 13–39.

Koontz, Dean. "Introduction: These Immigrants Don't Need No Stinking Green Cards." In McCarthy and Gorman, *Invasion of the Body Snatchers: A Tribute*, 7–12.

LaValley, Al. "*Invasion of the Body Snatchers:* Politics, Psychology, Sociology." In *Invasion of the Body Snatchers: Don Siegel, Director*, 3–17. New Brunswick, NJ: Rutgers University Press, 1989.

Lim, Dennis. "A Second Look: *Invasion of the Body Snatchers*." *Los Angeles Times*. July 20, 2012. articles.latimes.com/2012/jul/20/entertainment/la-et-mn-second-look-20120722.

McCarthy, Kevin, and Ed Gorman. *Invasion of the Body Snatchers: A Tribute*. Eureka, CA: Stark House Publishers, 2006.

Nelson, Erika. "*Invasion of the Body Snatchers:* Gender and Sexuality in Four Film Adaptations." *Extrapolation* 52, no 1. (Spring 2001), 51.

Smith, Frank. *Joining the Literacy Club*. Portsmouth, NH: Boynton/Cook Heinemann, 1987.

Smith, Michael W., and Jeffrey D. Wilhelm. *Fresh Takes on Teaching Literary Elements*. New York: Scholastic Press, 2010.

Stutler, Susan Lee. "From *The Twilight Zone* to *Avatar:* Science Fiction Engages the Intellect, Touches the Emotions, and Fuels the Imagination of Gifted Learners." *Gifted Child Today* 34, no. 2 (Spring 2011). 45–49.

Sunflower Education, *The Literary Terms Handbook*. Lexington, KY: Sunflower Education, 2013.

The Invasion. DVD. Directed by Oliver Hirschbiegel. Burbank, CA: Warner Home Video, 2007.

"The Ultimate Apocalyst." The Apocalypse Issue. *Entertainment Weekly*. July 4, 2014, 44.

Timpone, Anthony. "The Unseen Body Snatchers." In *Invasion of the Body Snatchers: A Tribute.* Eureka, CA: Stark House Press, 2006.

Versaci, Rocco. "How Comic Books Can Change the Way Our Students See Literature: One Teacher's Perspective." *English Journal* 91, November (2001). 61–67.

Chapter Six

Hacker Heuretics and Intertextuality in Video Games and English Language Arts

Hannah R. Gerber

THE SET-UP

Video games are a form of popular culture media that have existed for over half a century, with the first video game a simplistic analog simulation of a tennis match called *Tennis for Two* created by Richard Higginbotham in 1958. This game was developed at the Brookhaven National Laboratory by Higginbotham to, as he stated, "liven up the place to have a game that people could play, and which would convey the meaning that our scientific endeavors have relevance for society."[1]

The game required two players to play a simulated game of tennis in a two-dimensional space. Players engaged in play by taking turns serving and volleying the ball in a competitive game of simulated tennis. The game was well received, drawing hundreds of visitors to the laboratory to try their hand at playing the game.

Since the days of *Tennis for Two*, video games have evolved. Today's video games are complex three-dimensional digital spaces often following complicated storylines and plot development requiring gamers to engage in developing a deeper awareness of themselves as well as of their fellow gamers. These connections also aid them in solving problems and connecting the learning and knowledge gained in game environments to situations outside of the game environment.[2] Additionally, video games serve as platforms for engaging youth in reading and writing spaces that exist outside of the video game itself, often in venues that are not sanctioned in school spaces.[3]

The video game is a dynamic, engaging, multimedia environment that deserves deeper exploration for how it can be employed in classroom learning. Understanding these connections can allow teachers, researchers, and curriculum developers to see that, "Video games are a new form of art. They will not replace books; they will sit alongside them, interact with them, and change them and their role in society in various ways."[4] This concept points to the idea that the video game is a valid form of literacy, one that can foster deep and meaningful learning and literacy experiences for students.

By better understanding the video game as a literate practice we can begin to conceptualize methods to incorporate the multiple facets of learning that occur within video game environments and learn ways to employ these facets within classroom instruction. Of particular interest are the collaborative and cross-disciplinary intertextual meaning-making methods that gamers employ when they engage in learning and dialogue with other gamers in game environments and increasingly when embedded in school environments.[5]

Research, however, posits that gamers often do not see their interactions as related to school learning.[6] It is in better understanding these interactions and how these collaborative methods of interaction shape gamer engagement that will inform teachers about the methods gamers use to make sense of their game worlds as well as further their own experience in game environments.

Making sense of game environments through interactions with the game environment, as well as interactions with other gamers, is an important part of the video gaming–meaning-making process. By their very nature, games encourage gamers to engage in meaning-making across modalities, as well as to create and recreate game elements to further their own game experience. These game-related interactions are referred to as appropriation, remixing, hacking, and modding, and come out of a concept called hacker heuretics.[7]

Hacker heuretics allow the gamer/user to shape and change the user experience for others by relying on changing part of the structure of game play. It is with this frame of hacker heuretics, by incorporating the multiple literacy practices that adolescents learn in their game environments into classroom instruction, where new learning methods might begin to occur. Hacker heuretics, through the concept of allowing youth to remix and modify texts related to video games, will serve as a frame for exploring two popular game franchises: *Uncharted* (Naughty Dog Studios) and *Elder Scrolls* series (Bethesda Studios) and examine how they might be used in classroom instruction.

Discussing how gamers hack/appropriate/remix these environments and then subsequently connect these "hackings" to experiences across multiple modalities will support teachers as they begin to create lessons using video games.

REVIEW OF THE LITERATURE

Video games provide diverse spaces that often encourage play and experimentation,[8] as well as appropriation and modification of existing elements within the game structure. The idea of hacking the game, as in hacker heuretics, relies heavily upon concepts of play, experimentation, appropriation, and modding, short for modification. These concepts are important to consider because they allow us to see how video game spaces operate, which, in turn, provides insight into how gaming literacies inform traditional learning spaces. Play is important to learning because it allows groups and individuals the opportunity to learn in environments that are relatively free from risk of failure.[9]

Experimentation allows individuals the opportunity to try out new things and new methods, play with ideas, and try on new identities. Appropriation and modding both involve play and experimentation, and in gaming these elements are brought to the forefront as appropriation and modding in gaming involves youth taking material that is not originally theirs and changing it, playing with it, and experimenting with new ideas to make it their own.[10]

These concepts of play, experimentation, appropriation, and modding are related to hacking in its original sense: the idea of a hack in computing. Hacking within computer environments is defined as taking existing elements and modifying them to become something outside of the creator's original intent in order to improve the original work. Heuretics, on the other hand, refers to the branch of logic concerned with discovery or invention. According to Holmevik, hacker heuretics, in relation to game play, means inventing new forms and practices through a gamer's playful interactions (interventions) with a medium, to help create and shape the digital tools that are being used and played with on a daily basis.

Hacks, in this sense make technologies better and more easily accessible for people to engage with on a regular basis. Therefore, when we examine the hack, we can see that hacking is nothing more than a production that relies upon play, experimentation, appropriation, and modification. These concepts move us from the idea that hacking is insidious behavior, to the idea that hacking is a necessary and needed element of any gaming culture in order to improve the experience for the user(s).

In the game world, the type of above actions are known as "mods," short for modifications, or in the active voice known as "modding," and are undertaken by gamers who want to appropriate, change, and recreate game elements. Mods are defined as "digital artefacts [sic] that avid gamers design by tinkering with their favourite games."[11] When gamers create mods they are in fact entering into a type of playful engagement in passionate affinity groups.[12]

Play and experimentation in gaming are integral to the experience because these actions help gamers to remix and add their voice and opinion to a piece of work. Hacking (remix) is not a new practice, rather it is something that has existed across the ages as individuals read, respond, and critique others' works.[13] It is this hybridization of work that is directly related to the intertextual interactions and meaning-making activities in which gamers partake.

Video game spaces are complex; they are more than simply the action of playing the game. The video game space is the environment in which gamers interact with the various elements of game play, including online and offline affinity spaces, and appropriate and modify it for their own purposes.[14] Affinity spaces are those areas (existing across space and time, or in a third space) where people with similar interests and discourses[15] come together around a topic or passion.

Often referred to as passionate affinity groups,[16] these spaces allow productive meaning-making to occur, and they give individuals the opportunity to collectively work towards solutions and to engage in collaborative and creative endeavors. This enables an individual's engagement in a variety of interactions with peers by providing multiple routes of participation and access to other individuals with multiple levels and areas of expertise.

Video games are about more than just play within the game environment, although the play within the game environment is still a crucial and important part of the game. Video games are complex spaces where interactions within spaces with people outside of immediate game play are important and allow gamers to engage in multiple modes of communication such as reading, writing, listening, speaking, viewing, and presenting or representing.[17]

Through these communicative acts, and in concert with gaming venues, affinity spaces are developed and strengthened. By examining the way that these communicative acts in these multiple venues both inform game play and are informed by game play, one can begin to see areas where pedagogical connections can be made.

In particular, video games have strong ties to English language arts (ELA) and the standards, strands, and benchmarks that are deemed integral to reading and writing instruction.[18] These connections have been said to afford a "constellation of literacy practices"[19] and a constellation of information.[20] This provides a venue for deep exploration of the connections between texts and modes of communication, leading to a "constellation of connections."[21] This constellation of connections stresses the idea of intertextual meaning-making and further supports the Gee's concept of multiple routes to participation through the process involved in making meaning within these spaces.

Video games encourage gamers to interact across modalities and to construct meaning among literacy events fostering cross-literate connections. This means that there will be gamers who will, while playing a game, refer to strategy guides, while pulling up walkthrough videos on YouTube, and sketching storylines for fan fiction. In other instances, other gamers may refer to different strategies, such as wiki creation and adaptation, to engage in meaning-making and literacy practices, thus supporting the idea that different gamers use different strategies to succeed in the game that they are undertaking.[22]

This idea is supported by the idea that gamers are, in effect, engaging in metamediating[23] to more deeply engage in learning and meaning-making within digital spaces. Metamediating is the practice of interweaving multiple communicative acts simultaneously (reading, writing, listening, speaking, viewing, and representing) while also engaging in intertextual meaning-making.

Metamediating also posits that multitasking is not necessarily what is occurring in multimedia environments, particularly gaming environments, because gamers are not conducting disparate unrelated tasks, rather the activities that gamers are engaging in are related to each other and further the activity in which they are engaging. The ideas of metamediating, intertexuality, and cross-literate connections allow us to see how gaming can be used as a platform to engage students in the modern ELA classroom.

Amid multiple calls to create twenty-first-century literacy and English language arts classrooms that are media and technology-rich, there still remains a challenge to create environments that truly pull from students' rich and varied literacies in their out-of-school lives.[24] This can, in part, be attributed to teachers feeling comfortable with their current teaching material, or lack of resources and administrative support to engage in new teaching methods.[25]

Additionally, teachers are increasingly faced with new mandates, new programs to implement, and new initiatives on a near-daily basis. This leads to initiative fatigue, or the taxing of a teacher's personal-professional bandwidth.[26] Often teachers are asked to pick up the latest technology or strategy, embed it into their teaching repertoire, and are given limited support or resources to undertake the newest task—meanwhile, all before the next new media, technology, or strategy is introduced, thus making the former obsolete.

With these stressors in mind, there need to be methods and concepts that are embraced by administrators, districts, curriculum developers, and policy makers that allow teachers to tap into the types of lessons and pedagogy that are needed for a twenty-first-century literacy and English language arts classrooms without creating undo stress on the teacher needing to learn the next new technology that comes around.

This support lends itself to creating a learning climate that embraces students' ability to engage in the type of learning evidenced through hacker heuretics (experimentation, appropriation, and play) while providing peer and teacher support within classroom environments that embrace media, technology, and a student's home life. A connected learning frame provides just that type of learning framework.[27]

Connected learning is a supportive learning framework that allows youth to engage in learning that is socially connected, interest-driven, and oriented towards political opportunity and civic engagement through peer connection and the guidance of caring teachers. What this means for the ELA and literacy classroom is that students are given the opportunity to engage in learning that is relevant and impactful to learning situations that encourage students to be flexible in their approach to meaning-making and to engage in multi-sourced and layered literacy practices.[28] This connects with the idea of game-based learning as previously discussed, by allowing students to engage in multidimensional and multifaceted literacy experiences.

CLASSROOM CONNECTIONS

As evidenced in the review of the literature, video games are unique and dynamic multimedia environments that deserve unique analysis as to how they can be used as a pedagogical tool. As seen, video games encourage individuals to engage in activities that showcase the ability to recreate and appropriate through modding and hacking, the ability to engage in metamediating across multiple platforms in order to make sense intertextually and cross-literately. These activities, or practices, can be incorporated in classroom learning spaces through several popular game franchises.

The two games franchises discussed in this chapter are games that suggest mass appeal based upon sales and awards received from multiple groups, including Game of the Year for games in both franchises. The following section will explore the popular franchises of *Uncharted* and *Elder Scrolls*, and will walk through a variety of ways that fans of these series connect to affinity spaces related to these games through appropriation, intertextual meaning-making, cross-literate learning experiences, and metamediating.

Of particular interest are the methods and ways that paratexts support, augment, and inspire creative experiences amongst gamers. Paratexts are those texts, either commercial or fan created, that surround and support the main texts. In the case of video games, the commercial video game is the main text and the paratexts are those texts that are used by gamers to support their game play, such as walkthroughs, game guides, machinima, trade literature, game wikis, and fan fiction.

Walkthroughs and game guides serve the function of providing players detailed information about the game, such as backstory, instructions on how to navigate through difficult scenarios, as well as detailed character sketches. Machinima (a portmanteau between machine and cinema) are creations that rely on screen captures, sound, and dialogue and are created using elements from the game engine with an original story/script.

Game wikis are fan created and maintained sites that provide complex history, backstory, definitions, and other pertinent information and details about a game. Fan fiction are stories that are created by fans of a commercial game or novel where the fan-author furthers or changes elements of the game or story to create a new text.

Apperley and Walsh,[29] found that paratexts have strong ties to classroom literacy practices through intersections in four quadrants: actions, designs, situations, and systems. These literacy practices are important to note as Gerber and Price[30] posit that video game paratexts are prime platforms for engaging reluctant writers in writing instruction by encouraging exploration and a deeper understanding of writing for multiple audiences for diverse purposes. Additionally, other research[31] posits that the paratexts that youth consume are complex texts that are generally written above grade level, quite often written above high school graduate level, yet students often have deeper comprehension of these game-texts than they do of school-based content subject material.

Uncharted Series

Uncharted is a series of action-adventure video games produced by Naughty Dog Studios. The first game was released in 2007. Action-adventure video games rely on series of logic puzzles, as well as action sequences, to engage players within the video game environment. Currently, the *Uncharted* series is available on PlayStation 3, as well as the handheld PlayStation Vita. The games in the series chronicle the treasure hunting exploits of adventurer Nathan Drake, heir to the legendary seafarer Sir Francis Drake.

The games in this series take on the third-person perspective allowing the player to see the avatar of Nathan Drake on the screen as he or she negotiates game play. This series has strong ties to Indiana Jones, Lara Croft, and Benjamin Gates (*National Treasure*), thus supporting the idea of an intertextual story, while also tying into fan communities and strong commercial productions, thus giving the franchise many quality paratexts from which to pull.

Examining the fan-created paratexts that emerge from the *Uncharted* series shows a deep, yet broad, connection with multiple opportunities to read, write, and critique both written texts and multimodal creations that stem from the game. Fan fiction, is one of the paratexts connected to the *Uncharted* community. As of this writing, there are 132 different stories related to the *Uncharted* series on www.fanfiction.net.

These stories are all written by fans of the game and are broad in how they connect with the original game franchise: some focus on main characters from the game, such as Nathan Drake; others have a focus on minor characters; others base their fan fiction on other paratexts released by the publishers, such as fan fiction based off of the motion comic *Eye of Indra* that was released in 2009 alongside the release of *Uncharted 2*.

To implement lessons using *Uncharted* games that employ intertextual and cross-literate connections through the concept of metamediation within a connected learning frame, a teacher might create a lesson where students are encouraged to recreate one of the scenes of the game through the eyes of one of the avatars (other than Nathan Drake) in a multimodal text (such as digital storytelling, machinima, or creating fan art of a scene). This will allow a student to work through the concepts of point of view, purpose, and audience.

The following lesson idea, the creation of fan art or fan fiction, is an easy way to bridge literacies. As with all new media, and popular culture, teachers must be careful not to co-opt students' out-of-school literacy practices, but rather allow students to choose to take part in the game-based lesson, or to choose another direction to go. Additionally, students who are not familiar with the game will have a difficult time constructing a story with different characters' viewpoints, therefore the teacher should be open to students pulling from other games with which they might be familiar.

The following list of directions will help a teacher tweak this idea to fit his or her class.

- First, introduce the concept of multiple viewpoints to students and then show them several cut-scenes from the game, such as clips from YouTube.
- Next, encourage students to think about the cut-scene from a perspective other than that of Nathan Drake.
- Have students jot down notes and ideas about how the character might be feeling, thinking, or what they might be plotting to do next. Additionally, the student will need to make a list of the character traits that the character has been shown to exhibit within the game. This process will help with assessment on their knowledge of the character.
- Students can also research, through game wikis as well as other resources, the global region that their scene is taking place in (since *Uncharted* games take place in multiple locations around the globe).
- Additionally, students should read existing fiction that surrounds the game, such as the *Uncharted*-related novels, such as *Eye of Indra*, so that they can begin to make intertextual connections.
- As a result of this activity, students will then create the new story extension, as fan fiction, from their character of choice. The student may choose to create fan art instead of fan fiction, which would allow them to craft, through images and pictures, a particular scene as it would look to the character they are representing.

This idea is just one that a teacher could use to teach about point of view in a manner that fosters cross-literate and intertextual connections with the game franchise. Students would be building their reading, critical thinking, and writing skills as a result of this activity. There are other ideas that a teacher might employ, depending on comfort level with the storyline of *Uncharted*.

Elder Scrolls Series

The *Elder Scrolls* franchise developed by Bethesda Studios, is a series of video games (currently five games in the series for consoles, as well as a massively multiplayer online game), that belong to the role-play genre. This means that to play the game a player will need to create an avatar and will assign traits and characteristics to the avatar that he or she feels will lend to success within the game.

Additionally, this game takes on the perspective of the first person, allowing the gamer to play the game through the eyes of his or her avatar. The games in the franchise are fantasy-based and players engage in battling orcs, mages, and dragons as part of the negotiation of the game space. This series has strong intertextual connections, tying in with such texts as *The Lord of the Rings* trilogy and various other forms of multimodal play, such as *Magic: The Gathering,* thus supporting the development and discussion of a diverse range of paratexts that can be employed in English classrooms.

While the *Elder Scrolls* series inspires fan fiction, machinima, and other related paratexts, another area of paratexts that deserve exploration is that of the game wiki. The *Elder Scrolls* Wiki (elderscrolls.wikia.com/wiki/The_Elder_Scrolls_Wiki) is but one of several fan-created wikis related to the franchise. Within the wiki, members release breaking news stories, updates on game patches, walkthroughs for quests, details about the character races, as well as fan art. The wiki is community run and community edited, thus providing an opportunity for collaborative inquiry to occur among gamers.

Instructors can tap into the power of the *Elder Scrolls* Wiki by allowing students who are familiar with the video game series to research particular elements of the game, such as the ten playable races within the *Skyrim* volume of the *Elder Scrolls* series. The student could research one or two of these races and add information to the wiki, and then do a comparison between races that exist in another fantasy series of books, such as *The Lord of the Rings* series, while also at the same time conducting research into the history of the time period in both the game and the book series, thus fostering intertextual and cross-literate connections.

Again, like with the *Uncharted* series above (and any popular culture or new media), caution should be used when bringing these lessons into the classroom so that students' out-of-school literacies and experiences do not become co-opted and stripped of enjoyment. Students should be allowed to opt into these types of lessons and teachers should have other lessons available from which students can choose that will provide the same learning objectives.

To implement the idea of wiki creation and intertextual game-based research projects into the classroom, the teacher should create an environment where students have the ability to navigate multiple game-related resources. This can be done by providing students with access to game manuals, an Internet-connected computer, and other resources, such as related fiction and novels. From there the student can determine what class from the series he or she plans to research and begin to collect data on this class of avatar. As the student begins to edit and revise information within the wiki, he or she will have to make sure to save documentation to show the teacher of the changes made to the wiki. This will help the teacher to track and verify the modifications made to wiki.

FINAL THOUGHTS

Video games foster literate practices that encourage gamers to take part in complex meaning-making activities through hacker heuretics, cross-literate, intertextual meaning-making, and metamediating. These complex practices occur naturally in video game affinity spaces and can be tapped into when teachers allow students to bring their video game knowledge and schema to the classroom.

It is important to stress that these literacies should not be co-opted; students should not be forced into engaging in English language arts lessons that use video games, but rather they should be given the opportunity to *choose* either format or the video game for maximum engagement in the project. Video games provide rich, deep, and detailed experiences that teachers can use to help gamers connect to classroom literacy practices, and they can provide opportunities for these students to explore and develop deeper connections to traditional classroom literacies.

NOTES

1. Sandra Schamroth Abrams, "Gaming Frame of Mind: Digital COntexts and Academic Implications" *Educational Media International* 46, no. 4 (2009).

2. Ibid; James Paul Gee, *What Video Games Have To Teach us About Learning and Literacy* (New York: Palgrave, 2007).

3. Hannah R. Gerber, "From the FPS to the RPG: Using Video Games to Encourage Reading YAL," *The ALAN Review* 36, no. 3 (2009); Hannah R. Gerber and Deborah P. Price, "Twenty-First Century Adolescents, Writing, and the New Media," *English Journal* 101, no. 2 (2011); Cynthia Selfe and Gail Hawisher, *Gaming Lives in the Twenty-First Century: Literate Connections* (New York: Palgrave Macmillan, 2007).

4. James Paul Gee and Elisabeth Hayes, *Language and Learning in the Digital Age* (New York: Routledge Press, 2011), 40.

5. Hannah R. Gerber, Sandra Schamroth Abrams, Anthony J. Onwuegbuzie, and Cindy Benge, "From Mario to FIFA: What Qualitative Case Study Research Suggests About Games-Based Learning in a U.S. Classroom," *Educational Media International* 51, no. 1 (2014).

6. Sandra Schamroth Abrams, Hannah Gerber, and Melissa Burgess, "Digital Worlds and Shifting Borders," *New Media Literacies and Participatory Popular Culture Across Borders* (New York: Routledge Press, 2012).

7. Jan Holmevik, *Inter/vention: Free Play in the Age of Electracy* (Cambridge, MA: MIT Press, 2012).

8. Henry Jenkins, *Convergence Culture: Where Old and New Media Collide* (Cambridge, MA: MIT Press, 2006); Kurt Squire, *Video Games and Learning: Teaching and Participatory Culture in the Digital Age* (New York: Teachers College Press, 2012).

9. Gee, *What Video Games Have to Teach Us About Learning and Literacy*; Brian Sutton-Smith, *The Ambiguity of Play* (Cambridge, MA: Harvard University Press, 2001).

10. Mizuko Ito, *Hanging Out, Messing Around, and Geeking Out: Kids Living and Learning with New Media* (Cambridge, MA: MIT Press, 2010).

11. Olli Sotamaa, "When the Game Is Not Enough: Motivations and Practices Among Computer Game Modding Culture," *Games and Culture* 5, no 3 (July 2010).

12. James Paul Gee and Elisabeth Hayes, *Women and Gaming: The Sims and Twenty-First Century Learning* (New York: Palgrave Macmillan, 2010).

13. Lawrence Lessing, *Free Culture: How Big Media Uses Technology and Law to Lock Down Culture and Control Creativity* (New York: Penguin Press, 2004).

14. Sandra Schamroth Abrams, "Association through Action: Identity Development through Real and Virtual Videogame Environments," *National Society for the Study of Education Yearbook 2011* (New York: Teachers College Press, 2011); Hannah R. Gerber, "New Literacies Studies: Intersections and Disjunctures Between In-School and Out-of-School Literacies Among Adolescent Males" (Tuscaloosa: University of Alabama, 2008), Dissertation; Jayne Lammers, "'Is the Hangout . . . The Hangout?': Exploring Tensions in an Online Gaming-Related Fan Site," in Elisabeth R. Hayes and Sean C. Duncan, *Learning in Videogames Affinity Spaces* (New York: Peter Lang, 2012).

15. James Paul Gee, *Situated Language and Learning: A Critique of Traditional Schooling* (New York: Routledge Press, 2004).

16. Gee and Hayes, *Language and Learning in the Digital Age*.

17. Gerber, "New Literacies Studies."

18. Abrams, "A Gaming Frame of Mind"; Gee and Hayes, *Language and Learning in the Digital Age*.

19. Constance Steinkuehler, "Massively Multi-player Online Gaming as a Constellation of Literacy Practices," in Shelton and Wiley, *The Design and Use of Simulation Computer Games in Education* (Rotterdam, The Netherlands: Sense Publishers, 2007).

20. Crystle Martin and Constance Steinkuehler, "Video Games, Identity, and the Constellation of Information," *Bulletin of Science, Technology, and Society* 32, no. 5 (2012).

21. Sandra Schamroth Abrams and Hannah Gerber, "Cross-Literate Digital Connections," *English Journal* 103, no. 4 (March 2014).

22. Abrams, "Association through Action."

23. Gerber, "New Literacies Studies."

24. Donna E. Alvermann and Kathleen Hinchman, *Reconceptualizing the Literacies in Adolescents' Lives* (New York: Routledge Press, 2012).

25. Gerber and Price, "Twenty-First Century."

26. Justin Olmanson and Sandra Schamroth Abrams, "Constellations of Support and Impediment: Understanding Early Implementation Dynamics in the Research and Development of Online Multimodal Writing and Peer Review Environment," *E-Learning and Digital Media* 10, no. 4, dx.doi.org/10.2304/elea.2013.10.4.357.

27. Ito, *Hanging Out, Messing Around, and Geeking Out*.

28. Sandra Schamroth Abrams, *Integrating Virtual and Traditional Learning in 6–12 Classrooms: A Layered Literacies Approach to Multimodal Meaning Making* (New York: Routledge Press, 2014).
29. Thomas Apperley and Christopher Walsh, "What Digital Games and Literacy Have in Common: A Heuristic for Understanding Pupils' Gaming Literacy," *Literacy* 46, no. 3 (November 2012).
30. Gerber and Price, "Twenty-First Century Adolescents, Writing, and the New Media."
31. Constance Steinkuehler, Catherine Compton-Lilly, and Elizabeth King, "Reading in the Context of Online Games," *International Conference of the Learning Sciences* (Chicago: ICLA, 2010).

BIBLIOGRAPHY

Abrams, Sandra Schamroth. "A Gaming Frame of Mind: Digital Contexts and Academic Implications." *Educational Media International* 46, no. 4 (2009): 335–47.
———. "Association through Action: Identity Development through Real and Virtual Videogame Environments." In *National Society for the Study of Education Yearbook 2011*. New York: Teachers College Press, 2011.
———. *Integrating Virtual and Traditional Learning in 6–12 Classrooms: A Layered Literacies Approach to Multimodal Meaning Making*. New York: Routledge, 2014.
Abrams, Sandra Schamroth, and Hannah Gerber. "Cross-Literate Digital Connections." *English Journal* 103, no. 4 (March 2014): 18–24.
Abrams, Sandra Schamroth, Hannah Gerber, and Melissa Burgess. "Digital Worlds and Shifting Borders." *New Media Literacies and Participatory Popular Culture Across Borders*. New York: Routledge Press, 2012.
Alvermann, Donna. E., and Kathleen Hinchman. *Reconceptualizing the Literacies in Adolescents' Lives*. 3rd edition. New York: Routledge, 2012.
Apperley, Thomas, and Christopher Walsh. "What Digital Games and Literacy Have in Common: A Heuristic for Understanding Pupils' Gaming Literacy." *Literacy* 46, no. 3 (2011): 115–22.
Gee, James Paul. *Situated Language and Learning: A Critique of Traditional Schooling*. New York: Routledge, 2004.
———. *What Video Games Have to Teach us About Learning and Literacy*. New York: Palgrave Macmillan, 2007.
Gee, James Paul, and Elisabeth Hayes. *Language and Learning in the Digital Age*. New York: Routledge, 2011.
———. *Women and Gaming: The Sims and Twenty-First Century Learning*. New York: Palgrave Macmillan, 2010.
Gerber, Hannah R. "Changing Literacies for Changing Times: Lessons Learned from the New Literacies." *English in Texas* 40, no. 2 (2010): 52–55.
———. "From the FPS to the RPG: Using Video Games to Encourage Reading YAL." *The ALAN Review* 36, no. 3 (2009): 87–91.
———. "New Literacies Studies: Intersections and Disjunctures Between In-School and Out-of-School Literacies Among Adolescent Males." Tuscaloosa: The University of Alabama, 2008. Unpublished Dissertation.
Gerber, Hannah R., Sandra Schamroth Abrams, Anthony J. Onwuegbuzie, and Cindy Benge. "From Mario to FIFA: What Qualitative Case Study Research Suggests About Games-Based Learning in a U.S. Classroom." *Educational Media International* 51, no. 1 (2014).
Gerber, Hannah R., and Debra P. Price, "Twenty-First Century Adolescents, Writing, and the New Media," *English Journal* 101, no. 2 (November 2011): 68–73.
Holmevik, Jan. *Inter/vention: Free Play in the Age of Electracy*. Cambridge, MA: MIT Press, 2012.
Ito, Mizuko. *Hanging Out, Messing Around, and Geeking Out: Kids Living and Learning with New Media*. Cambridge, MA: MIT Press, 2010.

Jenkins, Henry. *Convergence Culture: Where Old and New Media Collide.* Cambridge, MA: MIT Press, 2006.

Lammers, Jayne. "'Is the Hangout . . . the Hangout?': Exploring Tensions in an Online Gaming-Related Fan Site." In Elisabeth R. Hayes and Sean C. Duncan, *Learning in Video Game Affinity Spaces.* New York: Peter Lang, 2012. 23–50.

Lammers, Jayne, Jen Scott Curwood, and Alecia Magnifico. "Toward an Affinity Space Methodology: Considerations for Literacy Research." *English Teaching: Practice and Critique* 11, no. 2 (2012). 44–58.

Lankshear, Colin and Michele Knobel. *A New Literacies Sampler.* New York: Peter Lang Publishers, 2007.

Lessing, Lawrence. *Free Culture: How Big Media Uses Technology and Law to Lock Down Culture and Control Creativity.* New York: Penguin Press, 2004.

Magnifico, Alecia. "The Game of Neopian Writing." In Elisabeth R. Hayes and Sean C. Duncan, *Learning in Video Games Affinity Space.* New York: Peter Lang, 2012. 212–34.

Martin, Crystle, and Constance Steinkuehler. "Video Games, Identity, and the Constellation of Information." *Bulletin of Science, Technology, and Society* 32, no. 5. (2012).

Olmanson, Justin, and Sandra Schamroth Abrams. "Constellations of Support and Impediment: Understanding Early Implementation Dynamics in the Research and Development of an Online Multimodal Writing and Peer Review Environment." *E-Learning and Digital Media* 10, no. 4 (2013). dx.doi.org/10.2304/elea.2013.10.4.357.

Selfe, Cynthia, and Gail Hawisher. *Gaming Lives in the Twenty-First Century: Literate Connections.* New York: Palgrave Macmillan, 2007.

Sotamaa, Olli. 2008. "When the Game Is Not Enough: Motivations and Practices Among Computer Game Modding Culture." *Games and Culture* 5, no 3 (July 2010).

Squire, Kurt. 2012. *Video Games and Learning: Teaching and Participatory Culture in the Digital Age.* New York: Teachers College Press, 2012.

Steinkuehler, Constance. "Massively Multiplayer Online Gaming as a Constellation of Literacy Practices." In Brett E. Shelton and David A.Wiley, *The Design and Use of Simulation Computer Games in Education.* Rotterdam, The Netherlands: Sense Publishers, 2007.

Steinkuehler, Constance, Catherine Compton-Lilly, and Elizabeth King, "Reading in the Context of Online Games." International Conference of the Learning Sciences. Chicago: ICLA, 2010.

Sutton-Smith, Brian. *The Ambiguity of Play.* Cambridge, MA: Harvard University Press, 2001.

II

Developing Writing and Critical Thinking Skills with Popular Culture

Chapter Seven

Make It Work

What We Can Learn About the Writing Process from Watching Project Runway

April Brannon and Elle Yarborough

THE SET-UP

On the surface, *Project Runway* appears to be just another reality television show. With its eccentric contestants, glamorous prizes, and super model host, it certainly fits the bill. But if viewers look beyond the sequins and feathers, what they will find is a fascinating portrayal of the creative process, and since the writing process is a creative process, what *Project Runway* offers is a useful glimpse into the writing process.

In each episode, contestants are given a challenge to complete, and while it is true that they use a needle and thread rather than a pen and paper to complete their work, the process they undergo mimics writing. They pre-write in the form of sketches and fabric selection, they draft and revise as they sew, and when they send their finished garment down the runway, they submit their final draft.

Project Runway puts a human face on the creative process so that students can quite literally watch that process in all of its messy, recursive, complicated, frustrating, and exhilarating glory. Fisher and Frey argue that students need to be made privy to "the natural stutter steps made by someone who is deeply knowledgeable of the complexities of [a] topic."[1] Of course, students in an English class do not need to know about the intricacies of the fashion industry, but they do need to understand what the creative process entails and how to think through that process.

Certainly writing teachers can (and should) model the writing process for students. Teachers can show students examples of free-writing exercises they have completed, can explain the revisions made to their own written drafts, and can stage model writing workshops to give students an idea of how they should provide and receive feedback. All of these strategies are useful, even essential, components of writing instruction.

However, these strategies are limited in what they offer students. Take a free-writing exercise: once a teacher has laid out the strategy, she can either model it by writing with students or she can show students her previously created free-writing exercise. If she does the latter, she is talking about her process after-the-fact, so students do not actually see her create the draft. If she tries to model the actual act of free-writing for students by doing a think-aloud in class, besides being painfully slow for students to watch, the idea of free-writing—to write without inhibition—is lost.

By watching scenes from *Project Runway* together, teacher and students are able to view the shifting nature of the composing processes of the contestants. The classroom community can then use this shared experience of *Project Runway* to draw parallels between students' writing process and the contestants creating garments on the show.

What *Project Runway* offers is an opportunity to glimpse into contestants' composing processes and because of the magic of television editing, the pace of watching contestants work through those processes is both useful and interesting. It goes without saying that the show itself is highly produced—the creators have chosen key clips from their footage to demonstrate whatever storyline, real or constructed, that they want to emphasize—but that doesn't diminish the show's value as a pedagogical tool.

Episodes of *Project Runway* shouldn't be viewed as raw data from which to draw overarching conclusions about the creative process, nor should they be viewed as a how-to of the creative process. Rather, the show should be used as a springboard for students to reflect on their own creative processes so that they can develop an understanding of themselves as composers.

Project Runway can be used as a teaching tool to guide students through their composing process. The episode, "Eye Candy" (season 4 episode 6)[2] will serve as the basis of this discussion. In it, contestants are given five minutes and an unlimited budget to shop at the Hershey's store in Times Square. They frantically stuff their shopping baskets with Hershey's chocolate bars, Twizzlers, and Reese's peanut butter cups before returning to the workroom where they unwrap, glue, and sew their materials into dresses that are runway worthy.

For students who are not particularly interested in fashion, the inclusion of candy provides a way to pique curiosity, making this particular episode a good choice for classroom use. Moreover, the contestants provide a great deal of diversity in terms of gender, race, age, work style, and personality.

Certainly, more recent episodes or even clips from various episodes could be used to demonstrate the points discussed in this article, but as longtime *Project Runway* fans know, later seasons of the show tend to focus more on interpersonal drama and less on the design process, making them less classroom friendly.

REVIEW OF LITERATURE

When teaching writing, it used to be that students were assigned a paper, wrote it, got a grade, and that was the end of the story. This process started to change in the late sixties and early seventies when the field of composition studies began to grow. In her book, *The Composing Process of Twelfth Graders*, Janet Emig provided a detailed discussion of the components of the writing process,[3] and in 1972 Donald Murray published his seminal article "Teaching Writing as a Process not Product" in *The Leaflet* where he argued, "when we [instructors] teach composition we are not teaching a product, we are teaching a process."[4]

Emig and Murray, along with many other process scholars, revolutionized the teaching of writing, resulting in hundred of articles and books on process pedagogy and the transformation of writing instruction. It is now common practice in classrooms for students to engage in brainstorming, free-writing, outlining, clustering, and peer-review activities as they make their way through an assignment.

Yet, despite teachers' best efforts, sometimes process-related activities fall flat. It is as if students put on a smile, take a deep breath, and complete the required task while detaching themselves from their work. In other words, they *do* the writing process, but they aren't *engaged in* the writing process. One way to explain students' detachment is by turning to post-process theory.

Post-process scholars argue that pedagogies that emphasize pre-writing, drafting, and revision are not an adequate explanation of the actual act of composing. They reduce writing to what Olson calls a single "Theory of Writing."[5] In other words, the writing process is oversimplified into a series of lockstep stages. Moreover, because a process approach emphasizes the steps of the writing, the context of the writing situation is often marginalized or ignored.

Providing an opportunity for personal reflection on students' writing processes is one way to allow students to personalize their own unique writing processes. In their book, *Professional Experience and the Investigative Imagination*, Richard Winter, Alyson Buck, and Paula Sobiechowska argue for the use of written reflection to enhance learning. While their work deals with written reflection in the professional sphere, their points about the importance of written personal reflection speak directly to students' engagement with the writing process:

> the reflective paradigm emphasizes the creativity of human subjectivity: experience is not simply a succession of "actions" or "behavior" which can be "directly observed," but a complex process. . . . "Understanding," therefore, requires more than observation; it requires us to engage in a process of introspection leading to self clarification.[6]

In other words, students can learn about the writing process through lecture, observation, or practice, but they need to reflect on their own personal experience(s) with the writing process in order to really gain insight.

Bringle and Hatcher add to the argument on the importance of written reflection, noting, "Analysis through writing helps make challenging experiences less overwhelming, fosters problem solving, and facilitates the exploration of the relationship between past learning, current experiences, and future action."[7] Bringle and Hatcher's claim is particularly relevant for the writing teacher because students have to be able to apply what they learned in writing class to subsequent assignments and tasks as they make their way through the university and the broader world.

Scholars such as James Pennebaker, Ira Progoff, and Lynn Nelson (to name a few) argue for the use of written reflection to promote self discovery and to gain emotional understanding of experiences, while other scholars such as David Bartholomae,[8] Patricia Bizell,[9] Gerald Graff, and Andrew Hoberek[10] note advocate for directing student-writers to recognize and participate in social spheres that transcend the self. Of course, students should use writing to engage with a range of audiences, and they should complete assignments that allow for successful participation in and engagement with a variety of social contexts, both academic and professional.

However, it is important not to exclude students' unique personal writing experiences because as Nelson aptly points out, "Too often in school, we study language and writing in isolation, apart from the people who speak and write and apart from what happens when people speak and write."[11] Composition teachers must recognize that the writing classroom is likely the only place where students can engage in in-depth personal reflection on their own composing practices, and that such reflection is an essential conduit to learning, allowing for writing growth, regardless of the social context.

Because of the value of personal reflection in the writing process, many teacher-scholars are focusing their instruction on helping classroom authors reflect thoughtfully on their own processes rather than just providing a series of steps to follow. There are several composition anthologies, including two by Wendy Bishop entitled, *On Writing: A Process Reader*[12] and *Elements of Alternate Style: Essays on Writing and Revision*,[13] that seek to provide students with discussions about text-making from writers' points of view. These themed collections include essays about how and why authors actually go about the act of writing and provide insight into famous and not-so-famous authors' writing processes.

Watching an episode of *Project Runway* compliments the reading of essays like this because it allows students to literally see multiple composing processes in action. Moreover, a whole class viewing opens the door for students' own pre-writing practices because they talk about the episode with one another, and discussion is often an effective form of pre-writing. After the viewing, students draw parallels between the contestants' creative practices and the components of the writing process (i.e., pre-writing is akin to sketching, drafting is akin to sewing, etc.).

CLASSROOM CONNECTIONS

In his book, *Write for Insight*, Bill Strong argues that metaphorical thinking draws upon humans' image-making ability and makes it easier to understand big ideas. This type of thinking is particularly useful when thinking about writing because the logical language of composition—drafting, revising, proofreading, and so on—is, as Strong notes, "too crude an instrument for expressing subtle, complicated ideas."[14]

Getting Started with Metaphors

One efficient way to present metaphorical thinking to a class is by using "Trigger Concepts,"[15] which can be found in Strong's book. "Triggers" are a list of four hundred words that promote metaphorical and complex thinking, which includes words such as skeleton, valley, maze, tunnel, amoeba, root, battery, spice, bag, hinge, algebra, menu, pepper, rainbow, ice, liquid, nut, port, shadow, lever, meteor, perfume, room, fruit, and water (81–83). Students apply a single word from the list in order to create a simile or metaphor that explains the overarching idea of an abstract idea or concept.

To use trigger words in conjunction with *Project Runway*, students use them as a springboard for reflection on the writing process. After viewing an episode, they choose a word from the list that encapsulates a contestant's creative process. For example, if a student chose the trigger word "menu" in describing Elisa's writing process in the episode "Eye Candy," the student might respond with something like this:

> Elisa's writing process is like ordering from a menu. A menu is full of options for the creation of a wonderful dinner experience, and Elisa gathers many supplies to create her dress. But when ordering from menus, an individual must think carefully about how she will place her order.

Choosing heavy appetizers might leave her too full for her entrée while disregarding the ingredients of a main dish might set off a food allergy, and choosing bad wine could drown the taste buds and ruin the whole dinner before the food even makes it to the table.

The problem with Elisa's composing process was that she had too many ideas or main dishes—she wanted a "magical" garment and a "fairy tale" feeling, words that have positive connotations, but she also wanted a "macabre Gretl," which didn't fit with the whimsical feeling she initially set out to create. In the end, because she used all of her ideas, she ended up with a garment that was the equivalent to ordering steak, chicken, fish, and pork chops all in the same meal.

Depending on the sophistication of the students, it might be useful to provide a template to focus their comparisons:

> [Insert contestant's name here]'s creative process is like a . . .
> Just as [insert trigger word here] is like [insert contestant's name here]

Prior to this activity, students take notes on contestants' composing processes as they watch the show because it can be difficult for viewers to keep track of who is who if they are not already familiar with the contestants.

Ideally, once students have finished their contestant's metaphors, they begin an extended writing project and keep notes on their own process as they complete their drafts. Once finished, they create a metaphor for their own writing process. However, if an extended writing project doesn't fit within the context of the course design, students write metaphors based on their remembered experience of a recent experience with the writing process. Either way, students reflect on the process of writing rather than just engaging in prescribed steps.

Crafting Revision Activities

While thinking about the writing process as a whole is a valuable activity, it is also useful to address specific tasks related to writing. Revision is often a key component to the composing process, but it can be difficult for students to practice. When asked to describe the act of revising, professional authors speak in terms of global or comprehensive changes to a piece, but students tend to describe a series of superficial adjustments that are similar to editing and proofreading.[16] For teachers, such a shallow view of revision is problematic because it limits the types of changes to a draft that students are willing to make.

In order to expand students' notions of revision, an episode of *Project Runway* is helpful because a large portion of each episode is focused on the designers trying out ideas as they engage in the actual act of revision. Also, because viewers see the changes almost instantly, they gain very concrete ideas about how a designer's willingness to make changes to an idea influences the final product. For example, in "Eye Candy," Jillian is the only contestant to use food in her design. Initially, she is excited about the challenge but quickly finds that creating clothing from food is an extremely challenging task. As she struggles to glue Twizzlers onto the bodice of her dress, she states that she has "the most frustrated and devastated feeling," and wonders if she will even be able to finish the project.

In a voice-over, Chris, another contestant, explains that neither Jillian's idea nor the plan is working. Ultimately, she decides to sew, rather than glue, the Twizzlers to her dress, and her changes land her a spot in the top two during judging. Much in the same way Jillian is willing to revise her original plan and to substitute thread for glue, a writer must sometimes deviate from her original plan regardless of how exciting the original conception of the idea actually is.

Sweet P provides another example of the revision process, although her revisions are far less successful. She recognizes early failure after receiving feedback from Tim Gunn and somewhat revises her plan, reluctantly stating, "It's just not working. I don't want to start over, but I have to." However, she doesn't really start over. She keeps both the bodice and the cut from her original design, and changes only the fabric of the skirt. In the end, she is not eliminated, but she is in the bottom two of the competition and is criticized because her outfit is not judged as "inventive."

Sweet P's changes are the writing equivalents of moving a sentence or adding a few adjectives, but they are not meaningful alterations of her original idea. Had she created a different outfit, not just a slightly different version of her original idea, she probably would have fared much better. Similarly, Elisa makes only superficial changes to her garment after receiving Gunn's feedback—she adds puffy sleeves but keeps both the cut and concept she started with—and ultimately, her dress causes her elimination. Sweet P and Elisa make good cautionary tales because all creators have to be able to recognize when an idea is not working and make the necessary adjustments.

In his chapter in the book, *Acts of Revision*, Brock Dethier identified eight limiting beliefs about revision that writers (or any type of creators) might have, including the idea that revision is trivial, unnecessary, makes things worse, wastes time, that it is drudgery and a sign of failure, and that some writers do not revise due to lack of time or because they don't know how to revise.[17]

Requiring students to identify moments in the episode when beliefs from Dethier's list are demonstrated by the contestants is a useful exercise that will make them more aware of their own attitudes and behaviors surrounding revision. Because it is the designers on the show, not themselves, that students are critiquing, they have the critical distance necessary to recognize both the beliefs and their detrimental effects. This exercise brings revision to the forefront of students' attention, and thus emphasizes the role of revision in the writing process and opens a space for more meaningful acts of revision.

Moreover, *Project Runway* features contestants who literally cut and sew their creations together, take them apart, and sew them together in new ways. In many ways, this is what teachers ask their students to do when revising an essay for class. Another variation on using *Project Runway* as a model of hands-on revision is to involve students with a cut-and-paste activity using their drafts as raw materials, similar to how contestants on the show physically move the pieces of their creation around by cutting and sewing, taking away and adding more.

To incorporate a cut-and-paste revision session in class, students compose a fat draft (a draft approximately at least twice as long as the final essay should be) in response to an assignment. They bring a printed version to class, where each student is provided a piece of butcher paper and a pair of scissors. Students cut their essays up into paragraphs, which are reordered in a new way, some thrown away, some revised, and a new conclusion is written.

This revision activity helps students experience firsthand how the physical movement of paragraphs into a new order can create an entirely new, very different piece of writing. The physical moving of paragraphs also helps students to see that revision is more than the editing of writing and that it often involves a whole new way of seeing and composing an essay, thus making students more aware of the possibilities that revision offers them as they compose.

A discussion about the role of revision in students' work provides a nice conclusion to this activity. Potential questions include:

- Have there been times when you have been unable or unwilling to revise? What were the reasons for this?
- As writers, how can we know if we should take the suggestions given by others? Should all suggestions be included in a revision?
- How can we evaluate the feedback we are given and determine when it is appropriate to refrain from following a specific suggestion?

Watching and discussing the experiences of the contestants as they revise their designs provides students the chance to identify these limiting beliefs about revision and to discuss how the attitude each contestant had about revision impacted their ability to make use of the criticism offered. They can also see their own revision practices take hold as they make connections between their work and *Project Runway*.

Learning to Give Feedback

In the same way that students can become more open to revision simply by recognizing their beliefs about it, thinking about the importance of feedback is also a valuable opportunity for growth. Giving and receiving feedback during the drafting process is a common practice in writing classrooms. However, getting students to provide one another with valuable feedback is a challenge for teachers.

Often, they are reluctant to say anything critical to their classmates and offer only hollow comments such as "I liked it." Students who do give criticism tend to focus on usage and spelling errors or they commandeer their peers' work to fit into their vision of what a project should be. However, by watching an episode of *Project Runway*, students gain valuable insight into the act of giving meaningful feedback.

In terms of attitude and demeanor, Tim Gunn serves as an excellent model. He is an informed mentor who takes each contestant's work seriously, no matter how ill-conceived, and he is compassionate and positive when he speaks to the designers. That said, while Gunn is known for providing useful and thoughtful feedback to the designers, during the course of an actual episode, his remarks often appear to be somewhat hollow. For example, in "Eye Candy," he offers comments such as "There is tremendous potential here," and "I am concerned." Such comments are relevant but not particularly insightful, and they do not guide contestants to an improved vision of their design.

In "Eye Candy," it is useful to review the scene where Gunn responds to Elisa's design by saying, "Bring a critical eye and wow me." Here students think about what they would do with that feedback if they were in Elisa's shoes. They reflect on how they would change her design to make it "wow" him and asked themselves if the feedback was constructive (or not).

Students then make suggestions for what they think Elisa might do to improve upon her design and then compare the feedback that Gunn provides to the feedback that they would provide. They ask one another which suggestions seem more effective in order to draw some conclusions about the nature of feedback.

Since Gunn is not the focus of the show—the designers are—his extended comments do not regularly appear in episodes. However, he can be seen judging contestants on the *Project Runway* website. Clips of the designers' critiques are available for free, and throughout those clips, there are multiple examples of Gunn providing specific criticism that would be useful models on how to give feedback. Because "Eye Candy" is an older episode, it does not have extended judging clips, but a clip of a critique from any recent episode effectively demonstrates key points about providing feedback.

Once students consider ways to provide useful feedback, they create a list of guidelines for giving feedback, both from what they noticed in the show and from their own writing experiences. These guidelines can be used in future peer review sessions to help the class build a shared expectation of how peer feedback will be given and used in the classroom. For example, in conjunction with assigned essays, students compose reflection letters in which they address which aspects of the feedback from their classmates is useful and how they use the feedback. They also identify what feedback they chose not to use and why they believe this was the right choice for the final draft of their essay.

FINAL THOUGHTS

Why bother making this connection in the classroom? And is it really helpful to bring more television into students' lives? Many teachers and scholars believe it is. In their book, *Signs of Life in the U.S.A.: Readings on Popular Culture for Writers*, Sonia Maasik and Jack Solomon make the case for pop culture in the composition classroom and argue that the examination of popular culture is "what analytic writing is about: going beyond the surface of a text or issue toward an interpretation."[18]

Similarly, Karen Fitts uses popular culture to help students gain an understanding of the world that surrounds them, but also of the role of the author and the practice of authoring in shaping that world. She argues that the inclusion of popular culture provides the opportunity to validate students' experience outside academia because it "indicates to students the valuable connections between one's education and one's everyday life."[19]

By bringing pop culture, via *Project Runway*, into the classroom, teachers are able to connect to students and to provide the opportunity for students to watch real world uses of the creation process.

The episode "Eye Candy" is especially useful in the composition classroom because it so clearly displays the recursive process of creation, the way that feedback ties into revision, and how attitude about revision can lead to, or prevent, success. Using an episode of *Project Runway* as a springboard for activities and conversations about writing, revising, and offering feedback provides the class a shared frame of reference and a lexicon from which to reflect on their own work.

Project Runway also contributes to learning about the creative process in a way that traditional teaching cannot. It puts human faces on the composing process, allowing learners the opportunity to see how creative thinking unfolds, but more importantly, it creates opportunities for students to reflect on how their writing practices mirror or deviate from the revision methods of the show's contestants and thus serves as a vehicle for students to gain personal insight into their own composing practices. John Dewey, one of the most influential education scholars in history, points out that there is an "organic connection between education and personal experience,"[20] and advocates for drawing from students' personal knowledge to facilitate educational growth.

By thinking about *Project Runway* in relation to their own composing habits, writing students can learn to "make it work" for themselves.

NOTES

1. Douglas Fisher and Nancy Frey, "Modeling Expert Thinking," *Principal Leadership* 11, no. 3 (2010): 58–59.
2. "Eye Candy," *Project Runway* (television), written by Heidi Klum (2008; New York: The Weinstein Company, 2009).
3. Janet Emig, *The Composing Practices of Twelfth Graders* (Urbana: National Council of Teachers of English, 1971), 91–94.
4. Donald Murray, "Teaching Writing as a Process Not Product," in *Cross-Talk in Comp Theory,* 2nd ed., ed. Victor Villanueva (Urbana: National Council of Teachers of English, 2003), 3.
5. Gary Olson, "Toward a Post-Process Composition: Abandoning the Rhetoric of Assertion," in *Post-Process Theory: Beyond the Writing-Process Paradigm*, ed. Thomas Kent (Carbondale: Southern Illinois University Press, 1999), 7–15.
6. Richard Winter, Alyson Buck, and Paula Sobiechowska, *Professional Experience and the Investigative Imagination: The Art of Reflective Writing* (New York: Routledge, 1999), 106.
7. Robert Bringle and Julie Hatcher, "Reflection in Service Learning: Making Meaning of an Experience," *Educational Horizons* 77, no. 44 (1999): 71.
8. David Bartholomae, "Inventing the University," in *Cross-Talk in Comp Theory: A Reader*, ed. Victor Villanueva (Urbana: National Council of Teachers of English, 2003), 623–54.
9. Patricia Bizell, "Arguing about Literacy," *College English* 50, no. 2 (1988): 141–53.
10. Gerald Graff and Ander Hoberek, "Hiding it from the Kids (with Apologies to Simon and Garfunkel)," *College English* 62, no. 2 (1999): 242–53.
11. G. Lynn Nelson, *Writing and Being* (San Francisco: Inner Ocean Publishing, Inc, 2004), xii.
12. Wendy Bishop, *On Writing: A Process Reader,* 2nd ed. (New York: McGraw-Hill Higher Education, 2007).
13. Wendy Bishop, *Elements of Alternate Style: Essays on Writing and Revision* (Portsmouth: Boynton/Cook, 1997).
14. William Strong, *Write for Insight* (Boston: Pearson, 2006), 81–83; 179–81.
15. Strong, 81.
16. Nancy Sommers, "Revision Strategies of Student Writers and Experienced Adult Writers," *College Composition and Communication* 31, no. 4 (1980): 378–88.
17. Brock Dethier, "Revising Attitudes," in *Acts of Revision: A Guide for Writers,* ed. Wendy Bishop (Portsmouth: Heinemann, 2004), 2–3.
18. Sonia Maasik and Jack Solomon, introduction to *Signs of Life in the U.S.A.: Readings on Popular Culture for Writers*, ed. Sonia Maasik and Jack Solomon (Boston: Bedford, 1994), 9.
19. Karen Fitts, "Ideology, Life Practices, and Pop Culture: So Why is this Called Writing Class?" *The Journal of General Education* 54, no. 2 (2005): 91.
20. John Dewey, *Experience and Education* (New York: Simon and Schuster, 1938), 25.

BIBLIOGRAPHY

Bartholomae, David. "Inventing the University." In *Cross-Talk in Comp Theory: A Reader*, edited by Victor Villanueva, 623–54. Urbana: National Council of Teachers of English, 2003.

Bishop, Wendy. *Elements of Alternate Style: Essays on Writing and Revision.* Portsmouth: Boynton/Cook, 1997.

———. *On Writing: A Process Reader.* 2nd Edition. New York: McGraw-Hill Higher Education, 2007.

Bizell, Patricia. "Arguing about Literacy," *College English* 50, no. 2 (1988): 141–53.

Bringle, Robert, and Julie Hatcher. "Reflection in Service Learning: Making Meaning of Experience," *Educational Horizons* 77, no. 4 (1999): 179–85.

Dethier, Brock. "Revising Attitudes." In *Acts of Revision: A Guide for Writers*, edited by Wendy Bishop, 1–11. Portsmouth: Heinemann, 2004.

Dewey, John. *Experience and Education.* New York: Simon and Schuster, 1938.

Emig, Janet. *The Composing Process of Twelfth Graders.* Urbana: National Council of Teachers of English, 1968.

"Eye Candy." *Project Runway.* First broadcast January 2, 2008, by Bravo. Written by Heidi Klum.

Fisher, Douglas, and Nancy Frey. "Modeling Expert Thinking." *Principal Leadership* 11.3 (2010): 58–59.

Fitts, Karen. "Ideology, Life Practices, and Pop Culture: So Why is this Called Writing Class?" *The Journal of General Education* 54, no. 2 (2005): 90–105.

Graff, Gerald, and Andrew Hoberek. "Hiding It From the Kids (with Apologies to Simon and Garfunkel)." *College English* 62, no. 2 (1999), 242–54.

Maasik, Sonia, and Jack Solomon. Introduction to *Signs of Life in the U.S.A.: Readings on Popular Culture for Writers*. Edited by Sonia Maasik and Jack Solomon. Boston: Bedford, 1994.

Murray, Donald. "Teach Writing as a Process Not Product." 1972. Reprinted in *Cross-Talk in Comp Theory*, 2nd ed. Edited by Victor Villanueva. Urbana: National Council of Teachers of English, 2003.

Nelson, G. Lynn. *Writing and Being.* San Francisco: Inner Ocean Publishing, Inc., 2004.

Olson, Gary. "Toward a Post-Process Composition: Abandoning the Rhetoric of Assertion." In *Post-Process Theory: Beyond the Writing-Process Paradigm*. Edited by Thomas Kent, 7–15. Carbondale: Southern Illinois University Press, 1999.

Pennebaker, James. *Opening Up.* New York: William Morrow and Company, Inc., 1990.

Progoff, Ira. *At a Journal Workshop.* New York: Penguin, 1975.

Sommers, Nancy. "Revision Strategies of Student Writers and Experienced Adult Writers." *College Composition and Communication* 31, no. 4 (1980): 378–88.

Strong, William. *Write for Insight: Empowering Content Area Learning.* Boston: Pearson Allyn and Bacon, 2006.

Winter, Richard, Alyson Buck, and Paula Sobiechowska. *Professional Experience and the Investigative Imagination: The Art of Reflective Writing.* New York: Routledge, 1999.

Chapter Eight

Up, Up, and Away

Superman in the Composition Classroom

Alex Romagnoli

THE SET-UP

The influence of graphic novels in the English classroom has become profound in the last decade. Graphic novels are highlighted by a multimodality of visuals and texts that promotes a literacy that expands beyond the typical boundaries of traditional prose, poetry, plays, and other staples of the English classroom. Research has shown that graphic novels are a productive method to access students' multiliteracies[1] and multiple intelligences[2] as the reading of graphic novels is subject to what one researcher has termed "outsider literacy."[3] Graphic novels represent an evolution in the ways stories and experiences are shared and discussed in the English classroom.

However, the academic evolution of texts that is the graphic novel has hit a crossroads of sorts. The medium of comic art, which is nearly one hundred years old, has strayed from its roots when it comes to academics. The academy has supported an insular understanding of which style of graphic novels are appropriate inside the English classroom. This style of graphic novel exists in stark contrast to the traditions and the pop culture popularity of the medium. Specifically, the academic usage of graphic novels has become personified by a certain genre.

Where are the superheroes? Where are the Sunday funnies? Where are the characters that made the medium of comics a fun and inviting world? Instead of the classic characters and stories that made the graphic novel even possible, English classrooms have taken the medium of comic art and focused its gaze upon a very narrow window.

Maus by Art Spiegelman,[4] *Persepolis* by Marjane Satrapi,[5] and *A Contract with God* by Will Eisner[6] are now representative of what graphic novels have to offer academics. A story about the holocaust, a story about a young Iranian girl struggling through the Islamic Revolution in the 1970s, and a story about a rabbi struggling with the death of his adopted daughter are now the stories that students are exposed to in academic usages of graphic novels.

At the same time, the medium of graphic storytelling, or what Will Eisner calls "sequential art,"[7] is traditionally a narrative vehicle born out of colorful characters whose exploits could be detailed in lively and interactive ways. Peanuts, Superman, Spider-Man, Garfield, and countless other popular characters are left in the academic dust in favor of stories that focus on much more serious narratives.

This is not to say that graphic novels with more mature and serious subject matter are to be ignored or relegated; graphic novels such as *Maus*, *Persepolis*, and *Contract with God* are invaluable teaching tools, which have elevated the medium of "sequential art" to unprecedented levels of artistry. The point here is that these styles of stories seem to be the predominant choice for English teachers when using graphic novels.

The following chapter is not a complete deconstruction of the graphic novel's canon in academic contexts, for that has been discussed at length in *Enter the Superheroes: American Values, Culture, and the Canon of Superhero Literature*.[8] However, the blatant relegation of superhero literature in academic contexts represents the academic world's resistance to texts that reflect a more juvenile style of narrative. Looking at the history of the comic medium, though, there is a dissonance between academia's embracing of "sequential art" and the selective nature of the texts privileged:

> The medium of comics, which was born out of the colorful heroes who brightened lives one dime at a time, is now predominantly recognized in academic circles only when the medium purposefully distances itself from its heroic origins in order to explore themes that more typically reflect academic concerns about social equity, the horrors of war, and the troubles of existence.[9]

Even the superhero graphic novel that is predominantly embraced by academia, *Watchmen* by Alan Moore and Dave Gibbons, is a superhero graphic novel about a world where superheroes don't work.[10] Superhero comic books and graphic novels are less valued in academic contexts even though the medium of comic books and graphic novels is currently experiencing a rise in popularity at the academic level.

However, this chapter takes a different stance, focusing on graphic novels in the English classroom beyond the now-established set often preferred by teachers. The superhero genre, which springboarded the medium to new heights throughout the twentieth century, will be explored as a way to encourage reflection and exploration in a college level or high school English class, and when the world thinks of superheroes, it undoubtedly thinks of the Man of Steel. Using popular graphic novels like *Superman* will not only connect with students, it will also help build reading and language arts skills.

REVIEW OF LITERATURE

Superman was created in 1938[11] by Jerry Siegel and Joe Shuster and became the flagship character of DC Comics (then National Periodicals). His story has become one of the quintessential American success stories. Born on the planet Krypton and jettisoned to Earth by his father Jor-El and his mother Lara before Krypton was destroyed, Kal-El (Superman) was found on Earth in the cornfields of Smallville, Kansas, by the kindly couple of Jonathan and Martha Kent.

The Kents adopted the young Kryptonian as their own, named him Clark, and raised him as a human. Upon discovering he had enhanced physical abilities due to Earth's yellow Sun, Clark Kent took it upon himself to become Superman. He moved to Metropolis and worked in the offices of *The Daily Planet*, the world's most respected paper so as to be at the hub of information in order to help those in need.

This is the essence of the world's premiere superhero: he fights a never-ending battle for truth, justice, and the American way. His physical presence is overshadowed only by his unyielding morality, which provides a standard that even the noblest of people would have a difficult time attaining. He is also the most popular and recognizable superhero.

For an English class looking to expand its scope in graphic literature, Superman is an excellent place to begin. The character is recognizable to generations of readers making introduction to the character relatively simple. There would likely be a summative review of the character and his backstory, but it would be much simpler than other texts in the typical English classroom to introduce as the presence of the character in popular culture and popular media is significant.

A typical text in an English curriculum includes themes such as heroism, bravery, altruism, and journeys. *The Odyssey*[12] is a text required in many curriculums. Homer's epic poem provides students with a rich story, ancient mythology, and an examination of the hero's journey home. It is, without a doubt, one of the most important works a high school student, or any student for that matter, could be exposed to and stands as one of the most significant stories in human history.

However, *The Odyssey* is incredibly dense. It is important to look at some aspects of the story that would need to be covered even before the students jumped into the actual reading and discussion of the text:

- The Battle of Troy
- A map of ancient Greece
- The concept of "hubris" and its implications for a hero
- The dynamics of Odysseus's family
- An explanation of how the Greek gods work within the constructs of epic poetry
- Why killing was an acceptable act by a hero in that time

This is only a handful of topics that would need to be covered in a typical English class before *The Odyssey* could even begin to be read by students. Quite frankly, any one of those could be the focus of a dissertation, let alone a ten to fifteen minute review for high school students. Stories such as *The Odyssey* represent traditional means for students to explore humanity's complexities, and Homer's epic poem is in the curriculum for good reason.

Yet, high school and collegiate classrooms constantly revisit *The Odyssey* and other stories, which to some extent, are socioculturally anachronistic. In comparing ancient mythological characters to modern heroes, it is important to note there may exist some anachronistic qualities: "While Achilles's morality and actions are much more in tune with modern audiences, Superman's morality and actions are much more relatable than those of Achilles because Superman's actions are much more in tune with modern culture's moral standards."[13]

Achilles and Odysseus kill people with regularity, but Superman does not traditionally kill his enemies despite the controversial choice of Zack Snyder and David Goyer having Superman kill General Zod at the end of 2013's *Man of Steel* motion picture.[14] That issue, though, is a book chapter unto itself.

Literary critic Harold Bloom[15] would probably find this blasphemous, but some Superman texts are just as capable of exploring issues of heroism, bravery, and journeys as well as *The Odyssey*. This is not to say that Superman is in any way superior to *The Odyssey* in terms of content or opportunities for academic discourse. Instead, Superman represents a more modern means to explore issues that transcend time, generations, and audiences. Additionally, Superman's traditional medium, the comic book, is reflective of what The New London Group termed multiliteracies.

The New London Group's assertion is that as media evolves through technology, the ways in which audiences interact with media also changes. Instead of readers possessing a singular mode of literacy, there are multiple literacies that can be utilized during any given interaction with a medium.

This can include traditional literacy (print/textual), visual, audio, or even digital. Traditional texts in English classrooms subscribe mainly to print literacy, which best represents the established skill sets that state standards and college curriculums expect of students. Graphic novels are an alternative to traditional texts, and they "offer important, unique, and timely multi-literacy experiences."[16]

Superman's presence as a pop culture and literary icon, coupled with his profound presence in the unique medium of "sequential art" provides an opportunity for academic discussions that are influenced by both popular culture and by timeless literary themes of heroism and bravery. The issue then becomes which of the multiple Superman titles would be appropriate for late high school and early college students to write in conjunction with.

Superman's story has evolved over the seventy-five years it has been in publication leading to a mythology that is ripe with complicated continuity. Since his first appearance in 1938, Superman has married, died, come back to life, changed his signature suit, and found his long-lost cousin from Krypton. The Man of Steel has had his fair share of experiences in his fictional existence, but those experiences have all been interconnected in what the genre of superhero literature calls continuity. Italian semiotician Umberto Eco referred to Superman never reaching what he called "final consumption,"[17] or the point at which readers resolve the events of the character's fictional life in their own minds. Superman's story never truly ends.

Long-time fans and readers of Superman are able to sift through all of the interconnected stories and interpret the exploits of the character in both the context of a singular story and the much larger world of its continuity. All superheroes, whether they are DC or Marvel, share this unique trait in their mythologies; their stories are simultaneously insular and interconnected through both narrative and metatextuality. For high school and college students, using a graphic novel from a superhero's mythology can be tricky because most superhero stories are connected to larger storylines that necessitate a reading of past material in order to understand the events of the current story.

The most common exception to this in superhero literature is the origin story of a character, which can exist on its own as it is the beginning of the larger and interconnected narrative. Superman's origin is quite popular though. There have been other origin stories written since his first appearance including *The Man of Steel* by John Byrne and Dick Giordano,[18] *Superman: Birthright* by Mark Waid and Leinil Francis Yu,[19] and *Superman: Earth One* by J. Michael Straczynski and Shane Davis.[20] All of them are excellent graphic novels and would make great companion pieces to any academic discussions of heroism. However, the Superman graphic novel that this chapter will focus on will be *All-Star Superman* by Grant Morrison and Frank Quitely.[21]

DC's "All-Star" concept was simple yet profound: what if famous creators were given the opportunity to write superhero stories that were not affected by continuity? In other words, creators would have the chance to write superhero stories that could truly stand alone with readers only needing a general background of the character. For the first two forays into this concept, DC chose Frank Miller and Jim Lee to do *All-Star Batman and Robin*,[22] and Grant Morrison and Frank Quitely to do *All-Star Superman*.

Grant Morrison was an accomplished comic book writer famous for rejuvenating the X-Men franchise with *New X-Men*[23] in the early 2000s and writing edgy stories that drew on readers' abilities to follow storylines that were not always linear. Frank Quitely was known for art that went against the status quo in comic books. Quitely's tall and lean characters did not always look like typical comic book characters, and his action sequences looked almost as if they were actually moving on the page. Quitely and Morrison had teamed together before on titles such as *New X-Men* and *We3*,[24] and *All-Star Superman* became an immediate hit.

Consisting of twelve individual issues, which combined to tell a larger narrative, *All-Star Superman* told the story of a dying Superman getting his affairs in order as he accomplished final labors including giving Lois Lane superpowers for a day, saving a race of Bizarro people, saying goodbye to his father, and defeating Lex Luthor for the final time. More so than most Superman stories, Morrison and Quitely looked to humanize Superman in a way that had not really been attempted before. Morrison himself reflected on the project:

> We aimed for the pared-down clarity of folktales: stories of a world where intimate human dramas of love, jealousy, or grief were enacted upon a planetary scale by a group of characters whose decisions could shake worlds. In the grand arena of *All-Star Superman*, a broken heart, a tear, or a single good deed would inevitably unleash massive, cosmic consequences. *All-Star Superman* was a divine Everyman, Platonic man sweating out the drama of ordinary life on an extraordinary canvas.[25]

All-Star Superman acts as a story designed to humanize the Man of Steel in order to analyze human emotions and situations. The fact that Superman is dying throughout the story forces the demigod to face the pains, both physical and emotional, that all humans are subject to. As Superman is characterized as being physically and morally perfect, the way in which he addresses his problems can have readers reflect on how they address such issues in their own lives.

For high school and college English classes looking for a text with which to facilitate composition, *All-Star Superman* provides multiple opportunities for reflection, debate, and abstraction and can be a useful, productive artifact in English courses.

CLASSROOM CONNECTIONS

Journal Ideas

One of Superman's final tasks in the concluding weeks of his life is to set his affairs in order; this includes preparing the world for his departure and saying goodbye to the people he loves and cares about. For the Man of Steel, these people include his mother and father on Earth, Lois Lane, Jimmy Olsen, Perry White, Krypto the Superdog, and even Lex Luthor. One assignment for students working with *All-Star Superman* could be the following:

> In *All-Star Superman*, Superman makes it a point of saying goodbye to his loved ones before his inevitable end. One such person was Lois Lane, who was granted superpowers for a day in order to share a day in the world of Superman. If you could do anything with anyone in your life for one day, who would it be and what would you do?

This question is deeply personal, and it would serve as an excellent journal entry in class or as a starter on a day after the students had read that portion of the graphic novel. It can also be used as a springboard into other writing assignments. The point of asking students to consider such a profound notion is to have them reflect on the choices Superman makes in the graphic novel and how those choices in a fictional story are mirrors of what people struggle with in their own lives.

People struggle with the idea of mortality throughout their lives, both their own and their loved ones. It is a subject not many are comfortable discussing and understandably so. That is why the analysis of Superman's death is so profound and important. The Man of Steel, the man who cannot die, is the embodiment of what humans would aspire to be, given superpowers. Even he must face death and resolve its consequences in his own, fictional mind. Superman makes it his mission to leave Earth in better shape than before he arrived. People all live for a similar purpose, that of improving the world through their experiences; everyone shares Superman's final heroic act.

Writing Activities

While there were many themes discussed throughout the reading of the book, one strong prompt is to focus on the final labors of Superman and what our final labors would be before we die. This prompt can also be used as a way to work through the writing process.

> **Pre-Writing:** Students first list ideas concerning what they want to accomplish in their lives. Listing accomplishments helps students visualize where they see their lives going, and the lists the students compile

provide excellent opportunities for career researching during a later project. This could be done as a free-write in class or given as a homework assignment. Given the dynamic of a particular class, perhaps students could trade papers with one another and compare ideas. Also, encouraging students to come up with more "labors" than they will actually need for a given essay promotes strong research skills: always get more information than you will need as you are never sure if all of your sources are going to work in a given paper.

Outlining/Mapping: At this point, students begin to choose which labors they want to address in their essays. It is absolutely up to the teacher to decide on how many "labors" he or she wants his or her students to write about. With students narrowing down ideas and constructing the ways in which they could elaborate through their writing, more pre-writing strategies are utilized in the students' preparation. Even linking the ways in which Superman plans throughout the graphic novel and how students plan their own writing can be highlighted. Clark Kent may be a journalist, but Superman is not necessarily known as a writer. However, there is a scene of Superman writing his last will and testament with heat vision and a piece of metal.

Composing: This essay is about reflecting on one's life and how the final labors represent what we want most. Superman showed a strong compassion for the people in his life as well as humanity in general. Subsequently, his labors were quite selfless. In that selflessness is the true power of Superman: with all the power one might wish and hope to have, he used his near limitless resources to say goodbye to both the world and the people in it. By defining the final labors, students explore what is important to them in their world. What makes me who I am, and where do I see my value in this world?

Research: One way to expand the scope of this assignment is to turn it into a partial research project. Have students cite instances in the graphic novel that encourage or inspire them. Perhaps students might find some of Superman's final labors ridiculous and bombastic. Either reaction is productive though as it pushes students to analyze what they interact with: a necessary characteristic to have as a researcher. Additionally, having students find outside sources on how their final labors would be possible is a definite plus. It may not be enough for a student to say, "I want to take a boat around the world." That is a wonderful "labor" for a student to look into, but it's not enough to simply say that. What would be required to do that? Has anyone done that? Have you read about these other people? What will you do for food? Money? Will your boat be gas-powered or will it be a sailboat? One "labor" opens a Pandora's box of possibilities for the young researcher.

Editing: The traditional peer-editing session would be particularly beneficial to a project such as this. Not only would students get the chance to read about each other's "labors," it creates an audience where a young writer can learn to navigate the intricacies of personal reflection and the eventual sharing of those personal thoughts.

Beyond the concept of "final labors" and how those represent the essence of humanity, *All-Star Superman* also provides various themes that can be touched upon throughout the course of a composition or literature survey course.

Perhaps one of the more interesting themes of the book is Superman's continuing hope that Lex Luthor will redeem himself before the Man of Steel meets his end. During a particularly enlightening interview, Clark Kent is sent to Lex Luthor's jail cell to get one last interview with the criminal mastermind before he is sentenced to death for crimes against humanity.

During their conversation, which spans an entire chapter, Luthor and Clark Kent deconstruct the relationship between the two in heartbreaking detail. Luthor taunts Clark Kent about Lois Lane saying, "She'll never see past him to you!" and glorifying his own masculinity because it is not enhanced by the sun like Superman's: "Feel *that* Kent. *Real* muscles, not like *his*."[26] However, Luthor deconstructs the convoluted relationship between him and Superman to one profound comment saying, "There's no deep *psychology* behind the struggle between Superman and me. It's all very *simple*. How would *you* feel if someone *deliberately* stood in *your* way over and over again?"[27]

The perversion of Lex Luthor also serves as a foil for the hope that Superman exudes. Clark Kent is Superman, so Kent's interview with Luthor is a futile attempt for Superman to bring Luthor back from the brink of Hell. The duality of Luthor's depravity and Superman's hope serve as representations of humanity.

Analyzing a segment of *All-Star Superman* is something students at the high school and college level can do in a single class period or as an entire unit on the sociocultural constructs of "good" and "evil." Perhaps a prompt could help them get started: "Analyze the relationship between Superman and Lex Luthor throughout *All-Star Superman*. For each character, find three quotes that embody their perspectives on each other." That is only one other theme that can be explored, and *All-Star Superman* is full of them:

- Superman's trip to Bizarro's world could be studied as an analogy for otherness.
- Superman traveling back in time to say goodbye to his father is great for analyzing familial relationships.

- Chapter 10, where Superman constructs a microscopic alternate reality where he never existed parallels our own reality where Superman exists only as a fictional idea. Concepts such as metatextuality, historical fiction, and the influences that history and popular culture have on each other could be explored.

Nonprint Reflection and Writing Activities

Finally, tapping into students' multiliteracies through analysis of the images throughout the graphic novel promotes a privileging of the evolution of media. It is easy to fall into the trap of focusing on what characters actually say instead of how they are depicted. This is due in part to the traditional conditioning of English teachers to focus on the written word.

Naturally, we gravitate to text because that is what is predominantly outlined in standards and curriculums. However, the value of the graphic novel is rooted in what a creative team does with both spheres of communication. Working in tandem with one another, Morrison and Quitely present a narrative that honors and empowers each others' strengths. Unlike the comic books of old, Frank Quitely's art would take the storytelling reigns from Morrison during an action sequence and seamlessly hand them back a page or two later with no text to be seen.

Highlighting and emphasizing that narrative communication is profound for young and aspiring writers to recognize because it presents a new and different way to analyze the writing process. Yes, writing is about pounding out the words on a keyboard. What becomes apparent when reading *All-Star Superman* is that writing is not solely a written endeavor. Instead, it is taking life experiences and presenting them in their purest essence, whether that essence is textual, visual, or a combination of the two.

Students could write journals about their impressions of the characters as they see them in visual depictions. How do the images augment their perceptions of the characters? How is tone portrayed through both words and pictures? Brainstorming activities comparing—and actually *using*—the images will excite the students and provide additional opportunities for reflection and writing practice.

While the focus of this chapter has been on utilizing a superhero graphic novel as an artifact in a composition or traditional English course, the writings that students produce during their analyses of the graphic novel and its themes could be channeled into future projects that expand beyond the sphere of traditional composition. This chapter is not venturing into that realm, but *All-Star Superman*, as well as countless other graphic novels, can serve as creative springboards into new and promising worlds of creativity for students.

FINAL THOUGHTS

Incorporating a superhero graphic novel in an English class is still something quite exotic in the world of academics. Unfortunately, there is still a stigma attached to the medium that only youth and adolescents read comic books and that the superhero genre's roots of appealing only to children is still applicable. Famed comic book creator Frank Miller has said, though, that, "In comics, in comic books, in superhero comics, people have wasted an awful lot of creative energy and hard work looking for kids who aren't there."[28]

The idea of using Superman in an English class or a composition class or a literature class is not to appeal to some fabricated notion that the best way to engage with young learners is to give them books with pictures in them. Instead, using a Superman graphic novel in an English class is productive because he is one of the most significant heroes in the history of literature. Additionally, the character's relevance during the last seventy-five years is precedential. His exploits are also full of iconography that students of any age (adults included) can engage with and produce excellent conversations about.

All-Star Superman just happens to be one of many Superman texts that could be studied by students in a high school or college English course. There are other Superman stories that are powerful and challenge the notions of power, heroism, villainy, and even family. But *All-Star Superman* presents the character at his most elemental; he is the superhero that sacrifices his own body and utilizes his amazing abilities to help the world. Even beyond the essay prompts and the analyses and the understandable attention to academically structuring the usage and study of a superhero graphic novel in an English classroom, embracing and discussing the story of Superman as the sociocultural embodiment of a hero is a profound discussion in any class.

NOTES

1. The New London Group, "A Pedagogy of Multiliteracies: Designing Social Features," *Harvard Educational Review* 66, no. 1 (1996): 60–92.
2. Howard Gardner, *Frames of Mind: The Theory of Multiple Intelligences* (New York: Basic Books, 1983).
3. Marie Romanelli, "Exploring the Culture and Cognition of Outsider Literacy Practices in Adult Readers of Graphic Novels" (PhD dissertation, Indiana University of Pennsylvania, 2009).
4. Art Spiegelman, *The Complete Maus* (New York: Penguin, 2003).
5. Marjane Satrapi, *The Complete Persepolis* (New York: Pantheon, 2007).
6. Will Eisner, *A Contract with God* (New York: Baronet Books, 1978).
7. Will Eisner, *Comics & Sequential Art: Principles & Practice of the World's Most Popular Art Form* (Taramac, FL: Poorhouse Press, 1985).
8. Alex Romagnoli and Gian Pagnucci, *Enter the Superheroes: American Values, Culture, and the Canon of Superhero Literature* (Lanham: Scarecrow Press, 2013).

9. Romagnoli and Pagnucci, *Enter the Superheroes*, 32.
10. Ibid., 31.
11. Jerry Siegel and Joe Shuster, *Action Comics* 1, no. 1 (June 1938).
12. Homer, translated by Robert Fagles and Bernard Knox, *The Odyssey* (New York: Penguin Classics, 1997).
13. Romagnoli and Pagnucci, *Enter the Superheroes*, 15.
14. *Man of Steel* directed by Zack Snyder (Warner Brothers, 2013), DVD.
15. Harold Bloom, *The Western Canon: The Books and School of the Ages* (New York: Palgrave Macmillan, 2005).
16. James Bucky Carter, "Introduction: Carving a Niche: Graphic Novels in the English Language Arts Classroom," in *Building Literacy Connections with Graphic Novels: Page by Page, Panel by Panel*, ed. James Bucky Carter (Urbana: National Council of Teachers of English, 2007), 7.
17. Umberto Eco and Natalie Chilton, "The Myth of Superman," *Diacritics* 2, no. 1 (Spring 1972): 15.
18. John Byrne and Dick Giordano, *Superman: Man of Steel*, vol. 1 (New York: DC Comics, 1991).
19. Mark Waid and Leinil Francis Yu, *Superman: Birthright* (New York: DC Comics, 2005).
20. J. Michael Straczynski and Shane Davis, *Superman: Earth One* (New York: DC Comics, 2010).
21. Grant Morrison and Frank Quitely, *All-Star Superman* (New York: DC Comics, 2011).
22. Frank Miller and Jim Lee, *All-Star Batman and Robin, the Boy Wonder* (New York: DC Comics, 2009).
23. Grant Morrison, Frank Quitely, et al., *New X-Men*, vol. 1 (New York: Marvel Comics, 2008).
24. Grant Morrison and Frank Quitely, *We3* (New York: Vertigo, 2008).
25. Grant Morrison, *Supergods: What Masked Vigilantes, Miraculous Mutants, and a Sun God from Smallville Can Teach Us about Being Human* (New York: Spiegel & Grau, 2011), 411.
26. Morrison and Quitely, *All-Star Superman*, 110.
27. Morrison and Quitely, *All-Star Superman*, 124.
28. "The Man Without Fear: Creating Daredevil," *Daredevil*, directed by Mark Stephen Johnson (2003; 20th Century Fox, 2003), DVD. Documentary on DVD Extras.

BIBLIOGRAPHY

Bloom, Harold. *The Western Canon: The Books and School of the Ages.* New York: Riverhead Books, 1994.
Byrne, John, and Dick Giordano. *Superman: The Man of Steel.* New York: DC Comics, 1991.
Carter, James Bucky. "Introduction: Carving a Niche: Graphic Novels in the English Language Arts Classroom." In *Building Literacy Connections with Graphic Novels: Page by Page, Panel by Panel*, ed. James Bucky Carter, 1–25. Urbana: National Council of Teachers of English, 2007.
Eco, Umberto, and Natalie Chilton. "The Myth of Superman." *Diacritics* 2, no. 1 (1972). 14–22.
Eisner, Will. *Comics and Sequential Art: Principles & Practice of the World's Most Popular Art Form.* Taramac, FL: Poorhouse Press, 1985.
Eisner, Will. *A Contract with God.* New York: Baronet Books, 1978.
Gardner, Howard. *Frames of Mind: The Theory of Multiple Intelligences.* New York: Basic Books, 1983.
Homer. *The Odyssey.* Translated by Robert Fagles and Bernard Knox. New York: Penguin Classics, 1997.
Miller, Frank. "The Men Without Fear: Creating Daredevil." *Daredevil.* Directed by Mark Stephen Johnson. Los Angeles: 20th Century Fox, 2003.

Miller, Frank, and Jim Lee. *All-Star Batman and Robin, the Boy Wonder*. New York: DC Comics, 2009.
Morrison, Grant. *New X-Men*. Vol. 1. New York: Marvel Comics, 2008.
———. *Supergods: What Masked Vigilantes, Miraculous Mutants, and a Sun God from Smallville Can Teach Us About Being Human*. New York: Spiegel & Grau, 2011.
Morrison, Grant, and Frank Quitely. *All-Star Superman*. New York: DC Comics, 2011.
New London Group. "A Pedagogy of Multiliteracies: Designing Social Features." *Harvard Educational Review* 66, no. 1 (1996). 60–92.
Romagnoli, Alex, and Gian Pagnucci. *Enter the Superheroes: American Values, Culture, and the Canon of Superhero Literature*. Lanham: Scarecrow Press, 2013.
Romanelli, Marie. "Exploring the Culture and Cognition of Outside Literacy Practices in Adult Readers of Graphic Novels." PhD dissertation, Indiana University of Pennsylvania, 2009.
Satrapi, Marjane. *The Complete Persepolis*. New York: Pantheon, 2007.
Siegel, Jerry, and Joseph Shuster. *Action Comics* no. 1, June 1938.
Snyder, Zack. *Man of Steel*. DVD. Directed by Zack Snyder. Los Angeles: Warner Brothers, 2013.
Spiegelman, Art. *The Complete Maus*. New York: Penguin, 2003.
Straczynski, J. Michael, and Shane Davis. *Superman: Earth One*. New York: DC Comics, 2010.
Waid, Mark, and Leinil Francis Yu. *Superman: Birthright*. New York: DC Comics, 2005.

Chapter Nine

Popcorn and Movies for All

Four Reasons Films Work in Developmental Writing Classes

Salena Fehnel

THE SET-UP

Many instructors believe that showing movies is not an effective, academic strategy; the idea, then, of showing movies in developmental-level college writing classes to students who struggle with even a basic understanding of critical thinking and writing is considered out of the question. It seems that students have to "earn" the right to watch a film in class, and that teachers should recognize that developmental-level students simply have nothing to gain from watching movies.

Choosing to use feature films in developmental classes requires justification in an educational system that likes curriculum ties in every learning event. The use of films has moved from a taboo status to a more commonly understood method of connecting with current students—students who are using media on a daily basis to connect to life. The future of learning requires innovation and flexibility in the classroom, and willingness to integrate learning events that challenge students to grab onto new concepts using their prior knowledge bank and modern media.

Pairing movies with developmental curriculum accomplishes four major tasks: it motivates students who had never found motivation in the classroom, challenges preconceived notions about what a college education truly does for an individual, promotes critical and creative thinking that transfers directly to the learning outcomes of the course, and enhances students' self-awareness. In short, as one student stated during his first semester using this strategy: "I never knew I could learn like that. Nobody ever tried teaching me that way."

Regardless of the true worth of writing, the ways that it will eventually change and mold a student's educational prowess, for those who come from a background where they have tried and failed, or perhaps never tried at all, in the writing classroom, the notion of writing can be daunting. One way to soothe this and access prior knowledge is through the Known/Unknown pairing technique.

As an example: when teaching poetic devices, introduce the unknown (alliteration, for example) through a known medium (an Eminem verse). Once the students have demonstrated the ability to pick out these devices in the verse, give them a traditionally classic poem ("Annabel Lee") and ask them to do the same. This works because it makes the new, unfamiliar concepts appear familiar because of how they are being delivered. It also works because they are motivated to move into the lesson when it is introduced as a song they love to listen to, hence the positive experience of having a Known introduce a new concept.

Thirty years ago, classrooms were chalk and blackboards, brown-paper-bag book covers, and paper handouts for homework. Sure, some of this survives in today's classroom, but the landscape has changed dramatically. Teachers integrate social media, smartphones, tablets, videos, digital presentations, music, vlogs, blogs, and Twitter feeds into their lesson plans. Millennial students learn differently, and therefore, teachers must teach differently.

In developmental writing, the motivation to learn is only as strong as the teacher's willingness to step out of her own comfortable perception of what teaching truly is. For natural-born writers and teachers, the idea of writing itself is motivation to do the act, much like a strenuous workout is rewarding in itself to a natural-born athlete. But for those who struggle, thinking about the workout can be paralyzing.

Assignments shape students' ideas of higher education, particularly in schools where the majority of the students are from low-income school districts and homes where education is not prioritized. It also capitalizes on the idea of self-regulation within the developmental classroom. In her dissertation, "Metacognitive Awareness in Developmental Writing Students," Raffaella Negretti says that "Self-regulation is particularly important for developmental students if they wish to be successful in college, because they often lack the ability to monitor, evaluate, and modify the self-regulatory strategies they use."[1]

In many cases, the audience for a developmental writing classroom is markedly different than a traditional college. One of the charges of a developmental writing class is to build confidence in students who have negative or no experience with language. It's to challenge their gut reaction when they think of education and learning and what it has meant to them in the past.

Because developmental writing classes are often one of the first classes a student will take, this first step also means that teachers are shaping the way a student will feel about and will proceed with their higher education, and perhaps most importantly, how they will feel about themselves as students.

Developmental writing classes are also one of the first classes that incoming freshman take, and therefore hold the first impression card. The teacher's challenge is therefore upped from the "simple" task of getting students from point a to point b in the academic writing world to essentially defining a college education for them; and for students who are the first in their family to attend college, who have fought their whole lives through the education system, who have had nearly all negative experiences with learning, and who cringe at the word "essay," this is no small feat.

A teacher in one college with a high disadvantaged population implemented the strategy of using films in developmental writing classes. Many of the students in her class have struggled to get even the most basic of their needs met. In one journaling activity, a student who regularly came to class, participated, and turned in all assignments on time—in other words, raised no flags—wrote about how he had not eaten for two days, how the last food he was able to get was a slice of pizza, and how sometimes it's hard to not know when your next meal will be. This was an eye-opening moment for the teacher.

What was even more astounding was that in a class of eleven, every student showed empathy and compassion, and two other students voiced their own experience with hunger. In this same class, a female student in her mid-twenties described how much she missed her mom, and how she had begun living out of her car earlier in the semester, and was working two shifts at a gas station to get through her two-year program. She looked at the class when she finished reading, telling them, "This is my chance to change where I'm going. I need this. It's hard, but I need it."

After careful consideration in one developmental writing class, a teacher decided to try showing the movie *Gone Baby Gone*. This particular class was a hard-sell group. There were a number of nontraditional adult learners mixed in, and overall, they seemed unimpressed as a whole with everything the teacher had to offer. After working with this for a few weeks, he chose this film specifically to target their cynicism and attempt to introduce critical thinking as a practice rather than explaining it as a concept.

The movie *Gone Baby Gone* is a depiction of gritty, underworld Boston and a kidnapping investigation that appears to go terribly wrong. The students were riveted. When the movie had concluded, the students were given their assignment: to figure out alternatives to the investigation. Where did the detectives go wrong? What could they have done differently? Where was the film realistic versus unrealistic? Lastly, how was the ending just or unjust based on (a) a moral sense and (b) a legal sense? They were to consider these questions and write two to three pages answering them.

For the first time that semester, every student did his or her assignment. Most wrote more than two pages because they had so much to say—and their ideas were excellent, innovative, creative, and most of all, critical. They listed details of the investigation that even the teacher hadn't noticed. They examined motives, evidence, alibis, and characters.

On the day they brought their assignment in, a very loud debate broke out about whether or not the ending was just or unjust. Upon hearing how interested they were in discussing their opinions, the teacher split them into sides, gave them ten minutes to work together and write down their reasons for feeling the way they did, and then they staged a solid, organized debate. They spoke with confidence. They gathered information and listened to each other's views. Critical thinking skills are directly related to one's own belief that they are capable of them, and *Gone Baby Gone* tapped into each student's prior knowledge database of life experiences.

Film can be an easy warm-up that entices students to learn. This strategy has been observed in dozens of developmental writing classrooms, and to date, not a single group of students have been unenthusiastic when they see a film on the projector screen upon walking into the class. The tone of the class changes from regular to special, the students feel as though they are doing something "fun," and their attention is directed undivided to the front of the classroom. Integrating films into developmental writing classrooms as a learning tool does not simply foster motivation; it creates opportunity for prior-knowledge connections, critical thinking, long-term retention of ideas, and a basis of skill practice for developmental writers.

REVIEW OF LITERATURE

In his article, "Trust, Challenge, and Critical Thinking," David Miller discusses how developmental students truly doubt themselves and how this affects the ability to write:

> I have found that developmental writing students, in general, often question the validity of their personal experience and find it difficult to accept that it is as valid as anyone else's first-hand experience—in short, they do not trust the knowledge they already possess.[2]

This is, essentially, a deep-seated mistrust in one's own worth within an academic setting. Miller also mentions "writing scars." Students who carry these scars from bad experiences are fearful that they will be reopened or repeated, and therefore do not try because trying involves risk, and they have learned in language classrooms that risk results in failure and humiliation.[3]

One of the major outcomes of a developmental writing course is a demonstrated ability to use critical thinking and foster creative thinking. In his article, "Remedial Writing Courses: A Critique and a Proposal," Mike Rose connects the dots between critical thinking and writing.

> In any case—and this is why formal logic always failed in the composition classroom—"thinking skills" must not be taught as a set of abstract exercises (which, of course, they will be if they are not conceived of as being part of writing), but must be intimately connected to composition instruction. [4]

Rose argues that thinking skills are not easy to explain without sounding too unfamiliar and intimidating, so teachers need to craft activities that are natural to the assignments and foster growth.

Of course, the greatest fear of administrators (and hopefully dedicated teachers) is that students will perceive an in-class film as a "fluff" class in which they do not have to do anything or pay attention. And, truthfully, this is a possibility; but it is up to the teacher to create an active learning environment. Students will not view film-watching in the classroom as a free day if lesson plans are constructed around the central learning outcomes, with active learning emphasized before, during, and after the movie.

In the article, "Making Movies Active: Lessons from Simulations," this active learning strategy is emphasized in the form of well-planned activities surrounding the students from the moment they walk in, through the screening, to the assignment and discussion following the end.[5] The threat of passive learning is not present if the teacher engages the students in a pre-movie activity and follows the movie with critical thinking, active engagement, and discussion, along with an assignment that helps the students tie together the movie with the current learning goal.[6]

The other argument against movies in the classroom is that teachers are dumbing down the curriculum by removing the pairing of reading/writing and replacing it with watching/writing. In "The Missing 'R': A Reluctant Reader in a College Developmental Writing Class," John Young writes a truth for teachers everywhere, saying, "The fact is, however, that reading and writing are not always joined in harmony or in creative synergy within the classroom."[7]

Refusing to acknowledge this does little for the teacher and even less for the student. This antiquated view of learning is dangerous in three different capacities: one, because it prescribes a "correct" way of teaching students to write, leaving the door closed to innovation; two, because it leaves a large gap for students who have an aversion to reading but perhaps not to writing, truncating the opportunity to build student confidence before moving on to larger writing goals; and three, it dismisses film as valuable, critical text and experience within the classroom.

Young discusses how at the turn of the twentieth century, John Dewey broke the mold of standard pedagogy, which relied on instructors dispersing knowledge directly to students in a lecture-style, and students receiving it in a passive-style.[8] Considering the wildly different landscape of today's pedagogy—different teacher-training strategies today than what was even ten years ago—Dewey's pathway to the new and the innovative should be not only a model, but also a goal.

In their article, "Classrooms as Cinema: Using Film to Teach Sustainability," Bruce Clemens and Curt Hamakawa say, "Many of today's learners are more apt to respond favorably to the dominant stimuli in which they were raised—that is electronic media versus lecture and reading."[9] For the faint of heart and the diehard literature buffs, this approach does not mean that film should be the only type of text offered, only that it should be considered a useful and effective text within the classroom, and for the purposes of writing teachers, even within the walls of the developmental writing classrooms.

CLASSROOM CONNECTIONS

In each of the lesson plans below, a movie is used to focus the lesson on a learning outcome within a developmental writing class. The three lesson plans each include a choice of film, a brief summary of thematic ties, and the assignment strategy. Teachers also have the opportunity to select movies that they are personally familiar with and that would allow for a deeper connection to be made between human experience and writing. The goal of each of these activities is to broaden the minds and experiences of students while fostering critical thinking and writing skills in a way that is engaging to the student.

Five-Paragraph Organization

In this activity, students will watch *The Blindside* and then write a five-paragraph essay organized around a central idea as the follow-up assignment. The movie is based on the real-life adoption story of Michael Oher and his path from the violent streets to the warmth of a family who believes he can go anywhere in life. This film's themes include courage, overcoming adversity and one's background circumstances, kindness, gang culture, socioeconomic stereotypes, and teamwork. An alternative film to use with this same lesson plan is *The Pursuit of Happyness*.

Step 1: Ice breaker activity—give students an index card when they come into class. Ask them to write down the phrase "Change your stars" on one side, and on the other side, write down what that phrase means to them. Spend a few minutes sharing and discussing their answers.

Step 2: Preface the movie by giving some biographical information on Michael Oher. Explain that the movie is based on the true story of a teenage boy who grew up to play for the NFL.

Step 3: Screen the movie with them in class.

Step 4: At the end of class, provide students with a written assignment such as this one:

> Decide on a topic to compose an essay on from the following choices:
>
> - The meaning of family
> - Overcoming life circumstances
> - Class stereotypes
> - Perseverance and resilience
> - A topic of your own
>
> Form a single sentence (a thesis statement) using examples from the film. Choose three different ideas about the topic to discuss. This essay may use personal thoughts and feelings as well as examples from the film. This essay will be five paragraphs: an introduction, three body paragraphs (one for each idea), and a conclusion.

Step 5: Students should bring a complete draft of their paper for the next class.

For closure, ask students to complete a Ticket Out, where they write down their topics and any questions they have on an index card before they leave the classroom.

This lesson plan works best when paired with drafting and peer-editing. Ideally, the students will return with full drafts of their papers on *The Blindside* and a brief teacher-led workshop followed by peer-editing can take place to help them "move the pieces" into the correct places for their essay organization goals. The follow-up to this would be allowing them their final draft rewrite due the following class.

Writing a Character Analysis

In this activity, students will watch *Lars and the Real Girl* and then write a two- to three-page character analysis based on a character of their choice. This movie is unique and most people have not seen it, so it provides a new experience. The plot centers on a man with some emotional issues who introduces a life-size doll to his family, church, and community as his girlfriend, insisting that she is a real woman. The themes include depression, family, community, facing fears, death awareness, and overcoming personal barriers. An alternative film to use with this lesson plan is *The Great Gatsby* (2013).

Step 1: Ask the students to take out a piece of notebook paper and write their name on the top line, then draw a line down the middle. In the left column, ask them to write "What I'm Like." Tell them to list their personality traits and words they would use to describe themselves. Instructors can model this activity on the board to break the ice, making sure to include both positive and negative character traits.

When students have finished their own, ask them to write "What People Think I'm Like" on the right side. Have them write common perceptions and misperceptions above themselves. When everyone has listed a few items in each column, discuss openly, layering in follow-up questions so that students can explore both their own perceptions of themselves as well as how they believe others also perceive them.

Step 2: Introduce the idea of character by having them note the differences between their two columns.

Step 3: Screen the movie with them, having them take notes on the character just as they did with the warm-up activity.

Step 4: After the film, have students write about character based on their viewing of the movie. Encourage them to use their judgment based on the character's actions, words, mannerisms, and interactions with others.

The assignment should focus on blending the notes on character with the film. Students should brainstorm on the following questions:

- What are the character's strengths and flaws?
- How does the character make you feel about him or her? How does he or she make you feel about the world in general?
- How does the character influence the other characters around him?
- How does this character change and grow from beginning to end?

If the informal writing activity and discussion work well, the last stage would be to have students move to a longer paper, writing a two- to three-page essay with an introduction paragraph, one paragraph for each of the questions above, and a conclusion.

Students would begin the activity by writing about themselves, working from a comfortable starting point. Then, after watching the film, students can blend their thoughts about the film as a basis for the paper. This lesson plan is designed to work some higher-level critical thinking skills and literary vocabulary into the developmental writing class.

FINAL THOUGHTS

In the age of stunning visuals and shocking plot twists, film can be viewed as pure entertainment, but negating the power of film as a text of its own sells teachers short of a great opportunity to integrate a powerful media into their classrooms. The rigidity of outdated pedagogy and cookie-cutter writing instruction will not reach today's students, and as all teachers know, creativity is the base of success when it comes to dispersing knowledge.

Entertaining is not a dirty word in the classroom. Most likely, teachers more than most know the importance of keeping students engaged. This is why pedagogy has moved away from what it was one hundred years ago, why students do not simply read textbook paragraphs in-class and call it a day. Film is the next generation of creative, engaging pedagogy.

This approach, of course, does not argue that teachers should water down curriculum; rather, film can be a powerful way to help students dive in more deeply. Visual text in the form of films offers students the opportunity to write based on a text that motivates them, connects with them, and opens their minds to new ideas. Upper-level classrooms in universities around the world use film as an educational tool. Developmental writing students can benefit just as much, if not more, if given the chance to learn using films that they find interesting, thought-provoking, and, yes, entertaining.

NOTES

1. Raffaella Negretti, "Metacognitive Awareness in Developmental Writing Students," Order No. 3367918 (University of Hawai'i at Manoa, 2009), 10.
2. David Miller, "Developmental Writing: Trust, Challenge, and Critical Thinking," *Journal of Basic Writing* 21, no. 2 (Fall 2002): 94.
3. Janet Kirchner, "Student Experiences of the Community College Developmental Writing Classroom," Order No. 3618268 (The University of Nebraska–Lincoln, 2014).
4. Mike Rose, *Lives on the Boundary* (New York: Penguin, 1990); and "Remedial Writing Courses: A Critique and a Proposal," in *A Sourcebook for Basic Writing Teachers*, ed. Theresa Enos (New York: Random, 1987), 113.
5. Sheri Sunderland, et al., "Making Movies Active: Lessons from Simulations," *PS, Political Science & Politics* 42, no. 3 (2009): 543.
6. Ibid., 544.
7. John P. Young, "The Missing 'R': A Reluctant Reader in a College Developmental Writing Class," Order No. 1503018 (Prescott College, 2011), 11.
8. Ibid., 12.
9. Bruce Clemens and Curt Hamakawa, "Classroom as Cinema: Using Film to Teach Sustainability," *Academy of Management Learning & Education* 9, no. 3 (September 1, 2010): 562.

BIBLIOGRAPHY

Clemens, Bruce, and Curt Hamakawa. "Classroom as Cinema: Using Film to Teach Sustainability." *Academy of Management Learning & Education* 9, no. 3 (September 1, 2010): 561–63.

Frieden, James A., and Deborah W. Elliott. "Teach with Movies: Using the Storytelling Power of Movies to Motivate Students." *Teacher Librarian* 34, no. 3 (2007): 61–62.

Golden, Freida. "Strategies for Teaching Writing: An ASCD Action Tool." *Journal of Adolescent & Adult Literacy* 49, no. 6 (2006): 551–52.

Gone Baby Gone. DVD. Directed by Alan Ladd. Burbank, CA: Miramax Home Entertainment, 2008.

Kirchner, Janet. "Student Experiences of the Community College Developmental Writing Classroom." Order No. 3618268, The University of Nebraska–Lincoln, 2014.

Lars and the Real Girl. DVD. Directed by Adam Kimmel. Beverly Hills, CA: 20th Century Fox Home Entertainment, 2008.

Miller, David. "Developmental Writing: Trust, Challenge, and Critical Thinking." *Journal of Basic Writing* 21, no. 2 (Fall 2002): 92–105.

Negretti, Raffaella. "Metacognitive Awareness in Developmental Writing Students." Order No. 3367918, University of Hawai'i at Manoa, 2009.

Perin, Dolores. "Repetition and the Informational Writing of Developmental Students." *Journal of Developmental Education* 26, no. 1 (Fall, 2002): 2.

Rose, Mike. *Lives on the Boundary.* New York: Penguin, 1990.

———. "Remedial Writing Courses: A Critique and a Proposal." *A Sourcebook for Basic Writing Teachers.* Edited by Theresa Enos. New York: Random, 1987. 104–24.

Safran, Stephen P. "Using Movies to Teach Students about Disabilities." *Teaching Exceptional Children* 32, no. 3 (Jan. 2000): 44.

Sunderland, Sheri, Jonathan C. Rothermel, and Adam Lusk. "Making Movies Active: Lessons from Simulations." *PS, Political Science & Politics* 42, no. 3 (2009): 543–47.

The Blindside. DVD. Directed by John Lee Hancock. Warner Bros. Entertainment, 2009.

The Pursuit of Happyness. DVD. Directed by Todd Black. Culver City, CA: Columbia Pictures Industries, 2007.

Young, John P. "The Missing 'R': A Reluctant Reader in a College Developmental Writing Class." Order No. 1503018, Prescott College, 2011.

Chapter Ten

The Heroine's Journey

Writing and Buffy the Vampire Slayer

Jennifer Marmo

THE SET-UP

An archetype is "a typical character, an action or a situation that seems to represent such universal patterns of human nature."[1] One such archetype is that of hero: "a character who predominantly exhibits goodness and struggles against evil in order to restore harmony and justice to society."[2] Joss Whedon, the creator of *Buffy the Vampire Slayer,* envisioned a modern version of this hero: a female role model for the nineties generation.

His creation was one that seemed to not just be a version of the archetypal hero, but also a version that seemed to defy easy categorization; his hero was reluctant, obsessed with boys and clothes, and wielded a stake as her weapon of choice. When Buffy Summers fought her first vampire on screen on the television show in 1997, viewers across the nation were exposed to a petite, pretty, blonde hero who could not only master martial arts but also craft the perfect manicure. Seeing her as an archetype, then, requires looking beyond the surface and making deeper comparisons.

Typically, including in classical mythology, a hero was a male who showed strength and courage. Females were not generally depicted as heroes. Even Joseph Campbell—the creator of the idea of the monomythic archetypal hero—references only the male hero in his book, *The Hero with a Thousand Faces.*

The archetypal hero of the monomyth is "a hero who ventures forth from the world of common day to a region of supernatural wonder: fabulous forces are there encountered and a decisive victory is won: the hero comes back from this mysterious adventure with the power to bestow boons on his fellow man."[3] Campbell's theory has been used since it was published in 1949 in classrooms across the country.

Even screenwriters and filmmakers have turned to Campbell for inspiration regarding heroes. People like George Lucas have credited Campbell with helping to create Luke Skywalker and the others in the *Star Wars* universe. It is no surprise then that people who study *Buffy the Vampire Slayer* compare Buffy with the monomythic archetypal hero depicted in Campbell's Hero's Journey. In an article titled *"Buffy the Vampire Slayer: The Greek Hero Revisited"* written by Laurel Bowman, the show about the Chosen One is closely linked to the ideas presented by Campbell.

A narrative prologue introduced the television audience each week to not only the character of Buffy but also the show and the idea behind it: "To each generation, a Slayer is born, one girl in all the world, a chosen one, born with the . . . strength and skill to hunt the vampires, stop the spread of their evil."[4] It is always a female that is expected to save the world and sacrifice her life for humanity.

This idea is different than much of the literature that is taught in English classrooms across the country. Most of the curriculum is male-based, and therefore makes it difficult for young women to connect with the characters and ideals. Common Core State Standards describe what students should know and be able to do with the English language. They provide the targets for instruction and student learning essential for success in all academic areas. In order to develop higher-order thinking skills, teachers must help students connect the outside world with the school world.

One way to make this connection is through literature and media, such as *Buffy the Vampire Slayer*. As a foundation, students need to read and discuss Campbell's Hero's Journey; then, teachers can help students better understand the work with popular culture. Ultimately, the goal will be to transfer this learning to classical heroes. Once teachers have helped facilitate this thought process for students, it is time to move on to visual media, such as television episodes, so that students can begin to use their higher-order thinking skills and write about what they are seeing and understand.

By using *Buffy the Vampire Slayer* in the high school classroom, a teacher can help students develop both their higher-order thinking skills and their overall writing skills.

REVIEW OF LITERATURE

Campbell's monomyth is widely used across academia and pop culture to show the connections between heroes. According to his theory, there are three stages to the mythological journey: the departure, which starts with the call to adventure and "signifies that destiny has summoned the hero";[5] the initiation where the hero "must survive a succession of trials";[6] and the return where it is the responsibility of the hero to return with his newly acquired knowledge and aid his home.

Valerie Estelle Frankel studied Campbell in depth and developed the idea of the heroine's journey. Her work mirrors Campbell's ideas, but instead of the "feminine being the 'goal' of the quest—the princess needing rescue,"[7] Frankel asserts "the heroine's true role is to be neither hero nor his prize"[8] but to be "dynamic, valiant, [and] thoroughly feminine."[9]

Frankel describes not only modern females but also those in ancient myths, such as Brunnhild and Scheherazade. She focuses on women who have existed through time to battle through the darkness—just as Buffy Summers consistently does in *Buffy the Vampire Slayer*. Brunnhild was a Valkyrie in Germanic mythology. She was so moved by two lovers that she refused to take a warrior to Valhalla. Brunnhild was punished for this and was banished to earth. She stood behind her beliefs and went against her orders. Frankel considers Brunnhild's actions to be a refusal of her call.

According to Frankel, Scheherazade's tale fits in with the sacred marriage. The frame story of *Arabian Nights* tells the tale of Scheherazade and how she "changes the king, but within the dictates of her society."[10] Here is a female main character that uses not force but cultivates understanding through storytelling. She is heroic in that she not only saves her own life but "rescues all the young women of the kingdom."[11]

Jennifer K. Stuller provides a study of female heroes that begins with the Amazons of Greek mythology, and includes the famous Wonder Woman, and follows through to modern heroines such as Buffy Summers. Stuller writes that "he [Whedon] created a new heroic archetype with the character of Buffy and the mythology of the Buffyverse"[12] and "therefore, while Wonder Woman will always remain a symbol of female empowerment, Amazons now have sisters in Slayers."[13] So, through Frankel and Stuller, one begins to see how Buffy Summers fulfills the role of archetypal hero in modern day.

There are several academic pieces that focus on the relevancy of Buffy as an iconic feminist character in today's society and how she fits with the academic study of the hero. Zoe-Jane Playden writes that for Buffy "there is an endless production-line of vampires, more than she could possibly ever kill"[14] but "that to try is enough, that intention rather than achievement"[15] is what makes a hero. Playden writes that "in spiritual terms, the transgression of boundaries is exemplified by"[16] Campbell's Hero's Journey and that Buffy fits that monomyth.

However, the heroic structure set up through classic mythology is shaken by the addition of Buffy Summers. Laurel Bowman writes that although Buffy Summers fits the "stereotypical 'victim' of the genre"[17] she actually "shows strong parallels to the patterns of classical heroic myth."[18] The problem is that "she has her work cut out for her. The will toward worshipping

Olympians and demigods still roils within us."[19] So, even though Buffy may fit the archetypal hero pattern that Campbell outlined, she is so much more—she is a modern teenager that the high school, and college, student can relate to as she deals with typical teen issues like dating and dealing with parents.

Each season of *Buffy the Vampire Slayer* follows the steps of Campbell's journey. However, "in the last five episodes [of the series], this model expanded to create a mini-epic, or Journey, of its own."[20] and can be examined separately to illustrate the hero's journey. This television show, featuring modern actors from the not-too-distant past, can help today's students understand the concept of the hero and the journey she must undertake.

Buffy the Vampire Slayer easily bridges the gap from contemporary literature/media to ancient, classical literature. Buffy is a hero that students can easily recognize and connect with; she is a young woman who they have a lot in common with. Buffy is not some superhero, like Wonder Woman or Superman, but an every woman; a teenager who struggles with all aspects of her life, including her identity.

By studying the monomyth, students can learn about language, power, and what it means to be human. The choices that heroes make show their humanity and can hold deep meaning for the audience. When students

> understand *Buffy*, they understand that myth explains where we come from, determines how we act in and upon the world, and shapes who we will become. If they understand *Buffy*, they understand that power resides in language, in the very words we use to create our realities. If they understand *Buffy*, they understand that *we*—like Buffy herself—are always already story embodied. We are our own myths become flesh.[21]

Therefore, by pairing *Buffy* and classical literature such as *Beowulf* and *The Odyssey*, students will be able to better understand the characteristics of the hero myth.

CLASSROOM CONNECTIONS

This unit is designed to build upon other readings of classic heroic texts and would be situated after exposure to the literature—but before a major paper or project. This unit would run for several weeks, but depending on the number of episodes and the amount of time available, it could be modified to meet various time frames.

Modern Definition Warm-Up

Students would write down their working definition of a hero on an index card using their notes and Joseph Campbell's Hero's Journey. Classroom discussion will help students complete or revise their working definition to have for later work in the unit.

Students will next craft a communal list of modern hero characteristics based on their note cards. One student can record all responses the class can offer on the board or other visual source. Using the list, the teacher and students will review each item with the students to make sure it not only is correct, but also to begin a tighter list of characteristics that will make a short, crisp definition of a modern hero. One characteristic that is sure to appear is one of Campbell's key items—gender. Although students can include this characteristic on the list, teachers can now have an interesting discussion about gender roles and open the door to talk about women as heroes as well.

Hero Free-Write

Next, consider using Buffy's character as a visual example. Show either the episode or a clip from "Becoming, Part One" from season 2 of *Buffy the Vampire Slayer.* One specific flashback shows Buffy pre-vampire slaying. She was a fifteen-year-old girl who, like many, only cared about boys and clothes until she almost accidentally stumbles upon her fate by killing a vampire. Buffy is confused and upset, returning home to a fractured household where her parents fight about her. Students would be able to relate to this scene as a metaphor for the confusing times teens face.

At the close of the scene or episode, have students do a free-write on Buffy. Students can tackle one general question or several specific ones such as the following:

- What are your first impressions of Buffy?
- In what ways does Buffy demonstrate the characteristics of a hero?
- In what ways does Buffy differ from your hero definition?
- Do you think that Buffy will be a hero?

Students can share their writings with the class, or the instructor can collect them. Using the episode clip, and the free-write, can help students compare and contrast the characteristics listed on the board/chart paper.

Venn Diagram

One great way to compare and contrast is with a Venn Diagram. Have the students read—either for homework on in class—David Brin's "Buffy vs. the Old-Fashioned Hero." This chapter, from the anthology *Seven Seasons of Buffy: Science Fiction and Fantasy Writers Discuss Their Favorite Television Show,* will help students build more knowledge on and then discuss, in small groups, how Buffy is similar and different to what is typically known as a hero. The students would then create a Venn Diagram (for each group) showing these attributes.

The Venn Diagrams from each group would be similar but slightly different in wording and form, allowing students to see other ways to use the vocabulary that they would be building with this unit. As a follow-up, students could then compose a short paper that selects three of the characteristics that they believe both the traditional hero and Buffy Summers share. Not only would this paper allow them to explore the vocabulary, it would also be a productive mid-unit assessment on their grasp of the material before a final paper or exam.

Three-Quarter Book Foldable

The students would break into small groups and read "The Hero's and Heroine's Journey" from *Buffy and the Heroine's Journey: Vampire Slayer as Feminine Chosen One*. Each group would discuss the differences and similarities between the two and how they relate to Buffy Summers. At this point, students would create a Three-Quarter Book Foldable, with Buffy's major character traits listed on the left side and then the traits of a hero on the front of the right tab and the traits of a heroine on the bottom of the right tab.

This activity will help students not only practice their writing skills, but also work together to compare/contrast their definitions of mythology and heroes. In addition, students can make written records of the changes in the definition of a hero over time. Once the foldable is created, the students can share and then they can be displayed in the classroom.

Dialectical Journals

Have students watch "Welcome to the Hellmouth." Buffy in this episode has worked as a slayer and has chosen to begin a new life in Los Angeles. However, as the study of heroes has shown the students, a hero can refuse the call to adventure, but she will eventually fulfill her destiny and prove herself as a hero. After watching this episode, it is time to reconvene the groups so students can document the evolution of Buffy.

Students will then be expected to independently read a summary of the next ten episodes of the season. Students can also independently watch the episodes if there is time. While reading, or watching, students will document using a dialectical journal. They will have to pull specific information from the reading/watching to support how Buffy fits, or does not fit, the role of a hero. It is important not only for students to document the characteristics that prove Buffy is a hero but those that separate her from the archetypal hero.

After reading their notes, students will write a one-paragraph reflection, based upon those notes that they will share with a partner. Both the dialectical journal and the reflection will help students to think critically about the reading/watching. This way, they can synthesize not only what they have read on their own, but also what they have heard/seen so far in the classroom. Students will then watch "Prophecy Girl" and discuss how this episode also fits the hero's journey with the ritual death of the hero.

Dialectical journals "support different pedagogical objectives: responding to and documenting sources in the course of research; identifying central ideas in complex readings; or synthesizing ideas from reading and course lectures."[22] Students can use the journals to gather evidence, evaluate it, and then use the evidence to support an argument in a later paper.

Article Jigsaw Activity

At this point in the unit, the students will be warmed-up to both the characteristics of a hero and Buffy's journey. Have students read "Heroism on the Hellmouth: Teaching Morality through *Buffy*" from *Buffy in the Classroom: Essays on Teaching with the Vampire Slayer* either in class or as homework. This activity will tie into their dialectical journals, as it builds on their work with the episode "Prophesy Girl."

This reading "examines the concept of personal sacrifice in the hero character."[23] It is here where the class will see that the "tension between Buffy's recognition of her duty and her reluctance to fulfill that duty is in full swing."[24] Students can now document in their dialectical journals how Buffy is refusing the call of the Heroic Journey.

The class will then be broken into four small groups to read about seasons 2 through 5 (except for the season 5 finale). Each group will take a season and they will use the jigsaw technique to learn about the seasons. The jigsaw technique will allow a smaller group of students to read the material and focus on the major events and characters of that season. The benefits of the jigsaw technique include direct engagement with the material, practice in self-teaching and peer teaching, and participation in cooperative learning.

Each student in the group will independently read the summary of the season and highlight or underline the major events and characters that she feels the rest of the class should know. The group members will then meet together to discuss what has been highlighted/underlined. They will then decide as a group what ideas to share with the rest of the class. One member of the group will put the season number at the top of a poster and then list the major events and characters. The information will then be presented to the class with all group members participating to make sure the rest of the class understands the information that has been listed and shared.

Once all the groups have shared, it is time to watch "The Gift" where the audience is once again shown sacrifice, in the form of Buffy giving her life so that her sister, Dawn, and the rest of the world can live. Closing discussions would use both the journal and the jigsaw artifacts to help them reflect on the heroic element of sacrifice.

Three-Column Chart

At this point, students should work on a Three-Column Chart that delineates the Departure, Initiation, and Return of the heroic vampire slayer. This chart helps students develop note-taking skills as they record details. They will use all information gathered so far to match the various attributes of each part of the journey. This information includes any notes that have been given by the teacher, any charts that have been developed, whatever they have seen or read both independently and as a class, and any personal insights they might have at this point.

For example, Buffy has many companions or helpers on her journey. She would not have been able to accomplish her feats without the loyalty and friendship of Willow Rosenberg, Xander Harris, and Rupert Giles. Buffy also returns multiple times "from the Master's lair, from the Hellmouth, from the grave."[25] Students should meet in small groups to go over the charts on the three parts of the hero's journey. The class will then reconvene to clarify each aspect.

Mini-Essay

Next, students will independently read, and take notes on, the chapters "Pain as Bright as Steel: Mythic Striving and Light as Pain" and "When Harry Met Buffy: Buffy Summers, Harry Potter, and Heroism" from *Why Buffy Matters*. Both chapters reflect on sacrifice and how Buffy does not always fit the archetypal hero developed by Campbell.

Another reading on sacrifice, specifically of Buffy's in "Prophecy Girl," is titled "Be a Hero, Even When You'd Rather Go to the Mall" from *What Would Buffy Do? The Vampire Slayer as Spiritual Guide*. The title of the chapter is a perfect analogy for Buffy since she mentions, especially in the early seasons, how she would rather go shopping than slay vampires.

This chapter focuses on how Buffy's role as the Chosen One sometimes interferes with her life but that she also makes the decision to put others before herself; fitting right along with the hero reluctantly taking on the journey and then changing along the way. After reading and taking notes on the three chapters, it is integral to have a full class discussion to be sure that students are getting the idea of how Buffy fits the monomyth.

Students will then write a Mini-Essay in which they incorporate two of the chapters that have just been read and the ideas that the students have drawn from the readings. Mini-Essays, or microthemes, are very short essays that can be used to "practice and refine writing skills."[26]

This actually does not even have to be graded but students can give each other feedback, either in class or for homework. It is a type of low-stakes writing that will work on various skills such as peer groups and the writing process (specifically brainstorming and pre-writing.) This Mini-Essay allows the students to pull together their thoughts and information on a microtheme that will assist them for the final essay.

Cooperative Learning Groups

Once everyone understands that five seasons of *Buffy the Vampire Slayer* have managed to cover the hero's journey in several ways (both fulfilling the arc in each season but then throughout the five seasons), it is time to break into four groups to research and discuss seasons 6 and 7 (except for the finale, "Chosen"). Two groups will focus on the characters (one group for season 6 and one group for season 7).

The groups should specifically focus on the changes they have undergone since "The Gift." The last two groups will focus on the events (one group for season 6 and one group for season 7.) The groups should specifically focus on events that fit into the hero's journey path and how they have impacted the life of Buffy Summers.

Once the groups have had time to research and chart the characters and events in the two seasons, they will share their findings with one another. This should be done on chart paper so that all students can see the information and write it down within their own notes. The teacher can fill in any gaps that may have been missed.

Focused Free-Write

Now, it is time to view "Chosen" and then have students write their reactions to the end of the series. Once students have had a chance to write their reactions, the class will share those reactions. They will then independently read two chapters from *Seven Seasons of Buffy: Science Fiction and Fantasy Writers Discuss Their Favorite Television Show*: Jacqueline Lichtenberg's "Power of Becoming" and Nancy Holder's "Slayers of the Last Arc."

Both chapters manage to classify Buffy's story as that of great literature and classical mythology. Once students have read these chapters, they should do a focused free-write on the idea that Buffy fits the Campbellian monomyth. These focused free-writes will then be shared in pairs with the idea that students will give feedback to one another about the ideas in the free-write.

Unit Essay

For the last activity as a class, students will once again revisit their chart with the three major components of the hero's journey: departure, initiation, and return. As a class, with the teacher as facilitator, they will read an essay by David Fritts featured in *Buffy Meets the Academy: Essays on the Episodes and Scripts as Texts.* This essay, "Buffy's Seven-Season Initiation," provides another look into the journey of the vampire slayer. It will give students a final idea to focus on before moving onto the last independent activity: an essay.

This essay should compare the events of the series to Campbell's Hero's Journey. This essay should be multiple paragraphs that incorporate the readings, viewings, and discussions about Buffy Summers and her destiny as the Chosen One. Students will be expected to create an outline and, if time allows, to participate in an independent conference with the instructor. Students will then draft, with another meeting with the teacher if needed but also with peer revision. Once someone else has read the essay and given feedback, students will work on the final draft.

The ultimate goal of this unit is to answer the question "How is Buffy a hero?" However, the question will evolve into "How is Buffy another type of a hero?" Although they should be able to see many ways that Buffy possesses the same characteristics as traditional heroes, she is also different. She is a girl; she is flawed. Most of all, she is modern—which students will be able to relate to.

FINAL THOUGHTS

The study of Buffy Summers and her role as a hero allows students to see beyond the traditional concept of a hero. The idea of a female teenager being the savior of the world is not common. Traditionally, women needed to be saved. They were sacrificed and used as pawns. Women have not been the hero. Buffy Summers changed that ideal for a generation of young women. She forged the way for other young female heroes. Buffy has the power to continue that change, which is why *Buffy the Vampire Slayer* should be studied.

Through this unit, students will learn to work together in order to understand. This cooperative learning will enable them to not only peer-teach but learn how to self-teach. The beginning of the unit starts with the teacher in the traditional mode of sharing the information; however, by the end, the students are the ones imparting the information with the teacher as the facilitator. In addition, students will learn various note-taking methods and comprehension skills as they not only read and listen but watch.

Further, they will learn how to use visual media as literature and to think critically about it. Students will be able to make connections between classical literature and modern text. Finally, students will learn that myths explain where we come from and shape who we become and that is where they can find the value in studying mythology, heroes, and *Buffy the Vampire Slayer* since Buffy follows the Campbellian monomyth.

By using *Buffy the Vampire Slayer* to build critical thinking and writing skills, a teacher allows growth within the students. Students will learn to evaluate and analyze not only written work but also visual media. This will allow them to go from being the students to being the teachers as they learn to work with one another and present the material that they have become the experts in. They will learn logical reasoning where they will draw inferences that are supported by evidence. They will then be able to transform this knowledge from elsewhere—everything they learned from viewing, listening, conferring, and reading—into their own words in written form.

Their writing skills will improve through the various strategies that will be utilized throughout the unit. From lists and free-writes to mini-essays, students will work on writing consistently, which will enable them to hone their skills. As students work through pre-writing and brainstorming, they will use their critical thinking skills to improve their writing. By providing feedback and editing for one another, they will not only help each other but themselves.

Through conferences with the teacher, students will learn to look in their work for consistent errors and they will learn how to fix those errors. Students will no longer be dependent on the teacher for assistance in each step of their learning. They will be like Buffy Summers, at the end of season 7, when she is finally able to tell Rupert Giles, her Watcher and father figure, that he has taught her all she needs to know.

That is the true lesson here: take a teenager and give her all the tools she needs to succeed. For Buffy, it took loss and sacrifice, friends and lovers, and finally, a choice to share her power. For the students in this class, it will take collaboration and critical thinking, peers and teacher, and finally, the ability to form their own thoughts and put them down on paper. *Buffy the Vampire Slayer* not only joins the past and the present, but also the future in that the students can now think critically and write more effectively.

NOTES

1. "Archetype—Definition and Examples," *Literary Devices: Definition and Examples of Literary Terms* (2014), literarydevices.net/archetype/.
2. Ibid.
3. Joseph Campbell, *The Hero with a Thousand Faces* (New York: MJF Books, 1949), 30.
4. *Buffy the Vampire Slayer,* "Welcome to the Hellmouth (Part One)," The WB Television Network (New York, NY: WPIX, March 10, 1997).

5. Joseph Campbell, *The Hero with a Thousand Faces* (New York: MJF Books, 1949), 58.
6. Ibid., 97.
7. Valerie Estelle Frankel, *From Girl to Goddess: The Heroine's Journey through Myth and Legend* (Jefferson: McFarland & Company, Inc., 2010), 3.
8. Ibid.
9. Ibid.
10. Ibid., 107.
11. Ibid., 106.
12. Jennifer K. Stuller, *Ink-Stained Amazons and Cinematic Warriors: Superwomen in Modern Mythology* (New York: I. B. Tauris & Co. Ltd., 2010), 78.
13. Ibid.
14. Zoe-Jane Playden, "What You Are, What's to Come: Feminisms, Citizenship, and the Divine," in *Reading the Vampire Slayer: An Unofficial Critical Companion to Buffy and Angel*, ed. Roz Kaveney (New York: Tauris Parke Paperbacks, 2001), 145.
15. Ibid.
16. Ibid., 144.
17. Laurel Bowman, "Buffy the Vampire Slayer: The Greek Hero Revisited,"*Academia.edu*, last modified February 23, 2002, www.academia.edu/1119683/Buffy_the_Vampire_Slayer_The_Greek_Hero_Revisited.
18. Ibid.
19. David Brin, "Buffy vs. The Old-Fashioned 'Hero,'" in *Seven Seasons of Buffy: Science Fiction and Fantasy Writers Discuss Their Favorite Television Show*, ed. Glenn Yeffeth (Dallas: BenBella Books, 2003), 2.
20. Nancy Holder, "Slayers of the Last Arc," in *Seven Seasons of Buffy: Science Fiction and Fantasy Writers Discuss Their Favorite Television Show*, ed. Glenn Yeffeth (Dallas: BenBella Books, 2003), 199.
21. Tanya R. Cochran, "And the Myth Becomes Flesh," in *Buffy in the Classroom: Essays on Teaching with the Vampire Slayer*, ed. Jodie A. Kreider and Meghan K. Winchell (Jefferson: McFarland & Co., Inc., 2010), 35.
22. "Writing Across the Curriculum," *Lehman College-Writing Across the Curriculum: Resources for Faculty: Using Writing to Promote Critical Reading,* last modified March 13, 2012, www.lehman.edu/academics/wac/critical-reading.php.
23. K. Dale Koontz, "Heroism on the Hellmouth: Teaching Morality through *Buffy*," in *Buffy in the Classroom: Essays on Teaching with the Vampire Slayer*, ed. Jodie A. Kreider and Meghan K. Winchell (Jefferson: McFarland & Co., Inc., 2010), 62.
24. Ibid., 63.
25. Ibid., 42.
26. "Mini-Essays (Microthemes)," *University Writing Center* (2014), writingcenter.tamu.edu/Faculty/Teaching-Writing-or-Public-Speaking/Developing-Your-Method-of-Instruction/Low-stakes-Writing-and-Speaking/Mini-Essays.

BIBLIOGRAPHY

"Archetype—Definition and Examples." *Literary Devices: Definition and Examples of Literary Terms.* 2014. literarydevices.net/archetype/.
Bowman, Laurel. "Buffy the Vampire Slayer: The Greek Hero Revisited."*Academia.edu.* Last modified February 23, 2002. www.academia.edu/1119683/Buffy_the_Vampire_Slayer_The_Greek_Hero_Revisited.
Buffy the Vampire Slayer. "Becoming (Part One)." The WB Television Network. New York, NY: WPIX, 1998.
———. "Chosen." United Paramount Network. New York: WWOR, 2003.
———. "Prophecy Girl." The WB Television Network. New York: WPIX, 1997.
———. "The Gift." The WB Television Network. New York: WPIX, 2001.
———. "Welcome to the Hellmouth (Part One)." The WB Television Network. New York: WPIX, 1997.

Campbell, Joseph. *The Hero with a Thousand Faces.* New York: MJF Books, 1949.
Durand, Kevin K. *Buffy Meets the Academy: Essays on the Episodes and Scripts as Texts.* Jefferson: McFarland & Company, 2009.
Frankel, Valerie Estelle. *Buffy and the Heroine's Journey: Vampire Slayer as Feminine Chosen One.* Jefferson: McFarland & Company, 2012.
———. *From Girl to Goddess: The Heroine's Journey through Myth and Legend.* North Carolina: McFarland & Company, 2010.
Kaveney, Roz. *Reading the Vampire Slayer: An Unofficial Critical Companion to Buffy and Angel.* New York: St. Martin's Press, 2001.
Kreider, Jodie A., and Meghan K. Winchell. *Buffy in the Classroom: Essays on Teaching with the Vampire Slayer.* Jefferson: McFarland & Company, 2010.
Riess, Jana. *What Would Buffy Do? The Vampire Slayer as Spiritual Guide.* San Francisco: John Wiley & Sons, Inc., 2004.
Stafford, Nikki. *Bite Me! The Unofficial Guide to Buffy the Vampire Slayer: The Chosen Edition.* The chosen ed. Toronto: ECW Press, 2007.
Stuller, Jennifer K. *Ink-Stained Amazons and Cinematic Warriors.* New York: Palgrave Macmillan, 2010.
"Why Use Jigsaws." *Teaching Methods: A Collection of Pedagogic Techniques and Example Activities.* Last Modified August 11, 2009. serc.carleton.edu/NAGTworkshops/teaching_methods/jigsaws/why.html.
Wilcox, Rhonda, and David Lavery. *Why Buffy Matters: The Art of Buffy the Vampire Slayer.* New York: I. B. Tauris & Co. Ltd., 2005.
Yeffeth, Glenn. *Seven Seasons of Buffy: Science Fiction and Fantasy Writers Discuss Their Favorite Television Show.* Dallas: BenBella Books, 2003.

Chapter Eleven

Speed Dating an iPad until the Break of Dawn

Creative Techno-Feminist Pedagogy for Stephenie Meyer's Twilight Saga

Laura Patterson

THE SET-UP

Some educators might wonder why anyone would teach the *Twilight* series at all—to students of any age. Certainly instructors do not want to encourage that kind of "bad" writing. Also, perhaps it would make more sense to teach students something they are less likely to read on their own. However, *Twilight* can spark discussions of literary canon formation and the traditional power structures that privilege certain kinds of authors over others. Students can interrogate high and low culture categories using the lens of postmodernism.

Offering a framework that allows for the serious analysis of pop culture often gives students permission to take pop culture seriously. Similarly, inviting students to analyze a text with which they are already familiar, or a text that has a voice within their culture, grants students insider or expert status and gives them permission to take themselves seriously as literary critics. Students' comfort with the texts also makes it easier to incorporate other new approaches, such as feminist theory, feminist pedagogy, and meaningful uses of technology.

In these ways, teaching the *Twilight* novels offers an entry point into the world of literature and an opportunity to build skills and ideas that transfer to the critical reading of canonical literature. This chapter focuses on a study of a college course taught at a small liberal arts institution with the intent of drawing students into feminist theory via a familiar text. To that end, the instructor frontloaded the syllabus with student-friendly feminist theory that would provide an analytical framework, including texts such as *Manifesta* (Richards and Baumgardner), *Feminism: A Short History of a Big Idea* (Hannam), and *Feminism and Pop Culture* (Zeisler).

Technology was also a primary feature of the course, and the instructor's technological goal was to enhance student-to-student interaction and to deepen analysis of the texts. To facilitate these goals, the instructor initiated a "speed dating" classroom activity, which asks students to share ideas within pairs or small groups during brief timed intervals. Because the timed intervals were no longer than a few minutes, students shared ideas with most or all of their classmates, including those who did not usually speak voluntarily within a larger discussion, during a single class period.

The course's particular twist on speed dating asked students to use iPads to record their insights in response to a set of predetermined discussion questions, creating a log of their ideas. Later in the same class period, students brought those insights back to a large group discussion and commented on which ideas they found most meaningful.

A speed dating activity like this one meshes well with feminist theory and literary criticism because it promotes student leadership, a nonhierarchical classroom, and the co-construction of knowledge, goals often aligned with feminist pedagogy. This chapter offers a detailed explanation and assessment of speed dating as a classroom activity, how to use the technology, and an analysis of how this activity increased writing and supported the goals of using both feminist pedagogy and a feminist critical lens to examine a facet of popular culture.

REVIEW OF LITERATURE

As bell hooks notes, "Student resistance to forms of learning that are not based on rote memory or predictable assignments has almost become a norm because of the fixation on degrees rather than education."[1] Yet whenever instructors teach popular culture texts, they are already shaking up some students' expectations of sticking to more canonical texts. In this climate of shifting expectations, creative pedagogy often becomes more appealing. Since the class is already experimenting with texts outside the norms of literature classes, why not also experiment with pedagogy?

In teaching popular texts at all, one risks something akin to what Jared Stein calls the "creepy treehouse"[2] phenomenon in academic technology: when a professor (or an institution) co-opts social environments for educational purposes, taking away the fun and open aspects of these technologies. Or, as Stein defines it: "Any institutionally created, operated, or controlled environment in which participants are lured in either by mimicking preexisting open or naturally formed environments, or by force, through a system of punishments or rewards."[3] An example of a "creepy treehouse" would be forcing students to post to a classroom Facebook page.

Although "creepy treehouse" usually refers to social media, in some senses, these books, along with their online and face-to-face fan communities, have become a social environment of their own, possibly one to which the "adults" have not been invited. As Leonard Sax notes, unlike the Harry Potter series, "the 'Twilight' books target a much narrower demographic: teenage girls and young women."[4] For these reasons, teaching a nontraditional text provides the ideal opportunity to experiment with creative pedagogy, but not in ways that encroach on students' personal spaces or on their own communities devoted to enjoying popular culture.

In *Feminism and Pop Culture*, Andi Zeisler comments on the vanishing lines between high and low culture: "Pop culture informs our understanding of political issues that on first glance seem to have nothing to do with pop culture; it also makes us see how something meant as pure entertainment can have everything to do with politics."[5] Zeisler links the postmodernist cultural studies urge to strike down the binaries of high and low culture with the resistance toward designating cultural products as "feminist" and "not feminist." Her comments also point to popular culture's potential for teaching political concepts through entertainment.

Despite its critical reputation, the *Twilight* saga is rife with the kinds of political issues Zeisler explores. According to *Seduced by Twilight* author Natalie Wilson, the novels echo "the world in which [fans] live—a landscape replete with conflicting messages about abstinence and sexuality, about femininity and masculinity, about race, class, morality, and religion," and these messages are "as unstable as Bella's mood."[6] Wilson emphasizes the shifting nature of the novels' messages to show that there are many ways to engage with the novels' gendered themes and that the novels resist strictly binary readings because of their complex nature.

The "instability"[7] that Wilson notes is a positive quality in a feminist sense because readers are exposed to something other than conventional moral messages about their culture. This cultural instability also provides fissures in the walls of what Pierre Bourdieu would term "the reproduction of the structure of power"[8] by way of the reproduction of the dominant culture. These fissures, these cracks in the text—its inconsistencies and mixed messages about crucial cultural issues—allow students a starting place for a feminist exploration that has meaning in their own lives.

To capitalize on student-created meaning, courses such as "Twilight: Feminist Readings" can use feminist pedagogy, including the creation of a less hierarchal classroom, with the instructor in a facilitator role rather than a lecturer role. Feminist pedagogy strives for "consciousness raising, social action, and social transformation." It employs concepts such as student empowerment, personal experience as a valid way of knowing, communal knowledge production, an integration of personal and academic lives, a participatory learning environment, and social responsibility.[9]

Carol Gilligan promotes an "ethic of care" in feminist pedagogy, while bell hooks notes the need for love in the classroom.[10] hooks also asserts, "the first paradigm that shaped my pedagogy was the idea that the classroom should be an exciting place, never boring," adding that "if boredom should prevail, then pedagogical strategies [are] needed that [will] intervene, alter, even disrupt the atmosphere."[11] Like that of many feminist scholars, hooks's classroom practice draws from critical and anticolonial pedagogies.[12]

Furthermore, feminist classrooms disrupt conventional wisdom, including those same binaries that postmodernism deconstructs: "Feminist classrooms create environments where students and teachers examine relationships of power in culture, where dichotomies of either-or can be rejected and replaced with the ability to problematize common-sense viewpoints, discover similarities within difference, and learn to understand phenomena through multiple lenses."[13] This kind of nonbinary critical thinking benefits students across the curriculum, not only in courses related to literature or popular culture.

CLASSROOM CONNECTIONS

Part 1: Opening Discussion Activities

A course, or even a unit, on a popular text may create confusion among students. Some students may be excited about the prospect of "easy" reading; others may take the traditional stance that popular texts are not as important to study as classic literature. It may be a good idea for the instructor embarking on a unit using a text such as *Twilight* to allow assumptions about the text to take center stage as an opening discussion activity. The instructor can ask students what their assumptions are about the text at hand and whether or not popular literature should have a place in the classroom.

As another way of opening the class and introducing the pop culture text, the instructor might list several popular texts appropriate to the students' age, and ask students to rank them in order of literary merit. The conversation that follows can uncover hidden assumptions about what makes a text worth reading or worth categorizing as "real" literature. It can also be interesting to ask students what kind of response they receive from friends, acquaintances, and parents when they are seen reading certain popular texts. Do others imply that they should spend their time reading something more "worthwhile"?

Additional opening discussion activities could include conversations about expectations for learning during the pop culture unit or course. It is useful for the instructor to explicitly list his or her learning objectives for the text. Many teachers probably already use classroom contracts of some kind, and the popular text expectations can be an extension of these. Another way to think about expectations is to have students decide how they want to self-monitor to keep the conversation on a scholarly level and not allow class time to devolve into a casual talk show or book group discussion atmosphere.

One way of encouraging students to respond candidly but critically to texts is for the instructor to model this behavior. At the beginning of the course, the modeling might take the form of self-disclosure on the part of the instructor. If the instructor has ambivalence about teaching a popular text, or if the instructor has any kind of mixed reactions to the text itself, it makes sense to share these thoughts from the beginning. Such a disclosure models productive ambiguities, internal intellectual struggles, and the importance of self-reflection and questioning.

Begin the unit with open discussion on their conceptions of the course. This dialogue will help to establish boundaries for the course and consciously decide on a group identity. One student proclaimed, "I am not interested in taking a course that is likely to be filled with *Twilight* fangirls. There are probably only going to be a few people who are willing to hear different opinions about the books and the discussion does not promise to be intelligent. I think that while it is possible for this course to go beyond *Twilight*, it probably won't because *Twilight* is too big a phenomenon."[14]

To avoid misperceptions, engage in a goal-oriented discussion. "What do you want this course to be? Why are you here?" In the sample study, student responses varied: some were there to fulfill requirements; others were true twihards, still others were curious or had taken previous courses with the instructor. Therefore, students had different ideas of how the course might work or what might be discussed, and some had no idea at all.

Through this type of preliminary activity, students can reach a general consensus about their identity as a class. For example, in this case, the class reached several consensuses: students did not want the class to devolve into Team Jacob versus Team Edward. They could put aside biases (either for or against the books, and including the embedded cultural biases we brought to the texts before reading) to view the books critically, as scholars, without judging each other on reading tastes.

When students have established a rapport and a consensus about class identity, the instructor can add her own identity as a critical reader to the mix. At this point, the instructor lets students know that she felt deeply ambivalent about the series. She confessed that her pleasure reading self was swept into the Edward/Bella romance and the secret world of vampires. On the other hand, her feminist literary critic self was taken aback by the gender politics at play in the novels. This confessional moment seemed to open a space for sharing ambivalent and contradictory reader responses.

Part 2: Getting Ready for a Speed Date

At any time after the opening discussion activities are complete, the instructor can introduce a speed dating activity as a way of creating more student-to-student interaction. The basic premise of a speed dating classroom activity is that students will share short bursts of information in pairs, then move on to a different pairing and share different information, recording the shared information as they move about the room. The class is divided into two groups. Desks can be arranged into an inner and an outer circle or in two lines with the desks back to back, depending on the space in the classroom and size of the group.

In the case of a line of desks, one group will move to the left and the other to the right. In the case of an inner and outer circle of desks, the group on the inside will rotate around the desks clockwise, and the outer group will rotate counterclockwise (or vice versa). Since the idea of speed dating in the classroom is well-established, a quick Internet search will turn up many similar activities and other ways of arranging the classroom space as well. Speed dating may aid in student-to-student interactions, making the classroom a less instructor-focused space, and thus aligning with feminist pedagogy.

The speed dating activity could be applied to nearly any level of student and to a variety of classroom situations. While the iPad or another electronic tablet is convenient and fun to use for sharing information in this activity, it would be possible to use laptops or paper, or even actual sticky notes, provided they were big enough to contain students' comments. If using paper for this activity, it might work well to ask students to transfer their speed dating discussion notes into an electronic format so that the class could have a record of the discussions on a class web site or learning management system.

In the *Twilight* course, the instructor took advantage of tablets' key virtues for classroom use:

- the ability to create digital visuals quickly
- a size and portability that take the awkwardness out of sharing screens
- the ability to transfer information quickly while moving around the classroom

Speed dating and the iPad are a good fit because students can have a rapid-fire exchange of ideas with their peers in a one-on-one format, but they can also create a visual record of the conversations that could be referenced in subsequent "dates." In other words, students have not only their own partner to draw on, but also the writing on the wall (or in this case, iPad) from past dater.

The first step in preparing a speed dating activity is to create several questions to which students will respond as they move around the room. The instructor may want to predetermine half or more of these questions in order to provide students with models of the kinds of questions that might be useful. After viewing the instructor's questions about the text, students can engage in free-writing for a few minutes as a way of generating three additional questions for the list. Once students have had time to free-write (perhaps ten minutes or so), the instructor leads the students in a discussion about their free-writing with the goal of reaching a consensus about which additional questions should go on the list.

For example, in the *Twilight* course, the instructor projected the following handout on the screen at the beginning of class:

- If you were going to rewrite the first half of *Breaking Dawn* (the part we've read so far), what would you change? Why?
- Are Bella's pregnancy and the birth of Renesmee portrayed in what you would call a feminist manner? Why or why not?
- What is your opinion of Meyer's choice to include a section of the narrative in Jacob's voice? Were you surprised by this choice? Although we can never really know an author's true motivations (intentional fallacy), speculate on why Meyer might have made this choice. What does it do to the gender politics of the series?
- Your question here.
- Your question here.
- Your question here.

The instructor's questions were chosen with an eye to addressing a number of different factors in the classroom. For instance, several of the students were creative writers, and question one asks them to view the novel in light of their craft, in writerly terms. The second question addresses feminism directly, but also risks creating the kind of feminist/not feminist binary the course strove to eradicate. Earlier in the semester, this question would not have worked as well. At this point, however, students were alert to the course's growing theme that these texts, like most texts, were rarely fully progressive and rarely fully regressive in their gender politics.

Other questions can be designed to encourage deeper critical reading. For example, the third question asks students to think in terms of literary structure (the inclusion of a new narrator late in the text), and it encourages students to use a feminist literary critical lens, building on earlier discussions of literary structure and literary feminism and asking students to perform a meaningful synthesis of the two. It may be useful to highlight particularly astute responses to a complex question later in the large group discussion after the speed dating activity.

In the next phase of the activity, students completed a free-writing session to develop their own speed dating questions, increasing their personal investment in finding answers. The students wrote for about ten minutes, discussed their ideas briefly, then reached a consensus about adding the following three questions to the list:

- Do you think that if Bella were able to understand the ranting of the South American woman she would have reconsidered keeping the child?
- What is the reasoning behind Bella's change of mind about seeing her father? Why did she decide to let him in on everything?
- How do the gender dynamics of the novel change when Leah becomes a werewolf? Consider imprinting and pregnancy topics.

The students' questions are somewhat more plot-driven, with questions one and two focusing on characters and their choices. This is the kind of question that surfaces most frequently in mid-level college courses without prerequisites. Students often want to discuss why characters did this or that, with less thought toward the author who controls the strings.

Although the instructor might wish for greater complexity in the students' questions, it is essential to validate and find answers to students' own questions, particularly because these are the questions that come up when reading for pleasure, even if the critical lens is supposedly set aside. However, instructors may also want to balance the types of questions that students generate with questions that may ask for more critical thinking. As shown in the final question, students quickly begin to ask the same kinds of complex questions after seeing models for much of the semester.

Part 3: Let the Games Begin, or, Speed Dating in Action

Next, students arrange their chairs and desks into an inner and outer circle, or a line of paired desks, depending on the size of the class and classroom. Each pair of desks holds one device for recording the information (paper sticky note, iPad, laptop, etc.) If the class is using tablets or laptops, the instructor may want to email the questions to save time. One member of each student pair writes a particular question on her device. Sticky note applications work well and allow students to create or import text and to change the color, background, size, position, or font of the note. Additional notes can be added and color-coded to indicate different respondents.

At this point, students speed date. Each pair of desks is now equipped with one iPad or other device with one of the discussion questions above written on it on an electronic sticky note. The inner ring of students can move to the right; the outer ring can rotate left. At each "date," the pair discusses the question at hand for several minutes and then takes a few extra minutes to jot down their findings on a separate sticky note attached to the first.

As students move through the groups, the instructor can encourage them to read the previous responses to each question, and to agree or disagree by attaching their new note to one already in place. They can also be asked to use new colors of sticky notes to indicate a new pair of voices, increase writing, and prompt new discussion. Students rotate partners until everyone has a chance to discuss each question. The result is a visual record of all conversations about the questions, a record students can use to find ideas for their formal essay assignments or to study for their final exam.

Part 4: The Wrap-up

Find a way to post all records of the speed date conversation. If large paper sticky notes were used, these could go on the walls so students could "tour" them. If electronic apps were used, the students could capture their results and post on a course wiki or web site, or they could email their captures to the instructors, who might post them on a learning management system or course web site. The activity ends with a review of the writing, followed by a large group discussion of the ideas raised where the students are also asked to share ideas they learned from their peers' records of their conversations.

In the *Twilight* course, the activity generated more detailed answers, stronger critical thinking, and more debate about each question than starting a conversation "cold"—that is, by simply posting the questions on a screen and beginning a large group discussion. Instructors used to writing warm-up activities or "idea sparking" pair sessions will be familiar with the benefits of this methodology.

Within this course, students also mentioned that they enjoyed the speed dating activity a great deal, although one student did note that she did not "want to do it every single day," and she makes an important point. Activities like this can lose their impact and novelty if they are employed too frequently. Students also mentioned that they enjoyed the opportunity to move around the room, which can jog new idea patterns, and they noted that they liked the opportunity to hear the opinions of those they did not know well or those who didn't contribute to the large group discussion as regularly.

Part 5: Other Approaches to Teaching Twilight in a Feminist Context

For other approaches to teaching *Twilight*, instructors may want to choose activities that empower students and ask them to own the knowledge they have acquired and co-created throughout the semester. For example, in this course's final exam, students had the option of answering this essay question, which followed up on an activity in which we researched and compared signs of teen dating violence with scenes in the texts:

Imagine that you are creating the curriculum for a lesson on teen dating violence for a group of young girls who attend an afterschool academic program that you direct. The girls are twelve years old, and you know that about half of them are reading the *Twilight* books. How do you construct this lesson and present your wealth of knowledge on this topic? Do you bring up *Twilight*?

If so, how do you do so without alienating them or seeming like just another adult who does not get their favorite books? If you do not mention *Twilight* at all, explain why not. Your essay response should include detailed lesson plans with specific signs of teen dating violence included. Your lesson plans must be original and cannot include versions of the activities we did in class.

This question asks students to write in a genre other than the imaginary school-essay format and to take on a project they might face in the near future. It also imagines them not as students but as professionals in charge of other learners.

Students may feel more empowered when co-creating classroom content, whether generating discussion topics in small groups and bringing them back to the larger group or choosing which topics for discussion interested them most from a list created with the instructor. In this course, students also created written presentations on special topics such as the *Twilight* series and Christianity, music, erotica, fan fiction, teen pregnancy, tattoos, film parodies, anti-fan culture, *Twilight* moms, and *Twilight*'s influence on the young adult fiction market.

Students also found larger audiences for their thoughts by creating book reviews suitable for online posting. Discussions were lively and accomplished in-depth feminist textual analysis, with only minor forays into well-worn or clichéd territory, such as the familiar refrain of "What is *wrong* with Bella?" When the discussion did veer into this territory, other students or the instructor could gently reroute the conversation using the expectations created at the beginning of the semester.

FINAL THOUGHTS

In a sense, feminist content and pedagogy provided the second tricky layer to this course, with the other two layers being popular texts and technology. Yet in some ways, the feminist angle may have been the most difficult of all. Feminism is often known as "the other F-word," meaning that the word alone is radioactive for many people. In courses that explicitly introduce feminism, it may be necessary to explain that feminism is not a monolithic discourse; there is a brand of feminism for nearly anyone who holds basic beliefs in equality.

The instructor may need to work to make the feminist lens a friendly one, particularly when working with popular texts. In the context of a *Twilight* course, or a course on any other popular text, students may fear that the instructor will bang a feminist gavel and judge their favorite texts. Here, it may make sense to tread lightly, especially at first, to avoid giving the impression that one believes *Twilight* fans to be the "dribbling, insipid, Edward addicts they are often made out to be."[15] Students are often able to engage in gender-based analysis of their own fandom, as well as in a popular phenomenon more generally.

Teaching popular texts such as the *Twilight* series is about breaking down binaries and helping students find more than two sides of any given problem. This kind of multidimensional thinking founds nearly all other forms of critical thinking and problem solving. Courses such as this one may benefit from brief primers in postmodernist literary critique, as well as other critical modes that focus on deconstruction and nonbinary thinking. In this way, students can see that they are participating in a larger tradition of critical thinking modes.

Yet it is difficult to give students texts they have never seen before and ask them to perform new forms of analysis, as well as detailed forms of analysis that take a knowing-it-backwards-and-forwards familiarity with a text. Instructors may have this kind of familiarity with the texts they encountered in high school or college, then again in graduate school, then again for pleasure, and again when teaching in their own classrooms. It makes sense to offer students the same kinds of opportunities to show what they can achieve.

What they are able to achieve is often inspiring. While some may claim that teaching popular texts is a kind of "dumbing down" of the classroom or a way of pandering to the lowest common denominator, it is also a way of leveling the playing field. When students are reading a familiar text, they are empowered to reach higher levels of analysis and to become the experts in the room, which is certainly one of the central projects of feminist and other liberatory pedagogies, as well as one of education's key aims—to guide students to a level of thinking that makes the teachers obsolete.

ACKNOWLEDGMENTS

The author acknowledges Dr. Mary Ann Gawelek, provost of Seton Hill University, for the idea for this course. Thanks also go to colleague and friend, Dr. Susan Eichenberger, for introducing speed dating activities for the classroom. Dr. Rhonda Matthews organized "The Twilight Saga: Girls, Women, and Feminism in Popular Culture: An Academic Conference" at Edinboro University of Pennsylvania, and she and the other conference participants were helpful in critiquing early versions of the course syllabus.

NOTES

1. bell hooks, *Teaching Community: A Pedagogy of Hope* (New York: Routledge, 2003), 130.
2. Jared Stein, "Defining Creepy Treehouse," *Flexknowlogy* (blog), April 9, 2008, flexknowlogy.learningfield.org/2008/04/09/defining-creepy-tree-house/.
3. Ibid.
4. Leonard Sax, "'Twilight' Sinks Its Teeth Intro Feminism," *Washington Post*, August 17, 2008, www.washingtonpost.com/wp-dyn/content/article/2008/08/15/AR2008081503099.html.
5. Andi Zeisler, *Feminism and Pop Culture* (Berkeley: Seal, 2008), 7.
6. Natalie Wilson, *Seduced by Twilight* (Jefferson: McFarland, 2011), 2.
7. Ibid., 8.
8. Pierre Bourdieu, *Reproduction in Education, Society, and Culture* (London: Sage, 1977), 6.
9. Robbin Crabtree, David Alan Sapp, and Adela Licona, *Feminist Pedagogy: Looking Back to Move Forward* (Baltimore: Johns Hopkins University Press, 2009), 4.
10. Ibid., 4–5.
11. bell hooks, *Teaching to Transgress: Education as the Practice of Freedom* (New York: Routledge, 1994), 7.
12. Ibid., 10.
13. Robbin Crabtree, David Alan Sapp, and Adela Licona, *Feminist Pedagogy: Looking Back to Move Forward* (Baltimore: Johns Hopkins University Press, 2009), 6.
14. Richelle Dodaro, "Pop Culture and Feminism Through *Twilight*," *Setonian Online*, Seton Hill University, November 10, 2010, blogs.setonhill.edu/setonian/2010/11/10/pop_culture_and/.
15. Natalie Wilson, *Seduced by Twilight* (Jefferson: McFarland, 2011), 2.

BIBLIOGRAPHY

Bourdieu, Pierre. *Reproduction in Education, Society, and Culture*. London: Sage, 1977.
Crabtree, Robbin, David Alan Sapp, and Adela Licona. *Feminist Pedagogy: Looking Back to Move Forward*. Baltimore: Johns Hopkins University Press, 2009.
Dodaro, Richelle. "Pop Culture and Feminism Through *Twilight*." *Setonian Online*, Seton Hill University, November 10, 2010. blogs.setonhill.edu/setonian/2010/11/10/pop_culture_and/.
Hannam, June. *Feminism: A Short History of a Big Idea*. New York: Longman, 2006.
Haraway, Donna. *Simians, Cyborgs, and Women: The Reinvention of Nature*. New York: Routledge, 1991.
hooks, bell. *Teaching to Transgress: Education as the Practice of Freedom*. New York: Routledge, 1994.
———. *Teaching Community: A Pedagogy of Hope*. New York: Routledge, 2003.
Meyer, Stephenie. *Breaking Dawn*. New York: Little, Brown and Co., 2008.
Richards, Amy, and Jennifer Baumgardner. *Manifesta: Young Women, Feminism, and the Future*. New York: Farrar, Straus, and Giroux, 2001.
Sax, Leonard. "'Twilight' Sinks Its Teeth Intro Feminism." *Washington Post*, August 17, 2008. www.washingtonpost.com/wp-dyn/content/article/2008/08/15/AR2008081503099.html.
Stein, Jared. "Defining Creepy Treehouse." *Flexknowlogy* (blog). April 9, 2008. flexknowlogy.learningfield.org/2008/04/09/defining-creepy-tree-house/.
Wilson, Natalie. *Seduced by Twilight*. Jefferson: McFarland, 2011.
Zeisler, Andi. *Feminism and Pop Culture*. Berkeley: Seal, 2008.

Chapter Twelve

Composing Digital Found Poetry in Secondary English Language Arts Classrooms

F. Blake Tenore and Katelynn Collins-Hall

THE SET-UP

This chapter describes the possibilities and methods of a poetry lesson that integrates digital media literacy into three aspects of secondary language arts education: (1) reading and composing poetry; (2) critical literacy; and (3) visual literacies. Using found images, videos, online comics, and more, students will think critically about a social issue of their choice by creating a multimodal found poem.

A found poem[1] is a popular writing strategy in which students compose an original poem comprised of words borrowed from multiple texts that they (re)arrange to create a new poetic text. The chapter outlines a series of lessons designed to help students create a digital found poem that includes words, images, and video. The digital found poem supports students' participation in an intertextual, multimodal conversation with the original poetry and poet.

Critically reading and writing poetry in secondary ELA classrooms addresses two key components of the Common Core State Standards (CCSS):[2] students read increasingly complex texts and strengthen their abilities to analyze complex texts to determine meaning and authors' intentions. The particular emphasis on close textual analysis in the CCSS represents a narrowed conception of literacy and reading,[3] but engaging in literacy tasks in a framework of critical literacy infused with the twenty-first-century skills that visual literacy demands may broaden students' interactions with texts and help them engage English language arts in ways that incite creativity, exploration, and enjoyment.

While the lesson described in this chapter is designed to support students' developing textual analysis skills and composition abilities, it is also intended to help students and teachers break from the limitations of a narrow, skills-based moment in English language arts history that discourages readers' participation in meaning-making.[4] The exercises outlined here encourage students and teachers to focus on big ideas, important issues or concerns, and to delve into the ways that who they are as readers influences and contributes to both the potential meanings of texts they read and, therefore, write.

Rather than analyze, accept, and reproduce a text, critical literacy should result in students utilizing the text and its cues from the author to make inferences and draw meaning that goes beyond the text form to develop a dialogue between themselves, the author, and the text. Having students enter into a critical dialogue with various forms of texts requires that they call upon prior knowledge and experiences and actively engage with the text as they make meaning. In order to engage in critical literacy, students must engage in active reading and analysis.

Former NCTE president Leila Christenbury, upon her return to a high school English classroom, found that her students viewed English class as "a barren way station, . . . a locale to pass the time, turn the pages, and get credit."[5] Inviting and encouraging students to adopt a critical stance toward poetic texts may be one antidote to the malaise Christenbury experienced in her classroom.

Critically literate students are expected to not only read closely and analytically but to view ideas from multiple perspectives, value their own experiences and perspectives relative to the author's, and challenge and question assumptions embedded in any text. Critical literacy pushes beyond the expectation of informational regurgitation and positions students as generative, thoughtful, producers of meaning who talk back to, through, and with texts in place of simply being receivers and meaning-hunters.

Visual literacy can assist students in strengthening their critical literacy and analytic skills because, as with critical literacy, students should participate in a dialogue with the "thousand words" an image is conveying, just as they should with a print text bring their prior knowledge and experiences to make meaning. Reading poetry is challenging and, for many students who never imagined themselves as poets, writing it may simply be torturous.

Incorporating images into the analysis and production of complex poetic texts may increase students' engagement and interest, and, moreover, the digital component of this project can bring what may seem an archaic art form to some students into the present realities of their lives. Students are bombarded by images daily, and not only should they be taught how to view them critically, but they should have the opportunity to manipulate, generate, and contemplate them as thoughtful producers of texts as well.

With the contemporary expectations and challenges of English classrooms as the backdrop, this chapter begins with an outline of a conceptual framework to guide this lesson followed by a description of the project and the responsibilities of both teachers and students. Finally, steps for students to take to plan out their digital found poems, find and capture online images, compose, and publish are provided. Taken as a guideline for structuring this experience with poetry, students will be highly engaged and learn the power of the multimodal critical products they create.

REVIEW OF LITERATURE

Smith and Wilhelm[6] conceptualized students' study of literary themes as an exercise in identifying the broad conversation in which the author is participating and the particular literary piece as the author's turn at talk in that conversation. The poetry lesson presented here draws on two traditions of literacy theory to frame the exercise and guide students' to not only recognize the conversation taking place but to also take their own turn at talk in it.

First, a transactional approach[7] to secondary literature instruction positions readers as integral to the meaning-making process. Their experiences, purposes, and stances as readers make them co-creators of meaning with the words on the page. Thus, reading is not only an active process, but it is a productive one during which readers are encouraged to construct their own turns at talk as they respond to texts.

As Appleman[8] points out, however, reader-response theory[9] in practice risks tumbling into text-independent opinion sharing about works of literature. The objective of this lesson is to help students value and contend with their lived experiences in the presence of and in response to the words on the page. A critical literacy stance may help students keep both the text and their selves "in play" as meaning producers who interact with their chosen texts.

Critical literacy[10] also calls for students to be participants in the conversations taking place around them, not mere recipients of information. One aspect of a critical literacy approach is to help students understand how texts are used by powerful discourses[11] to position them, to identify them, and to present the values and ideology of a particular discourse.[12] Critically literate students read the word and the world and learn to identify and resist oppressive and hegemonic discourse. Another aspect of critical literacy invites students to write about the world around them, to use their own texts as venues for their voices to be heard. Students witness[13] the contexts in which they live from their own perspectives, and they wrestle with important social issues in their lives. Critically literate students also use texts to disrupt the commonplace and strive to view a situation from multiple points of view,[14] particularly those of persons or groups subjugated by the text.[15] Students may produce their digital projects as a way to represent alternative perspectives, to disrupt a common (mis)conception of a group of people, a situation, or an issue, or to witness the world through the lens of their own lived experiences.

Finally, cultivating students' visual literacies in the classroom is imperative in twenty-first-century English language arts classrooms. Images bombard students, and they should learn to bring the same responsive, critical stances to their reading of images—photos, videos, advertisements—as we ask them to bring to print texts.[16] And just as students learn to compose print texts, they should learn to manipulate and communicate visually with images.

At a moment in education history when emphasis is on informational texts and standardized testing, why poetry? Because we want students to be able to pause and immerse themselves in the experience of literature.[17] Reading poetry creates an opportunity, in a classroom world of time constraints and pressures, to lose oneself in a relatively short but rich and complex text. Reading poetry allows students to linger and ponder single words or images and engage in thoughtful talk about the choices writers make and why they make them.

CLASSROOM CONNECTIONS

This section describes the steps of the digital found poem project as part of a literacy program that takes a critical approach. Infinite adaptations, of course, are possible at each step along the way. Among the envisioned outcomes for this project is a digital composition that students will have created using text, images, and videos in response to or to critically comment upon a traditional print poem that addresses a social issue of interest to students.

Students' products will be visual, poetic, and represent their own critical contributions to an ongoing conversation with the poet and others who have thought deeply about the issues or topics students have chosen. At the beginning of each section, tables outline the responsibilities of the teacher and students and the materials needed for each task.

Selecting and Analyzing Poems

The first step is for teachers to guide students to select a poem that aligns with a specific topic or thematic unit (e.g., feminism, war, adolescents, race). Students should read with the intent of identifying the position the writers take on the topics through their poems. As they are reading the poem(s),

Table 12.1. Responsibilities and materials for initial poetry analysis

Teacher responsibilities	Student responsibilities	Materials
Provide topic choices	Select a poem that matches topic	Poems or resources for finding poems
Lead a discussion on critical approaches to literary analysis	Create T-chart or cluster	T-chart

instruct students to use one of the two following strategies to begin collecting words for their digital found poems.

The first strategy is for students to use a double-entry journal, or *T-chart* to identify specific words and phrases the poet uses to make statements about the topic. On one side of the journal or T-chart, students write the words and language that they identify in each stanza as important. On the other side of the paper the students briefly explain why the adjacent word or phrase is important, or simply why it appeals to them. Students' responses to their poems may be shared in small groups or as a class discussion to demonstrate the different critical analyses students are constructing and the type of language the authors are using.

A second strategy to support students' initial responses and analyses of their poems is *clustering*.[18] Students may identify important words in the poem and then begin to jot down words that they associate with that word. Through this process, students build a collection of words that help them express their interpretations of the poem(s), and they also begin to generate their own thinking about the topic with a list of words they may include in their own compositions later.

Analysis of Images

As students prepare to move to the next phase of their projects, teachers should model an analysis of an image or video clip that will serve as a guide for students through their own image selection processes. Beginning analysis of images (or video clips) should focus on two aspects: *syntax* and *semantics* of the image. Syntax refers to the individual components of an image, which may also include decisions the artist has made in the composition.[19] Examples of syntactic elements to notice in an analysis are: scale, color, light/shadow, shape, size, foreground/background, and perspective.

Semantics have to do with how images (and their composition) gain meaning in the world and how cultural discourses and expectations shape a viewer's construction of an image's meaning.[20] Some questions teachers might ask to help students begin to understand the semantics of an image are:

Table 12.2. Responsibilities and materials for analyzing found images

Teacher responsibilities	Student responsibilities	Materials
Provide model images	Practice image analysis	Images to practice analyzing
Demonstrate analysis of syntactic and semantic elements of images		Graphic organizer or template to support beginning analysis

Who created the image? Who paid for or published the image? In what context is the image used? Who is most likely to see the image? What aspects of a culture are conveyed in the image? Do syntactic elements of the image have particular significance or symbolic value in a particular culture or context?

Commercial images intended to persuade or attract viewers have syntactic and semantic elements that teachers and students might discuss together before students practice analyzing images on their own. Journalistic images, too, ostensibly neutral, are also thoughtful constructions of artists and photographers that capture only limited experiences of the world. Teachers may guide students in thinking about and discussing how syntactic elements such as perspective, focus, foreground/background are used to tell a story or convey particular meaning.

As students embark on searches for images to help them represent their stance on their chosen topics, teachers should encourage them to consider the syntactic components of images and videos they choose and support students' thinking about the semantic meanings they construct with the images.

Finding and Capturing Images

The order in which the steps of this project have been presented reflects a fairly traditional approach to literary analysis—students read a work, use language and print to support their thinking, and share their interpretations. The next phase, finding and selecting images, might also be useful in an earlier phase of the project.

Teachers may wish to first ask students to search for and collect images that they think are representative of a particular topic and then have them read and analyze poetry in light of the thinking they have done with their images. Whichever path teachers choose, students will need to have time to search for and create images or video clips to incorporate into their compositions. Using the Internet to collect images/videos requires teachers and students to have an understanding of copyright laws and fair use principles.

Table 12.3. Responsibilities and materials for finding and capturing images and video

Teacher responsibilities	Student responsibilities	Materials
Make a fair use/copyright guidelines handout	Abide by copyright law and fair use principles	Desktop or laptop computers
Provide students with a list of online tools and websites to use to find and capture images/video	Make a storage and organization plan for captured images/video	Internet access
Demonstrate search strategies		Online tools and space for students to store found images/videos
Support students' development of a storage and organization plan for captured images/video		

Teachers should be aware of laws about fair use of copyrighted material. In general, there are four guiding principles to think about when deciding if copyrighted material may be used in your classroom:[21]

- purpose and character of the use, including whether the use is of commercial or nonprofit/educational use;
- the nature of the copyrighted work;
- the amount and substantiality of the portion used in relation to the copyrighted work as a whole;
- the effect of the use on the potential market for or value of the copyrighted work.

In short, for a project of this nature, wherein students are not using copyrighted material for commercial use and the aim is to create a new composition, students' use of most images constitutes fair use. However, teachers should encourage students to create their own images, record their own videos, and play their own music whenever time and resources permit.

Not only does this eliminate concerns about copyright violation, it gives students an opportunity to participate more directly in the creative process and shape their final product in a way that is more customized and better fits their personal visions and the nature of their critical commentary. Richard Byrne, creator of the popular (and very useful) educational technology blog, *Free Technology for Teachers*,[22] recommends this simple list representing the order of preference for how students procure images: homegrown, creative commons, fair use.

CAPTURING IMAGES

Before students embark on the mission of finding and selecting images to incorporate into their compositions, teachers should help them make a plan for storage and organization of the images they may wish to use. One option, if students will use a wiki (more on this later) to compose their found digital poem, is to simply drag and drop images from the source onto their wiki page, save, and return to them later for organizing.

Another option, if, for example, students have not decided what software or application they will use to construct their finished product, is to simply have students create a desktop or USB folder into which they can drag images they find compelling. Finally, students might create a table in a word processing document to serve as an initial storyboard (more on this later, as well) and drop their images into fields of their table to be arranged later.

LOCATING IMAGES AND VIDEOS

After students have begun their analyses of poems, it may be time to begin brainstorming or searching for images and video to include in their found digital poems. The purpose of including images in students' compositions is to promote and refine students' understanding of how images carry meaning. Whether symbolic, metaphorical, or literal, images dominate our opportunities to construct meaning as literate participants in contemporary society.

Students should seek images that help them respond to the stance the poet has taken in the poem students have already analyzed. They may either strive to respond, dispute, or extend the position of the poet or make a connection from the poem to a personal or broader conceptualization of the social issue in question.

Students are probably familiar with using Google Images or Yahoo! Image search engines, and allowing this is fine, though they will have to pay particular attention to avoid using copyrighted materials if they are conducting general, unfiltered searches. One feature of these search engines that students may not be aware of, however, is the advanced search filtering options that limit image searches to public domain materials. Using Google Advanced Image Search (www.google.com/advanced_image_search) enables users to filter the images the search engine retrieves by usage rights, so students only access public domain images and artwork.

In addition to traditional search engines, several websites and blogs serve as clearinghouses for photographs and artwork freely available for students' use. Among them: search.creativecommons.org, morguefile.com, wylio.com, the World Images Kiosk at www.worldart.sjsu.edu, Image Base at imagebase.davidniblack.com/main.php, photos8.org, and picdrome.com.

Each of the sites, and many others, allow for click and drag downloads to students' desktops. Of course, both to avoid any copyright violations and to encourage students' image production, if and whenever possible, it is a great idea to have students take their own photographs and produce their own video clips for their final products.

If students wish to incorporate video into their compositions—either their own or fairly used from online—several websites may be useful. Of course, youtube.com is a vast repository of videos of all kinds, but, again, be wary of potential copyright violations. A video ripper application like www.saveyoutube.com enables students to download, edit, and save versions of videos from youtube.com. Creative Commons and Google Video are also excellent sources of fairly used video clips. Free online video editing tools such as magisto.com and loopster.com are user-friendly and can enable students to craft and select exactly the footage they want to include in their final products.

In addition to recording their own videos using digital cameras, DVRs, or their smartphones, students may find a site like animoto.com useful. Animoto.com allows users to upload photos or video clips and the application produces a video using the uploaded content.

JellyCam (www.ticklypictures.com/shop/jellycam/) is another free online application that enables users to create their own stop-motion videos using their webcams. Finally, xtranormal.com and zimmertwins.com are sites that make it fast and easy for students to create their own animated videos. Videos created at all of these sites can be exported for inclusion and manipulation in students' digital compositions.

Storyboarding

Storyboarding, or visually arranging words and images in a graphic organizer of cells like a comic strip, is a common method used by visual artists to plan and conceptualize their work. Students should have the opportunity to plan the arrangement of their words and images before embarking on their digital compositions (like pre-writing, nothing, of course, is set in stone).

Table 12.4. Responsibilities and materials for creating storyboards

Teacher responsibilities	Student responsibilities	Materials
Provide storyboard template handout	Create connections between words and pictures	Storyboard handout
Demonstrate storyboarding as pre-composing exercise	Plan digital found poem visually and spatially using storyboard template	Access to capture images/videos and texts

Students may want to arrange the words first, or choose to think about images that may best represent their response to the poem and issue first. The objective at this point of the process is for students to begin to try to rely on various images to convey their perspectives, arguments, or commentaries. In the storyboarding process, students should keep brief notes (in the storyboard spaces) as to why they selected the image and how they imagine it contributing to the critical commentary or narrative they wish to convey.

Students should have the opportunity to workshop their storyboards with peers and conference with the teacher to receive feedback throughout the process. Teachers should help students articulate how each image/film clip conveys meaning and how it interacts with other images and text(s) to build a commentary.

Sometimes a tendency of both teachers and students is to rely heavily on language to convey ideas at this point in the process. Strive to use images as much as possible and push students to allow images to drive the message or narrative they create. After students have spent time in the pre-composition/planning phase of the lesson, they are ready to begin producing their digital found poems.

Composing the Digital Found Poem

While there are assuredly countless tools that might support students' digital, multimodal compositions, four are outlined below. SMART Notebook, PowerPoint, Glogster, and wikis each may help teachers and students achieve the goals of the digital found poem project, but they offer different formats in which to do so. Again, teachers may wish to model the capabilities of each tool for students and then provide students with time to experiment as they envision their final products. Some possibly useful functions to model and practice may be capturing and embedding images from the Internet into

Table 12.5. Responsibilities and materials for composing digital found poems

Teacher responsibilities	Student responsibilities	Materials
Promote peer learning opportunities for using composition tools (e.g., jigsaw)	Select composition medium suited to his or her vision for the final product	Desktop or laptop computers
Guide and support students' compositional choices		Access to the Internet
Provide adequate in-class time for composition		Instructional handouts for using various composition tools

Notebook and PowerPoint, creating hyperlinks or captioned videos in a wiki, or creating visually appealing collages in Glogster.

SMART Notebook

The presentation software used with SMART brand interactive white boards offers exciting composition possibilities for a project like this. After students have embedded the words, images, and videos they intend to use in their compositions into a page of the Notebook software, the individual elements are easily manipulated and positioned in relation to one another. Students may work individually at desktop or laptop computers, but the additional interactivity afforded by an interactive white board seems especially appealing. Enabling students to physically arrange the elements of their composition to create a just-right effect may increase engagement and add the impression of hands-on work to the project.

PowerPoint

Minus the interactivity of the interactive white board, PowerPoint offers similar opportunities for digital composition. With the ability to embed images, video, and sound into a presentation, the software will not limit students. As with Notebook, PowerPoint presentations may be constructed as hypertexts wherein viewers/readers can experience a variety of pathways through the composition, or they may be put together more akin to digital stories with transitions of slides preprogrammed by the composer. Like Notebook, PowerPoint has the advantage of offering students multiple pages for their productions, while wikis and glogster.com are more suited to single-page compositions.

Wikis

A third option is to allow students to compose on their own pages in a class wiki space. Wikis support collaborative work and allow students to work together asynchronously from home. Wikispaces.com is an online wiki host used by many educators to provide spaces for students to contribute content or share work online. Again, wikis offer students a blank space in which they can manipulate the components of their composition with relative click and drag ease. Images and video clips are also quickly and easily embedded into compositions.

Glogster.com

Finally, glogster.com is an online digital poster-making tool. Like wikis, glogster.com posters support images, text, and video, and Glogster allows users to arrange content as they choose. Files are uploaded to the website and students compose within its boundaries. A possible shortcoming of this tool, however, is that it is viewable only through glogster.com and cannot be exported or shared.

With any of the tools described above, teachers may find it useful to allow students some experimental time to learn to manipulate images and incorporate the powerful functions of the applications. Each of the digital tools described will allow students to arrange and format combinations of words and images as they please and students will not be limited in their creativity or conceptualization of their work by the potential of the media.

Publishing Digital Found Poems

As with any composition project, digital found poems should be published, shared, and celebrated both within and beyond the classroom. The three tools that follow will allow teachers and students to view each other's work and in some cases share feedback.

One wonderful capability that technology and digital media have made available is that the compilation of multiple products and of multiple media forms can be accessed through one media site. Resources such as Facebook, wikis, and glogster.com are all free web sources that allow the publication and sharing of different media projects. Teachers can create a classroom Facebook, wiki, or Glogster page and give students the username and password. This requires a great deal of trust from the teacher as well as a great deal of respect, professionalism, and honesty among students. Some teachers use a contract that outlines professional responsibilities and conduct expected when using one of these sites that all students and the teacher signs.

Creating a group within a class Facebook page is a simple way to publish student work online. After creating this page and assigning a password, give both the username and password to the students to be used for submitting their projects. Glogster.com is another online space designed specifically for

Table 12.6. Responsibilities and materials for publishing digital found poems

Teacher responsibilities	Student responsibilities	Materials
Select a publication site/platform and set up an account	Publish or upload completed composition to class site	Desktop or laptop computers
Provide students with account information	Provide respectful, constructive feedback to peers as allowed by platform	
Monitor students' material uploaded or published		

classroom use. Teachers can sign up as an educator and students sign up as a student. However, the number of students, capabilities, and control of glogs ranges in price from free with ten students and the most basic features to $99 annually with up to two hundred students and includes all features. The package a teacher plans to use will greatly influence the use of the site for projects. However, using Glogster in similar ways to Facebook will allow students to create collages and embed videos.

A classroom wiki site has all of the same basic options that Facebook and Glogster offer. One benefit of a wiki that the others do not offer as easily is the ability to have multiple separate pages within the site. This capability could allow the teacher to set up multiple pages and designate with the students' names where they are expected to post their finished product. As with Glogster, students can choose to produce their product within the site itself or to upload or embed from a different site such as Google Docs or YouTube.

FINAL THOUGHTS

The series of lessons outlined in this chapter represent a method for supporting secondary English language arts through students' construction of a found digital poem. Valuable not only to build reading skills, found digital poetry is also beneficial to students as writers.

The conceptual framework values active reader participation in meaning construction and teaching students to adopt a critical stance as both readers and writers. The lesson supports students' engagement with complex poetry texts by using images and digital tools to scaffold their analysis of poems and their composition of a digital, visual text. Through participation in the exercise, students will use nontraditional tools to share their voices and their perspectives with their classmates and the world.

NOTES

1. "Found Poetry—Found Poem," Creative Writing Now , accessed September 8, 2012, www.creative-writing-now.com/found-poetry.html.
2. National Governors Association Center for Best Practices and the Council of Chief State School Officers, 2010.
3. Stergios Botzakis, Leslie D. Burns, and Leigh A. Hall, Literacy Reform and Common Core State Standards: Recycling the Autonomous Model, *Language Arts* 91, no. 4 (2014): 223–35.
4. Ibid.
5. Leila Christenbury, *Retracing the Journey: Teaching and Learning in an American High School*, Teachers College Press, 2007.
6. Michael W. Smith and Jeffrey D. Wilhelm, *Fresh Takes on Teaching Literary Elements: How to Teach what Really Matters about Character, Setting, Point of View, and Theme*, Scholastic, 2010.

7. Louise Rosenblatt, *The Reader, the Text, the Poem* (1978): 139.
8. Deborah Appleman, *Critical Encounters in High School English: Teaching Literacy Theory to Adolescents*, Teachers College Press, 2000.
9. Ibid.
10. Mitzi Lewison, Amy Seely Flint, and Katie Van Sluys, "Taking on Critical Literacy: The Journey of Newcomers and Novices," *Language Arts* (2002): 382–92.
11. James Paul Gee, *Social Linguistics and Literacies*, Routledge, 2007.
12. Norman Fairclough, *Language and Power*, Pearson Education, 2001.
13. Elizabeth Dutro and Kristien Zenkov, "Urban Students Testifying to Their Own Stories: Talking Back to Deficit Perspectives," in *57th Yearbook of the National Reading Conference*, Oak Creek, WI: National Reading Conference, Inc. (2008), 172–218.
14. Mitzi Lewison, Amy Seely Flint, and Katie Van Sluys, "Taking on Critical Literacy: The Journey of Newcomers and Novices," *Language Arts* (May 2002): 382–92.
15. Cynthia Lewis, "Critical issues: Limits of Identification: The Personal, Pleasurable, and Critical in Reader Response," *Journal of Literacy Research* 32, no. 2 (2000): 253–66.
16. Gunther Kress, *Literacy in the New Media Age*, Psychology Press, 2003; Carey Jewitt and Gunther R. Kress, *Multimodal Literacy*, New York: P. Lang, 2003; Frank Serafini, "Expanding Perspectives for Comprehending Visual Images in Multimodal Texts," *Journal of Adolescent & Adult Literacy* 54, no. 5 (2011): 342–50.
17. Jeffrey D. Wilhelm and Bruce Novak, *Teaching Literacy for Love and Wisdom: Being the Book and Being the Change*, Teachers College Press, 2011.
18. Gabriele L. Rico, *Writing the Natural Way: Using Right-Brain Techniques to Release Your Expressive Powers*, Los Angeles: J. P. Tarcher, 1983.
19. Anne Bamford, "The Visual Literacy White Paper," Adobe.com (2003), retrieved March 12, 2012, from www.images.adobe.com/content/dam/Adobe/en/education/pdfs/visual-literacy-wp.pdf.
20. Ibid.
21. Section 107, 1976 Copyright Act.
22. *Free Technology for Teachers*, retrieved October 9, 2012, from www.freetech4teachers.com.

BIBLIOGRAPHY

Appleman, Deborah. *Critical Encounters in High School English: Teaching Literacy Theory to Adolescents*. Teachers College Press, 2000.

Bamford, Anne. "The Visual Literacy White Paper." Adobe.com (2003). Retrieved March 12, 2012, from wwwimages.adobe.com/content/dam/Adobe/en/education/pdfs/visual-literacy-wp.pdf.

Botzakis, Stergios, Leslie D. Burns, and Leigh A. Hall. "Literacy Reform and Common Core State Standards: Recycling the Autonomous Model." *Language Arts* 91, no. 4 (2014): 223–35.

Byrne, Richard. "Free Technology for Teachers." *Free Technology for Teachers*. (n.d.). Retrieved October 9, 2012, from www.freetech4teachers.com.

Christenbury, Leila. *Retracing the Journey: Teaching and Learning in an American High School*. Teachers College Press, 2007.

Dutro, E., and K. Zenkov. "Urban Students Testifying to Their Own Stories: Talking Back to Deficit Perspectives." 57th Yearbook of the National Reading Conference (2008): 172–86.

Fairclough, Norman. *Language and Power*. Pearson Education, 2001.

Found Poetry—Found Poem. *Creative Writing Now*. (n.d.). Retrieved September 8, 2012, from www.creative-writing-now.com/found-poetry.html.

Gee, J. P. *Social Linguistics and Literacies: Ideology in Discourses*. London: Routledge, 2012.

Jewitt, Carey, and Gunther R. Kress. *Multimodal Literacy*. New York: P. Lang, 2003.

Kress, Gunther. *Literacy in the New Media Age*. Psychology Press, 2003.

Lewis, Cynthia. "Critical Issues: Limits of Identification: The Personal, Pleasurable, and Critical in Reader Response." *Journal of Literacy Research* 32, no. 2 (2000): 253–66.

Lewison, M., A. S. Flint, and K. Van Sluys. (2002). "Taking on Critical Literacy: The Journey of Newcomers and Novices." Language Arts 79, no. 5 (May 2002): 382–92.
National Governors Association Center for Best Practices and the Council of Chief State School Officers. (2010).
Rico, G. L. *Writing the Natural Way: Using Right-Brain Techniques to Release Your Expressive Powers*. Los Angeles: J. P. Tarcher, 1983.
Rosenblatt, L. M. *The Reader, the Text, the Poem: The Transactional Theory of the Literary Work*. Carbondale: Southern Illinois University Press, 1978.
Serafini, Frank. "Expanding Perspectives for Comprehending Visual Images in Multimodal Texts." *Journal of Adolescent & Adult Literacy* 54, no. 5 (2011): 342–50.

About the Contributors

EDITOR

Sandra Eckard has a PhD in rhetoric and linguistics from Indiana University of Pennsylvania. She is an associate professor of English at East Stroudsburg University where she teaches writing, works with English education students, and directs the Writing Studio, a tutoring spot for students. She specializes in teaching writing, tutoring writing, and using pop culture in the classroom. Dr. Eckard presents on tutoring and teaching several times a year, and in addition to articles, she has also published her dissertation, *The Ties That Bind: Storytelling as a Teaching Technique in Composition Classrooms and Writing Centers*.

CONTRIBUTORS

April Brannon is an assistant professor of English at California State University Fullerton, where she serves as the director of the English education program. She teaches writing and English methods classes and has published on both writing pedagogy and literature.

Mary T. Christel taught world literature as well as media and film studies at Adlai E. Stevenson High School. She has published numerous articles on teaching Shakespeare and has cowritten books on media literacy, including *Seeing and Believing: How to Teach Media Literacy in the English Classroom* with Ellen Krueger as well as coediting *Lesson Plans for Creating Media-Rich Classrooms* and *Lesson Plans for Developing Digital Literacies* with Scott Sullivan.

Katelynn Collins-Hall is an alumnus of Hartwick College in Oneonta, New York, where she majored in sociology and English while completing the education program in elementary and special education. She is currently a graduate student at Teachers College Columbia focusing on applied behavior analysis. Her teaching and research interests include special education, elementary education, multicultural, and equity education.

Salena Fehnel earned her Master's degree in creative writing from Wilkes University. She is a doctoral candidate at Drew University with a concentration in writing and global studies. She teaches developmental composition and writing through literature classes at Berkeley College in New Jersey and is the assistant director of academic support, where she runs peer-based and faculty-based tutoring for students. She has published fiction, poetry, and novels.

Hannah R. Gerber earned her PhD in secondary English education from the University of Alabama. She is an assistant professor of literacy studies at Sam Houston State University where she teaches graduate classes in virtual ethnography, digital literacies, and games studies. Her research focuses on videogames and the literacy connections that occur within gaming.

Carmela Delia Lanza is an assistant professor of English at Dakota State University in Madison, South Dakota, where she advises, mentors, and evaluates English education students. Her academic interests include gender studies, working-class theory, teaching methods, and the role of the arts in education. Her writing, which includes poetry, academic essays, and creative nonfiction, can be found in various journals and anthologies.

Jennifer Marmo earned her BA in English education at State University College at Oneonta in New York. She is an English teacher at East Stroudsburg High School North where she teaches tenth and twelfth grade English. In her early years as a writer, Jennifer published several poems.

Laura Sloan Patterson received her PhD in literature from Vanderbilt University. She is an associate professor of English and the director of undergraduate writing at Seton Hill University in Greensburg, Pennsylvania, where she specializes in American, southern, and women's literature, as well as composition. She is the author of numerous articles as well as *Stirring the Pot: The Kitchen and Domesticity in the Fiction of Southern Women*.

Carissa Pokorny-Golden received her PhD in American literature and composition from Temple University. She is an assistant professor of English at

Kutztown University of Pennsylvania, where she teaches composition, adolescent literature, methods of teaching English and practicum to English education undergraduate and graduate students. She specializes in literacy and teacher education.

Luke Rodesiler, a former high school English teacher, is currently a doctoral fellow in the School of Teaching and Learning at the University of Florida and a teacher consultant of the Red Cedar Writing Project at Michigan State University. His ideas related to using popular media in the English language arts classroom have appeared in various publications, including *The English Journal*.

Alex Romagnoli is an assistant professor of English education at Monmouth University. In 2013, he received his PhD in composition at Indiana University of Pennsylvania. He is the coauthor of *Enter the Superheroes: American Values, Culture, and the Canon of Superhero Literature*. Additionally, he received the IUP Composition and TESOL program's "Exemplary Teaching of Literacy and Language Award" in 2013. Dr. Romagnoli is currently coediting a special edition of the academic journal *Works and Days* with Dr. Gian Pagnucci. His research interests include multimodality, multiliteracies, utilizing graphic novels in academic contexts, and popular culture.

F. Blake Tenore is assistant professor of education at Hartwick College in Oneonta, New York, where he teaches literacy education courses for teacher candidates, grades 1–12. His teaching and research interests include teacher education, multicultural and equity education, literacies of diverse learners, and digital literacies as they pertain to teacher preparation and development.

Elle Yarborough has a PhD in English education from Arizona State University. She is a professor of English at Northern Essex Community College, where she teaches composition and film studies courses. Her teaching and research interests include teacher education, experimental literature, online composition instruction, using popular culture to increase student engagement, and the use of technology in the composition classroom.

www.ingramcontent.com/pod-product-compliance
Lightning Source LLC
Chambersburg PA
CBHW070638300426
44111CB00013B/2154